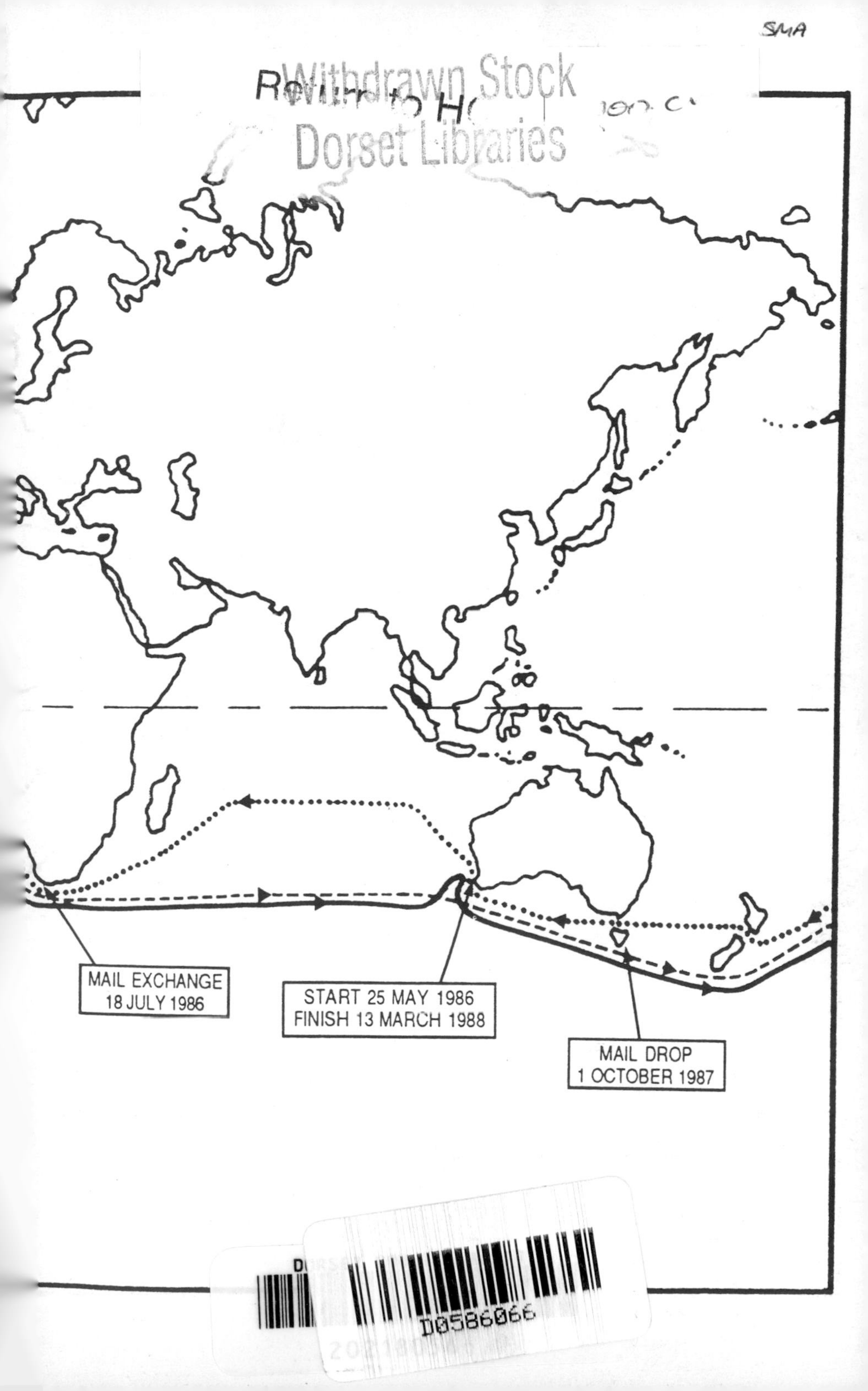
MAIL EXCHANGE
18 JULY 1986
START 25 MAY 1986
FINISH 13 MARCH 1988
MAIL DROP
1 OCTOBER 1987

SPECIAL MESSAGE TO READERS

This book is published by

THE ULVERSCROFT FOUNDATION,

a registered charity in the U.K., No. 264873

The Foundation was established in 1974 to provide funds to help towards research, diagnosis and treatment of eye diseases. Below are a few examples of contributions made by THE ULVERSCROFT FOUNDATION:

★ A new Children's Assessment Unit at Moorfield's Hospital, London.

★ Twin operating theatres at the Western Ophthalmic Hospital, London.

★ The Frederick Thorpe Ulverscroft Chair of Ophthalmology at the University of Leicester.

★ Eye Laser equipment to various eye hospitals.

If you would like to help further the work of the Foundation by making a donation or leaving a legacy, every contribution, no matter how small, is received with gratitude. Please write for details to:

THE ULVERSCROFT FOUNDATION,
The Green, Bradgate Road, Anstey,
Leicestershire, LE7 7FU. England.
Telephone: (0533) 364325

I've travelled the world twice over,
Met the famous: saints and sinners,
Poets and artists, kings and queens,
Old stars and hopeful beginners,
I've been where no-one's been before,
Learned secrets from writers and cooks
All with one library ticket
To the wonderful world of books.

SEXTANT, SEA AND SOLITUDE

What makes a man want to spend nearly two years alone on a small boat, with danger an almost constant companion, and security and comfort virtual strangers? For Western Australia's self-effacing solo yachtsman, Jon Sanders, the answers go deeper than the mere pursuit of records, or some spurious need to test the whims of fate. Nevertheless, this one-time shearing contractor with salt in his veins truly wrote himself into the annals of nautical history when he sailed home to a hero's welcome one sparkling March day in 1988. He had just completed the longest continuous voyage—658 days—ever undertaken.

Books by Jon Sanders
in the Ulverscroft Large Print Series:

LONE SAILOR
SEXTANT, SEA AND SOLITUDE

HUGH SCHMITT

SANDERS SEXTANT, SEA AND SOLITUDE

Complete and Unabridged

ULVERSCROFT
Leicester

First published in Australia in 1988 by
St. George Books,
a division of
Bell Publishing Group Pty. Ltd.,
Western Australia 6000

First Large Print Edition
published March 1990
by arrangement with
St. George Books,
a division of
Bell Publishing Group Pty. Ltd.,
Western Australia 6000

British Library CIP Data

Schmitt, Hugh
Sanders sextant, sea and solitude.—Large print ed.—
Ulverscroft large print series: non-fiction
1. World. Circumnavigation by yachts
I. Title
910.4′1

ISBN 0-7089-2160-4

Published by
F. A. Thorpe (Publishing) Ltd.
Anstey, Leicestershire

Set by Rowland Phototypesetting Ltd.
Bury St. Edmunds, Suffolk
Printed and bound in Great Britain by
T. J. Press (Padstow) Ltd., Padstow, Cornwall

To my daughter Cassandra

Foreword

SIR CHARLES COURT, AK, KCMG, OBE

WHEN I wrote the Foreword to his book *Lone Sailor*, I thought Jon Sanders had achieved the ultimate; there would be no sea epic of its kind to exceed his achievement.

How wrong I was.

I underestimated the physical and mental stamina of this remarkable man, already on a pedestal as somebody quite unique.

It is no surprise to me that he kept immaculate records during his triple circumnavigation of the world in *Parry Endeavour*. I also knew he would always maintain a healthy respect for the sea and the elements.

For lesser sailors, an encounter with a

large Taiwanese fishing vessel in the Atlantic probably would have signalled an ignominious end to their voyage. But not Jon Sanders. Although he was desperately in need of rest, he turned near disaster into a commendable demonstration of how a lone sailor can triumph over adversity.

The same applied when his satellite navigation gear and his radio failed. He was trained and ready to cope.

He has unwittingly written a textbook for long distance sailors of the future—whether alone or with others—where the objective is to complete the planned voyage safely and not be obsessed with speed or dramatic headlines.

The special type of courage required by people like Jon Sanders is quite different to that recorded on the field of battle, or in other spontaneous situations.

There was nothing spontaneous about contemplating a voyage to circumnavigate the world three times, and alone. Like those who went into orbit in the early days of space history, he had weeks and months to decide whether to face the dangers. During that time he could have withdrawn without any loss of reputation.

But, like those men in space, Jon Sanders went knowingly on his first double circumnavigation, and then on his triple circumnavigation of the world.

Just to make it more difficult for himself, he accepted some testing scientific assignments. It may have sounded ostentatious to do this on his little craft when you consider the type and size of vessels in comparable missions—and their array of sophisticated modern electronic equipment. Even Captain Cook had a sizeable ship and specialists in his crew when he went on his historic scientific expeditions.

But we have come to expect so much from Jon Sanders that we assumed that if anyone could do it on a small yacht, Jon Sanders was the one to succeed.

In all of this we should not overlook the faith shown in Jon Sanders by Kevin Parry. The fact that there was such reluctance on the part of other sponsors tells its own story.

In generations hence, I believe people will gain inspiration and wisdom from this book. Certainly, one lesson will emerge loud and clear—to be brave, successful and above all survive, you treat the sea and the elements with respect. No matter how long or hard the voyage might be, it is no place for the foolhardy!

Jon Sanders—we salute you!

To avoid confusing readers with the Beaufort Scale of wind forces, all wind speed estimates or readings in this book have been kept to knots rather than "forces". So that the reader can get some idea of the type of seas to be expected at certain wind speeds, the following table is included:

Knots	Descriptive	Sea Conditions
17–21	Fresh breeze	Moderate (about two metres) waves, taking a more pronounced long form; many white foam crests; may be some spray.
22–27	Strong breeze	Large waves begin to form, white foam crests more extensive, spray likely.
28–33	Near gale	Sea heaps up and white foam from breaking waves begins to be blown in streaks along the

		direction of the wind, spindrift begins.
34–40	Gale	Moderately high waves of greater length, edges of crests break into spin-drift, foam is blown in well-marked streaks along wind direction.
41–47	Strong gale	High waves, dense streaks of foam along direction of wind, crests of waves begin to topple, tumble and roll over, much spray.
48–55	Storm	Very high waves with long overhanging crests. The resulting foam in great patches is blown in dense white streaks along wind direction. Sea surface usually white and tumbling of sea be-comes heavy and shock-like.
56–63	Violent storm	Exceptionally high waves. Sea is completely covered with long white patches of foam. Everywhere the edges of the wave crests are blown into froth. Visi-bility reduced.

64–71	Hurricane	The air is filled with foam and spray. Sea completely white with driving spray, visibility poor.

Author's Note

WORKING with Jon Sanders on a book is like trying to catch a moonbeam. While he was sailing the ocean wastes of the world we always knew where he was—from his satellite reporting system—but on land he is difficult to pin down for interviews. But thanks to his meticulously kept logbooks, all five of them, plus some fleeting interviews and my long-time association with the remarkable sailor, I have been able to piece together an accurate account of his incredible odyssey.

Having worked with him on *Lone Sailor* in 1982, I was gratified when Jon asked me to write the story of his epic triple lone, non-stop circumnavigation. Because his logbook entries are revelatory of his way of thinking, his methodology of making long sea passages alone and his psyche, I have included copious excerpts from his log, which was written always in pencil and in a tiny scrawl.

I would like to thank the photographers who have contributed pictures to this book, and also Jack Seabrook, who monitored the epic voyage by radio as far as possible, and whose maps are reproduced inside.

Finally, I thank Jon Sanders for choosing me to write this book.

1

The Worst Day

The sea has no generosity. No display of manly qualities—courage, hardihood, endurance, faithfulness—has ever been known to touch its irresponsible consciousness of power.

Joseph Conrad, The Mirror of the Sea

THE lone sailor squinted through his ancient sextant towards the cloud-shrouded noonday sun as his 14.5–metre sloop corkscrewed down steep, breaking South Atlantic waves. Swathed in yellow foul-weather gear—and soaked to the skin—he sat precariously on the pushpit of the yacht with a sinewy arm hooked round one of the three backstays, to which his trusty safety harness had been closely clipped.

Navigators do not normally take sextant sightings when it is overcast; not unless they are desperate for a position fix, however vague. And Jonathan Sanders, on his 545th day at sea continuously and without stopping and without reprovisioning—and quite alone—badly needed to know where his sturdy, sea-stained yacht *Parry Endeavour* was on this grey November day.

He knew from sightings two days earlier that he must be within a few hundred nautical miles of the world's most famous, and infamous, ocean extremities—Cape Horn. And with the weather closing in, this third rounding of the Horn on his current incredible voyage promised to be the most hazardous.

His attempt to become the first man in history to sail round the world three times non-stop and alone had been fraught with setbacks, not the least of which was the failure of his sophisticated satellite-navigation equipment through condensation in the cabin of his yacht. Now it was a case of seat-of-the-pants navigation in one of the trickiest and roughest regions of any of the seven seas Sanders had wandered for two decades or more. *Parry Endeavour* was surfing down green-and-white-crested waves whipped up by the force nine gale that whistled and whined mournfully through the sloop's stout rigging. "These are the screaming fifties, worse than the Roaring Forties," the lone sailor told himself as he gripped the cold brass sextant with sore and frost-bitten fingers. "Why does it always have to be overcast just when I really need a sight?"

But clinging to the pushpit with aching legs, Sanders got a rough sight of the sun through a grey veil of cloud. Then painfully he eased his tall, gaunt frame through the boarded-up hatch leading to the comparative warmth of his cabin. He lit the spirit stove to warm his fingers before working out his position at the chart table. The stove was faulty, emitting acrid black smoke that filled the cabin and made the sailor cough.

Jon Sanders knew that his position could be a few miles out, because of the cartwheeling of the yacht in the steep, breaking seas and because of the overcast conditions. But he also knew from the experience of his previous non-stop lone double circumnavigation of the world that his "fix" would not be far out.

When his hands had thawed Sanders

translated the sextant reading on to his chart of the Tierra del Fuego region: Latitude 55 deg. 45.4 S; Longitude 73 deg. 39.7 W. This put him about 210 nautical miles west of Cape Horn. Over a cup of steaming hot cocoa he told himself he was in for a pasting this time round the Horn. That morning after breakfast he had noted in his meticulously kept logbook: *Oh dear, the wind is 35 to 45 knots from the northwest, despite the high barometer reading for the region—1008. Time for the last reef in the main*.

Soon after he had taken his rough sextant sight at noon at that day, 19 November 1987, he wrote: *Those were the roughest conditions this voyage that I have managed to take a celestial sight (sun). Normally I would not have bothered but I am now closing Tierra del Fuego and expect to pass between Ildefonso and Ramirez Islands and rocks tomorrow afternoon*.

The wind eased to thirty knots, but rain and hail were now falling and the forty-eight-year-old sailor rigged a canvas water bucket under the triple-reefed mainsail to catch some fresh water. His tanks were low.

At 5.10 p.m. he recorded in his log: *Wind increasing rapidly. It is really cold, bleak and damp—and very rough.*

After a scratchy meal of canned lasagna made slightly palatable by a can of peeled tomatoes, Sanders tried to tune his short-wave radio into the BBC news. The reception was bad and outside he could hear the thumping of the hull as it fell down wave faces, the roar of breaking waves and the whining of the wind in the rigging as the storm worsened.

He was wondering how much worse it could get when *Endeavour* suddenly became airborne and crashed on to its side in the trough of a wave, burying the mast tip in green water. A major knockdown! Plates, the remnants of his rushed meal, books, navigational instruments, charts and anything stowed high in the cabin went flying across the cabin, and gear stashed low in the cabin found higher lodgings. Water poured through a ceiling vent into the cabin as Sanders quickly pulled on his foul-weather gear over still-damp clothing. As the yacht slowly righted itself, the solo sailor climbed into the cockpit, clipped on his safety harness and looked for damage with his torch. It was ten minutes away from 11 p.m.

The rogue wave had broken the wind vane that controlled his self-steering, an eventuality for which he was prepared. With cold and aching fingers, he hauled in the broken vane and replaced it with a stubby vane he had cut down especially for the purpose. Quickly he climbed back into the shambles of his cabin. At least it was warmer there. After cleaning up some of the mess he scribbled into his logbook at midnight: *Gale continues. Wish it would go away*.

A sleepless hour later he wrote: *I think I had better change my tactics. This yacht is getting knocked over too often*. By this time he had the mainsail down and was surfing the big waves under bare mast. At 3 a.m. Sanders again ventured on deck to put out a sea brake—*Endeavour* was surfing too fast and threatened to nose-dive into a trough and possibly pitch-pole. He also raised a storm or spitfire jib, the smallest he had on board. While on the foredeck he glimpsed in the pre-dawn light a monstrous wave, terrifying in its very proximity, descending on his sloop with a thunderous roar. He grabbed the mast and hung on for grim life as it cascaded over him, seemingly bent on prising him from the yacht.

Back in his cabin a few minutes later he wrote with shaky hands: *Obviously the fjords of Tierra del Fuego cause tidal currents which make the ocean break . . . it is all very frightening. But the sea brake seems to help. I do wish the gale would let up*. He never suspected that his trial by storm had hardly started.

He snatched an hour's fitful sleep with the pounding of the specially-strengthened fibreglass hull and the roar of waves telling his subconscious that the storm was still raging. At dawn he recorded: *This awful gale keeps on keeping on*. He switched on his echo sounder and got a reading of seventy-five fathoms. This helped him establish his general whereabouts. But the storm worsened.

At 7 a.m. on Friday 27 November he logged: *Terrible storm . . . 60 knots or more*. He ventured once more into the wave-swept cockpit and his heart sank when he saw the sea brake line had got caught round his self-steering rudder. It had happened when a temporary malfunction in the self-steerer caused the yacht to broach sideways in the trough of a giant wave. He cut it free quickly with his sea knife and *Parry Endeavour* leapt forward, unfettered and storm-driven.

Jon Sanders' long experience told him that to run before this big, steep sea was courting disaster, especially without a sea brake. The yacht had already suffered several knockdowns and he had long since given up on tidying his damp cabin. He tried bringing the yacht thirty to forty degrees on to the wind flying only a spitfire jib. But with that sail up the yacht was not balanced and was going too fast.

He told himself it would be too dangerous to unfurl the mainsail at the moment. In these conditions the lone sailor always heaved-to with his mainsail fully reefed, but because the barometer was high—1008 millibars compared with 968 on previous roundings—he could not believe the gale would last or get worse. But it did.

Sanders now wished he had adopted

tactics he had successfully used in previous storms, tactics he had learnt four years earlier while riding out storms in his Sparkman & Stephens 34 *Perie Banou* during his double lone circumnavigation—hove to with a storm-reefed main. "I'll know better next time," he muttered to himself.

Outside the winds had reached almost hurricane force—sixty to seventy knots. About 9 a.m. *Endeavour* fell off the back of a huge wave with the worst crash of the eighteen month, 53,000–mile voyage to date. Sanders' teeth jarred with dizzying force.

How much longer could his yacht stand this punishment? Should he venture on deck to drop the spitfire jib and raise a fully-reefed main?

At noon he scribbled into his log: *This gale is absolutely terrible . . . rather difficult keeping track of where I am in this muck. The region is not famous for being kind to seafarers.* A bald entry an hour later: *Wind at hurricane strength.*

Jon Sanders rarely swears, even when confiding in his logbook. He wrote earlier that day: *I wish this bleep bleep gale would buzz off*. But at 2.25 p.m. he broke his no-swearing dictum when he logged: *This is the worst gale. Blow the bloody sea brake. I should now be riding with a fully reefed main instead of the storm jib. It is too rotten to risk changing. The main halyard is wrapped around a spreader.*

Parry Endeavour was now crashing off the biggest waves he had ever seen in six circumnavigations of the world. In his long association with the sea Sanders tended to play down wave dimensions, but in a letter describing this particular Cape Horn rounding (and plucked from his sloop by a Royal Navy helicopter) he said:

I have heard sailors talk of 100–foot waves and I just thought *bulltwang*, but 100 feet they were—or more. I judged them by the height of the mast and the length of the yacht. The sea was tiers of eerie plateaus. The spindrift off the waves were streaks of mist being blown horizontally . . . it was dreadful. I think I sprouted some new grey hairs . . .

Six months later, in the warmth of the author's living room, he explained how he estimated the wave sizes: "You're in a forty-six foot yacht climbing an almost-vertical wave in front of it. You can see the crest breaking twenty or thirty feet above you and if you looked behind you saw the trough the same distance astern. Some of them must have been more than a hundred feet."

On this awful November afternoon Sanders decided he must bite the bullet and take down the spitfire jib and raise a fully-reefed mainsail, though he knew it would be a long and dangerous manoeuvre in the frightful conditions. At 4.40 p.m. he logged: *Another knockdown. This is all so worrying . . . a wave just put the yacht about. Wind hurricane strength*.

During one knockdown his chart table lid flew ajar, emptying all his charts and navigational instruments across the cabin floor. As the yacht bumped and ground like a drunken striptease artiste, the solo sailor methodically put the gear back in place, ruefully reflecting that the door to his "office" had never before been forced open by a big wave. But half an hour later the same thing happened. "You're a slow learner," Sanders said to himself as again he lifted the contents back into the chart table, this time wedging it firmly closed.

Sanders decided something really bad would happen to *Endeavour* if he did not drop the storm jib to slow it down and put up the reefed main. "I wondered how long the boat could stand the battering it was getting," he said later. "I knew that heaving-to into the wind with a fully-reefed mainsail was the way to go, but accomplishing this in these monstrous seas was going to be a real chore, especially with the halyard wrapped around the spreader."

Taking a few deep breaths the lean, sunburnished sailor climbed out of his cabin into the cockpit—and caught the full fury of the hurricane. The spume was being blown horizontally off the top of the cresting waves. And *Parry Endeavour* was crashing under the power of a pocket handkerchief-sized jib.

He clipped his safety harness on to the forestay and waited for a chance to drop the storm jib. "I had to be careful when stuffing it down the for'ard hatch," he recalled later. "If a big wave hit while the hatch was open, it could have ripped the hatch away, and this would have been disastrous. I was also fearful that thousands of gallons of seawater would cascade down the hatch into the forepeak.

"Every time a wave broke I had to grab the mast and hang on for dear life as tonnes of water crashed over me. Somehow I managed to unhank the jib, take the sheets off it and get it down the hatch without the yacht taking hardly any water.

"I was now side-on to the sea and clinging to the mast. I didn't want to hoist the main while the jib was still up. The yacht was still moving super fast—too fast for safety. With every roar of a breaking wave I clung desperately to the mast as hundreds of gallons of icy water cascaded over me. I unfurled the main and freed the main halyard that was caught round the spreader. Then the unfurled main was wrapped to windward round the mast by the hurricane-force winds and my strength in comparison to the wind was puny.

"As I struggled to free the sail I kept a watch out of the corner of my eye for breaking waves. My hands were frozen and I could hardly feel anything with my fingers.

"Being near the mast was the best place to be—I had something to hang on to when a wave broke over the yacht. Somehow I managed to winch the sail gradually up the mast far enough so that it no longer caught in the rigging.

"Just as I got the sail up a rogue wave hit the boat and knocked it down again. It was a super squall of about eighty knots. The yacht slowly righted itself and I went below—cold and exhausted."

The lone sailor wrote in his log: *I did it! But it took more than an hour for a task that would normally take less than five minutes . . . the super squall was a wind change . . . I notice the barometer went up a point*.

At 9.40 p.m. he noted with obvious relief: *Lousy gale continues, but some lesser periods*. Though the sea was just as rough *Endeavour* was handling them well without the spitfire jib and Sanders felt "safe", despite still being soaked through.

He snatched an hour's sleep—albeit a fitful rest—and at 4.45 a.m. the following morning, Saturday 21 November, he decided to take the bull by the horns and square the storm-reefed mainsail. *I'm off*, he wrote in his log, adding *but rough as bags*.

As pale dawn lit the angry Antarctic seas, he logged: *Wind 25–35 knots. Yacht rolls in huge sea. Beginning to tidy up the cabin and sponge dry*.

He took time out to berate himself in his logbook: *If I had hove-to under mini-main instead of running under storm jib and sea brake at 0310 yesterday most of the knockdowns and mess in the cabin would not have happened. We tried all the storm tactics. There is only one—hove-to to fully reefed main*. Fully-reefed, the mainsail was very small and specially constructed for severe storm conditions.

His stove, which had been emitting acrid black smoke, was now working well and he decided to leave it burning to help dry out the cabin. At 6 a.m. he recorded: *The wind is moderating nicely, thank goodness. What a dreadful day yesterday was*. But ten minutes later he wrote: *Gosh, a wave just crashed over the yacht. Oh well, I fibbed*.

Jon Sanders is never likely to forget his fifth rounding of Cape Horn or the hurricane that gave him the worst day of his epic 82,000 nautical mile odyssey.

2

Dare to be Different

I must go down to the sea again,
to the vagrant gypsy life,
To the gull's way and the whale's
way where the wind's like a
whetted knife.

John Masefield, Sea Fever

WHEN Jonathan William Sanders sailed alone in his sloop *Parry Endeavour* through the heads of Fremantle Harbour into the teeth of a nor 'westerly gale on the wintry Sunday afternoon of 25 May 1986, he was following his mother's advice.

For whenever he got into trouble for giving up school cricket or football matches—sheer boredom to him—in favour of messing around in boats, his mother, prolific authoress Dorothy Sanders, advised him, "Son, who wants to be ordinary? Why don't you be original?"

Although Jon Sanders tried desperately hard to be "ordinary", he always seems to come up with "original" deeds. If attempting to circumnavigate the world three times single-handedly without stopping or reprovisioning is not being original, then he should not be credited by the *Guinness Book of Records* with a dozen single-handed sailing records.

If you asked the lone sailor extraordinaire why he would want to lock himself up in "solitary" in a cramped fibreglass prison for nearly two years while undergoing frightful privations much of the time, he would grin and state blandly: "Because I like it out there." If you pressed him for a better reason, he might say: "Because it's never been done before," or "Because they say I'm foolhardy to try it." When people queried his sanity, the tall, raven-haired sailor-navigator would respond with a shy grin: "Say what you like, I'm thick skinned."

Probably only long-time friends can truly appreciate the psyche of a man approaching middle age who is prepared to put his life on the line in solitary danger to conquer new frontiers.

It takes a special kind of person—and there is no doubt that Sanders *is* special. Those who do not know him well are usually struck by the penetrating steel-blue eyes of this strong, rangy six-footer. As an individualist and a loner, he is basically shy and tends to think carefully before he speaks, then does so nervously and rapidly. He is certainly gregarious, and garrulous, in the company of friends or people he knows he can trust.

Gentle and forgiving in nature, he does not harbour grudges. Rather than suffer fools or people who have irked him, he avoids their company. His crew and those close to him attest that he is a loyal friend and a fine skipper who will listen to any crewman who thinks he has a tactic to win a race. But he is quick to point out any shortcomings within his crew—usually in a diplomatic way.

His younger brother Colin says of him: "Jon finds difficulty in fitting in with the cocktail set and he doesn't have much capacity—or like—for small talk. He rolls through the community with a great deal of ease and doesn't want or expect much attention to be paid to him. He has stuck to his pursuits without much thought about costs or sensitivities to his family. He has shown great resoluteness, which at times caused concern to our parents. These traits were probably inherited from our maternal grandfather, Canon W. J. McClemans, an Irishman who showed the same determination to pursue the direction he had chosen."

Sanders' favourite subject is, naturally, the sea and feats of sailing and navigation. His boyhood idol was Captain James Cook, and it was fitting that not only was his 14.5–metre masthead sloop named after Cook's famous converted coal ship *Endeavour*, but one of the reasons for his triple-circumnavigation was to attempt to carry out scientific work started by Cook more than two centuries earlier.

It is reasonable to assume that when he returned to his home port of Fremantle in May, 1982 after twice circling the globe non-stop and alone in his S & S 34, *Perie Banou*—setting a dozen records for single-handed voyages along the way—he would settle down and rest on his considerable laurels. These included an Order of the British Empire from the Queen, the rarely-given (nine only) Chichester Award, a Superior Achievement Award from the United States Institute of Navigation and the Epic Achievement Award from the State of Western Australia. But Jon Sanders is a restless soul and a true loner. He had to do three "laps" of the world, as he calls them.

When people ask him if he is mad, he has a stock answer: "No, but it would help." And when he is inevitably asked, "Don't you get lonely out there?" he responds: "Not really, I get on very well with myself."

In any case he could not be talked out of going. Nobody who knew him tried. His adoring parents, both of whom died while he was circling the world, understood that their son must go and challenge the world's most tempestuous capes again. His beloved Aunt Sheila (Kenworthy), who had followed his 1981–82 double circumnavigation with intense interest, made desultory efforts to talk him out of the triple rounding, but she knew it was futile. She lived to watch his triumphant return twenty-three months after he set out, but died within three months of his home-coming.

Many people suggested that Jon Sanders should postpone his departure from Fremantle on 25 May 1986 because of the stormy weather. This amused the solo circumnavigator because he knew that the thirty-five to forty-knot gale whipping the tops off big swells outside Fremantle that day was puny compared with the tempests he would have to sail through in the journey ahead.

Months of meticulous preparation were at an end when *Parry Endeavour* (the Parry foretag was in deference to sponsor Kevin Parry, a wealthy businessman) plunged through choppy seas and driving rain to start the voyage. Despite the abysmal weather, about two hundred power boats and yachts gave him an enthusiastic escort out of the harbour and a rousing send-off. The honorary time-keeper as *Endeavour* crossed the harbour mouth was former West Australian Premier Sir Charles Court, a longtime friend of the lone sailor.

Sanders' young crew of his faithful *Perie Benou* sailed with him as far as the starting line where they shook hands emotionally and transferred to a chaseboat. "Jon seemed real happy he was at last under way," said his first mate, Richard Stainton. "I've never seen him so happy."

Endeavour was low in the water with the weight of three and a half tonnes of food, water and fuel. The manifest of groceries read like a supermarket inventory and the nautical hardware on board would have almost stocked a ship's providore's store.

Jon Sanders confessed to having a lump in his throat as he headed his sturdy sloop with a storm jib and reefed mainsail standing stiffly in the gale towards the north of Rottnest Island, the popular holiday resort eighteen kilometres off the coast of Perth. His first circumnavigation was to be west-about, his next two east-about.

The first lines in the first of five meticulously kept logbooks Sanders kept during his twenty-three month voyage read: *1300—cleared heads. Gale, rain—awful but okay*. Then he recapped on the feverish activity that preceded his start. After telling of how his young crew sailed *Parry*

Endeavour down to the harbour from Royal Perth Yacht Club, he logged: *I board Parry Endeavour; storm jib hoisted, three reefs in mainsail. I alone start in gale and rain . . . gun fired from [power cruiser] Sutherland by Kevin Parry . . . gun on naval patrol ship HMAS "Adroit" misfires . . . never mind. Sir Charles Court official timekeeper.*

When he completed his first circumnavigation off Fremantle on 29 January 1987, he received documents attesting that his voyage had officially begun at 1301 and forty-two seconds. It was signed by Richard Midford, commanding officer of *HMAS Adroit*.

The solo circumnavigator was glad to be alone at sea, despite the lumpy conditions. The voyage had already been delayed three weeks and the preparations had been tedious—as had the work in getting *Endeavour* ready for a two-year stint at sea.

Endeavour is four metres longer and much stronger than the S & S 34 *Perie Benou*, in which he made his double circumnavigation four years earlier. Formerly called *Challenger*, the yacht was designed by top West Australian naval architect Phil Curran, who has since achieved international acclaim for some of his luxury power yachts. It was designed for Parry Corporation boffin Dr. Jim Chute, who sailed her in the 1979 Parmelia race from Plymouth to Fremantle to celebrate Western Australia's 150th anniversary. Dr. Chute's boss at that time, self-made millionaire entrepreneur Kevin Parry, bought the sloop for Sanders' remarkable odyssey and sponsored him to the tune of $600,000. A caring man, Parry had many misgivings about the wisdom of helping a sailor who could be on a path of self-destruction. It took a lot of soul-searching before he agreed to bankroll the attempt.

The voyage was managed and came under the umbrella of the Centre for Marine Science and Technology at Perth's Curtin University. The centre's director, Associate Professor John Penrose, oversaw the university's role in the record-shattering voyage.

Endeavour was considerably modified for the voyage by veteran boatbuilder Des Piesse—himself a talented yachtsman—

and the rigging was specially shortened and strengthened by ace yachtsman-sail-maker Rolly Tasker. Sanders had cause to "bless" both Piesse and Tasker many times during the voyage as *Endeavour* survived more than a dozen knockdowns and one collision. Much of the design work for the strengthening of the hull, building a new (shortened) mast and a new keel was done by naval architects and engineers from Curtin University, led by Kim Klaka.

Jon Sanders dubbed his sloop the "floating fortress" as Piesse installed extra stringers, deck girders fore and aft, a forward collision bulkhead and watertight doors to form flotation chambers if the vessel was holed. Her keel was removed and rebolted on with double-strength bolts. All windows were replaced with double-sided acrylic. Sanders particularly liked the forward collision bulkhead, which would allow the yacht to stay afloat in the unthinkable event of a collision with a whale, an iceberg or another vessel.

At 3.15 p.m., two hours after he cleared Fremantle heads, Sanders took down the storm jib and put up a working jib, read a few telegrams and noted in his logbook: *Rough. WSW 30–40 knots with gusts 40 to 45 knots*. Before he took a nap on the first of 658 long nights at sea, the lone sailor logged: *Seas rough, but wind appears to be moderating—25–30 knots.* He felt a head cold coming on and cursed the germs on the shore he had just left behind. Away from land he was to spend nearly two years without even a sniffle.

After breakfast on his first full day at sea he pulled one of the three reefs out of the mainsail and pulled down the Royal Perth Yacht Club burgee and a Christ Church Grammar School football jumper that had also been run up the mast for his farewell the day before. As part of a sailor's superstition, Jon Sanders always hoists a guernsey from his alma mater's football team on departing or arriving home, a habit he acquired during earlier successful sea wanderings.

That afternoon he spoke by radio-telephone to newspaper reporters, Dr. John Penrose, and his radio mentor Jack Seabrook, a much-venerated former rear commodore of Royal Perth, who was to monitor closely most of his voyage by radio.

Tired from a hard day and restless night on departure day, he slept during the late afternoon and dosed himself for his wretched cold. That night he entered in his log: *Wind light, progress not fast, full main and working jib. Watched Gregory Peck in* The Sea Wolves *on video*.

So ended his first full day at sea.

Lying restlessly in his bunk that night, Jonathan Sanders took time out to reflect on a colourful career in sail that stretched over nearly forty years, one in which the insistent lure of the sea always managed to outweigh the weightier practicalities of terra firma.

At the age of eight he had taken over his cousin's four-metre canvas-covered canoe, which he paddled with explorative delight around the Swan River near Pelican Point —an undeveloped pristine area much loved by the bird-watching Duke of Edinburgh during Royal visits. He joined the sea cadets at thirteen, sailing his own dinghy down to Fremantle to enrol. "My mother promised me a sailing dinghy if I passed first grade piano," he once said, "and though I've never passed anything much, I passed the piano exam in short time."

When his father, Colsell Sanders, took a job with the British Foreign Office in West Germany during sabbatical leave, Jonathan was enrolled at Sloane Grammar School in Chelsea, London. There he started learning the violin and enjoyed playing in the school band. His love of music (later he played the fife at Christ Church Grammar School) served him well in many lonely months at sea, and a selection of good tapes is always high on his list of priorities.

On his family's return to Perth, Jon finished his schooling at Christ Church but, forever the daydreamer, found it difficult to concentrate on lessons when he knew that within a short walk lay the Swan River and the University of Western Australia campus, both adventure paradises for a boy in his early teens. The tug of interests see-sawed, and it was obvious which was the victor when the dreaded moment came to sit the annual Junior Certificate examinations. Sanders passed only three subjects—history, geography and physiology—and, in his own words, made "dubious school history" by amassing all of two per cent in the maths exam.

When it was time to leave school—his parents realised he was not going to be an academic like his younger brother Colin and sister Lucy-Anne—Colsell Sanders approached a close friend and chief general manager of Elder Smiths, the big wool and produce company, to see if he would give his son a job. Elders would have to waive a company rule that the minimum educational requirement for new staff was a Junior Certificate. Young Jonathan started work in the merchandising section of Elders' Fremantle store, delivering parcels to the railway station in a three-wheeler pushbike, keeping the petty cash, filing and buying the manager's lunches. "The boss would often forget to pay me, so I'd have to take the money from petty cash," he recalled. "That is, until the auditor complained."

Young Jonathan was transferred to Elders' wool department, and he spent a full day every week learning about wool and the art of woolbuying. "I amazed myself," he reflected. "I managed to get top marks in theory and second top in practical and second top of the school overall."

It was customary for Elders to send their budding young wool experts away to Western Australia's pastoral areas with shearing teams—an excellent way of gaining practical experience. It was considered a pretty tough breaking-in period, according to Sanders, and his workmates advised him against going because he was "too gentle" and wouldn't be able to cope.

"I decided to resign and go north off my own bat," he said. "I told a fib and said I was going to join the crayfishing industry."

So at the age of twenty-two he was off with a shearing team to learn woolclassing.

Sanders' paradoxical life of weekend sailing and working in shearing sheds often hundreds of miles from the sea he loved so much soon earnt him the sobriquet of the "sailing shearer" or, as a variant, the "shearing sailor". But life in the shearing shed was far from easy.

"I started as a rouseabout, picking

fleeces up off the shed floor and throwing them on to the woolclasser's table," he remembered. "For several months I wondered whether I was ailing for something, because every muscle in my body ached. But I soon realised it was because I was using muscles I'd never used much before."

Young Sanders quickly became an expert woolclasser, and his ambition grew; he hankered to have his own shearing team and do contract shearing all over Western Australia. His chance came when Ted and Frank Barrett-Lennard, who leased Mount Stuart, Nanutarra and Boolooloo stations, decided to change shearing contractors and asked the genteel young woolclasser if he would provide a team.

"They made it financially easy for me and my mother helped out with the finance. I bought a new Ford Fairlane in which to accompany my team, but this was probably a mistake. I got more respect later when I switched to an old utility."

The shearing sailor would work hard with his team all week and on Friday afternoon jump into his Ford and drive through the night (even as much as a thousand kilometres) to sail his yacht in weekend club races. On Sunday night the dusty car headed back to the sheep station, and as the Monday morning's stint in the woolshed began, Sanders found it hard to stifle his yawns.

"I had the unique honour of being the first shearing team boss to be prosecuted for allowing my shearers to use wide-comb shears," Sanders recalled. "The shearers would heat the combs and stretch them so they took a bigger swath of wool at every blow. The Australian Workers' Union, under which shearers work, claimed the wide-comb shears would shorten the working time in sheds and the shearers would suffer. New Zealand shearers were using the wide combs without any union trouble.

"My Aunt Sheila, who was a lawyer, suggested I phone the AWU counsel and tell him I would plead guilty to the charge and then act dumb—which was easy for me.

"I was the first of several shearing team owners charged to go before the Arbitration Commission. I explained to the commissioner that I was only the overseer and woolclasser and it was the shearers who were using the wide combs. He fined me $5, which set a precedent for the other employers who had hired themselves $200-a-day Queen's Counsels to defend them. My aunt would have charged them only $20 a day, and some of my colleagues were furious—I was lucky I didn't get a shearer's handpiece wrapped around my head."

Jon Sanders chose a shearing run that ended in October so that he could spend the off-season sailing. Often the sailing and shearing seasons clashed, which meant a lot of weekend travelling.

Evidently Sanders was a kind boss because his shearers stuck with him for years. It became a joke that whenever he took on a new hand, his colleagues would inquire "Who's died?" Although the yachtsman tried his hand at defleecing a few sheep, he never took up the back-breaking job. "I got a nice income from my shearing team and it allowed me to spend a lot of money on my favourite pastime—sailing," he explained.

But now he was far from the shearing sheds, and all of the hundreds of station owners, shearers and wool industry people he met during his shearing team days were anxiously following the exploits of the team boss with salt in his veins as he flirted with his mistress, the sea.

3

The Prime Minister's Biscuits

The sea! the sea! the open sea!
The blue, the fresh, the ever free.
Barry Cornwall, The Sea

ON day three Jon Sanders found himself out of wind and his sails slatting. He dropped his jib and started taking an inventory of his huge food stocks. To his amazement and consternation he found several important food items missing—most important being butter, margarine and cooking oil. "I know they were on the shopping list," the solo sailor muttered to himself. "Someone has goofed."

He could find no dried peas, beans, sweet corn or carrots and the instant potato was also AWL. *Rather disappointing* he told his logbook. *But cannot do anything about it*. Sanders was adamant that he would not take on any stores during the entire voyage. It would disqualify him—as would the placement of any equipment or sails on board *Parry Endeavour*. He took comfort in ascertaining that there seemed plenty of everything else, and later was relieved to find a small quantity of freeze-dried peas, beans, carrots and sweet corn—much less than had been ordered.

Sanders observed that his yacht had two companions—black and white sucker fish that usually follow or hitch a ride on sharks. He surmised that there could be a shark around, perhaps cruising under his yacht.

Late that afternoon he radio-telephoned Richard Stainton, his leading crewman back home, who had helped stow the food on board. Stainton said he believed there was some tinned butter on board, but it was never found. Sanders admitted in another call that it was going to be dull having to cook without oil, and not have anything to put on his bread. "I'll probably be healthier for it," he added philosophically. "I've got plenty of tomato juice and tinned tomatoes so I'll make up that way." It didn't take him long to improvise by "frying" eggs in tomato juice!

Later he discovered that another important food item, sugar, was also not on board. For a man who was used to having two or three teaspoonsful in his coffee, this was a blow. He rued the fact that he had not taken the time to supervise the checking of provisions as they were loaded on board.

At 10.17 p.m. he logged: *Just watched* Man With The Deadly Lens *on video. Nice. Wind, 15 knots SE, progress good.*

As his spanking white sloop headed across the Indian Ocean in the general direction of the Cocos Islands, he thought of his mother and father and wondered whether they would be at Fremantle harbour entrance to welcome him home in twenty-three months. He had always been close to his parents, both of whom fully supported and followed his many sea voyages with great interest—and, naturally, no little concern.

Sanders, with younger brother Colin and sister Lucy-Anne, lived his early life with his close-knit family in the genteel, leafy riverside suburb of Nedlands, just a few minutes' drive from Perth.

Young Jonathan's school was Christ Church Grammar, founded by his grandfather, Canon W. J. McClemans, a graduate of Trinity College, Dublin. When he came to Western Australia, this Church of England minister was concerned for prospectors living in primitive conditions on the goldfields, where they risked typhoid and other diseases. For the unlucky, death often came without a proper Christian burial. As Sanders recalled, the erstwhile Canon was rector at Boulder, the twin city of Kalgoorlie, during the early 1890s at a time when his opposite number in the Roman Catholic Church was a fellow-countryman. "The rivalry and oratory between the two ecclesiastics became a local legend," said the grandson.

Jon's mother, Lucy McClemans, was born in Boulder as the second of five daughters. She met Jon's father, Colsell Sanders, when she was teaching at the Northam State School where he was assistant headmaster. His father, who graduated with a Master of Arts (majoring in English Literature), later got his doctorate in child psychology. One of the University of Western Australia's most distinguished scholars and later professors, his career spanned being president of the Guild of Graduates to becoming the university's academic registrar and its professor of education. He was chairman of the State's Tertiary Education Commission for several years and was honoured with fellowships of both the British Psychological Society and the Australian Psychological Society. He was also awarded a Commander of the British Empire.

His mother, who wrote forty-two romantic novels under the pseudonym of Lucy Walker, loved the countryside that figured so much in her descriptive prose. Jonathan, her first son, often took her with him when he travelled north with his shearing teams. With him she visited homesteads, shearing sheds, outback towns and even some out-of-the-way pubs. Her books were published in hardback and paperback in Britain, the United States and other countries in six languages, and she sold millions of copies.

With a literary mother and a learned father who loved fine literature, Jonathan Sanders grew up with books. He started reading Enid Blyton at an early age before graduating to boys' adventure books like Biggles and Arthur Ransom's stories. Later he favoured escapism novels, particularly those by Hammond Innes and Alistair MacLean.

A slight astigmatism in one eye prevented young Jon from playing team ball sports, and in any case these bored him. He was much more at home exploring the bushland at the university campus, with its secret swamps, creeks and ponds. This, and the nearby river, was his true adventure land.

He remembers his mother sitting hunched over an old typewriter at the kitchen table working on her novels. She would work till the wee small hours and get up late. Dad was just the opposite—he would retire early and get up early.

If Jon Sanders lacked academic application, younger brother Colin and sister Lucy-Anne made up for it. Colin was a prefect at Christ Church, where he won trophies for hockey, and a graduate of the

University of Western Australia. Lucy-Anne excelled at school and played hockey for her home State and Australian teams.

The Sanders family were fully supportive of Jon's penchant for adventurous voyages round the world. "My parents helped financially with my long voyages, because when my shearing career got in the way of the long-distance sailing, I no longer had a regular income," he said.

Now, forging across the open sea and backed by a caring sponsor, Jon Sanders had no problem with finance. He was even being paid a retainer by Kevin Parry while doing what he liked to do most. But on day four of his incredible voyage he was far from happy with the situation on board *Parry Endeavour*.

Let his log tell the story: *There are no flares on board. I wonder who would be silly or mean enough to take the flare container off the yacht. It was certainly on board for my Sydney trip*. (He had sailed *Endeavour* to Sydney the month before he started his triple circumnavigation attempt to show her to the Australian Bicentennial Authority, which accepted the voyage as a designated Bicentennial project.) He consoled himself with the thought that in most of the regions his yacht would be traversing, there would be nobody to observe his flares if he got into trouble. (He was to find the flares a month later while fossicking in the forepeak for a headsail. They were under the sail.)

Sanders was also not feeling well on this day. His cold had developed into influenza with sore throat and chest and nasal congestion. But that night he tucked into a supper of curry and rice with curried egg, stewed (dried) fruit and custard, washed down with cordial.

The following day, with a blue sky and kindly sea, *Endeavour* was running nicely before a pleasant breeze with two reefs in the mainsail and the jib down. *Should have full main*, he told his logbook, *but barometer going down rapidly*. He filled in time photographing the cabin and deck of his yacht, studying the echo sounder that was to help him fulfil the scientific purpose of his voyage, and restowed gear. He also started both of the small diesel motors installed in *Endeavour* to keep his batteries charged and noted that the front motor was difficult to start. It was to be an ominous sign.

That night, as his sloop ploughed steadily along under a slatting mainsail, Sanders settled down with his mind at rest to watch another saga of human endeavour, the movie *Chariots of Fire* from his video collection.

For the most part, leisure time was a luxury for the lone sailor, and there was generally so much to attend to that he had little chance of becoming bored.

Sailing solo meant that he had to make frequent sail changes and running repairs, navigate the yacht, keep his logbooks and sometimes steer (as a supplement to the self-steering equipment), and on top of this he had cooking chores, cleaning, laundry and his personal hygiene to attend to. At sea Sanders is as fastidious about his personal appearance as he is on land. He shaved every day—except during storms—and washed or showered regularly as long as he had enough fresh water on board. If short, he used sea water scooped up by bucket on the foredeck.

He gave himself regular haircuts and, though his hirsute happenings left much to be desired, it kept Sanders' raven locks out of his eyes. "When wet hair hangs down continuously over your eyes, you risk infection," he said. "This happened to me once and from then on I kept my hair short."

His logbooks are so well documented they would act as a manual for any sailor bent on circumnavigating the world, or voyaging afar. They are laced with wry humour and sprinkled with quaint, old-fashioned expressions like "gosh", "oh dear", "golly", "heavens", "dear me" and "darn".

He often chided himself for carelessness. At noon on day six, for instance, he scolded himself for reading ten degrees out in his longitude reckoning after "shooting" the sun with his sextant. *Bit sloppy*, he logged. *Will find fault tomorrow. Alas, I forgot my plotting specs and the scale in the South Indian Ocean for plotting is ridiculous*.

At 10 p.m. the same day he wrote: *Just watched* Flying High *sequel on video and now eating some of Elsa Finn's lamingtons. Nice sailing, full main and working jib, 8–10 knots*.

Elsa Finn is the wife of veteran Perth yachtsman Merv Finn, who often raced against Sanders in bluewater classics off the West Australian coast. On each of Sanders' lone voyages, Mrs. Finn has put a batch of lamingtons—cubes of sponge cake coated in chocolate and desiccated coconut—on board his yacht. When *Perie Banou* reprovisioned off Plymouth during his double circumnavigation in 1981, a box of lamingtons was tossed on board his sloop after being airfreighted to England. Elsa Finn well knows the solo sailor's sweet tooth.

Many of Sanders' early radio-telephone calls were to, and from, Dr. (later Professor) John Penrose, director of the Centre for Marine Science and Technology at Perth's Curtin University, and the man who put together the scientific package on *Parry Endeavour*. One of the reasons the Australian Bicentennial Authority recognised Sanders' triple circumnavigation attempt as an official bicentenary project was his desire to complete scientific research started by his idol, Captain James Cook, and to emulate some of his navigational achievements.

The eighteenth century master navigator, whose accuracy of charting is still marvelled at, was no less a wanderer of the southern seas in his pursuit of the Great South Land which philosophers of the day speculated must exist to balance the northern hemisphere land masses.

Sanders too had the same motive, but his quest was for signs of a submerged land mass. Already United States' satellite programmes had revealed evidence of submarine protuberances jutting from the ocean floor east of New Zealand, and Sanders hoped to be able to confirm their existence for further study.

For this purpose *Endeavour* was fitted with a sophisticated depth-sounder enabling Sanders to probe the hidden ocean mass six kilometres down. The sturdy sloop was also equipped with a hydrophonic unit which enabled him to listen to and record sounds of the deep, particularly dolphin and whale "talk". There was a touch of irony in this, because one of Sanders' greatest fears was the threat of whales. "Like icebergs," he said, "they don't seem to have much boat sense. So I won't be going too close to them voluntarily. One flick of their tail and these normally gentle creatures can smash a small yacht to pieces."

After nine days of sailing he had completed his first 1000 nautical miles, and he noted in his log: *Sparkling fresh south-east wind 25 knots. Good progress. Yacht appears to be going comfortably fast.*

There were more mundane entries as well in this early period, but far from being minutia they are intriguing pointers to life at sea for a solo sailor, revealing how even the smallest detail takes on a special significance. Samples:

0850: Found retaining pin on self-steering upright support worn, so hove yacht to and replaced with a later model pin. Washed track suit trousers. 1350: Started front motor to re-charge batteries, started first flick, perhaps because I am now using the port fuel tank instead of starboard. Using port fuel and water tanks because yacht listed to port because of bias in water and kerosene tanks and in loading stores. Stowage is more to port. 1830: Supper—Maggi beef curry with curried fresh eggs and freeze-dried rice. Wind is much stronger (30 knots SE) and seas getting bigger.

The very next entry in his logbook contained the melancholy news of his father's death, only eleven days after his embarkation. He logged: *Colin came on* [to the radio] *to say Dad passed away today—poor old fellow. About the best Dad there ever could be*. The news was not altogether unexpected, because Colsell Sanders was in ill health when his restless son left port.

The following day, 6 June, he wrote: *A most enormous fin went past the yacht, like large dolphin—some type of whale. Put hydrophone out, nothing to record, just usual noises*. Two hours later he sighted another huge fin—or was it the same one? *About killer whale size*, he observed, *but not necessarily killer whale. Fin grey in colour*.

His echo sounder was starting to pick up the Indian Ocean seabed at a range of five kilometres. *Very good*, he told his log. But radio communication with his minder back-home, Jack Seabrook, and with Dr. Penrose was difficult and faint. But he did manage to get through to Penrose via

Perth Radio and give him his expected date of arrival off the Cape of Good Hope —9 July. The genial, bearded boffin told him some disquieting news—that Dr. Jim Chute, Parry Corporation's scientific adviser, wanted him to have an exchange of mail off Cape Town. Sanders logged: *I am not keen for mail exchange*.

Throughout his twenty-three month voyage, the stoical circumnavigator was always apprehensive of any contact with the "real" world for fear that some person in a spirit of goodwill might include some foodstuffs in a mail package, or someone might try to set foot on his yacht. As far as Sanders was concerned—and the *Guinness Book of Records* too—either eventuality would disqualify him under the rules of single-handed voyaging.

On day fourteen at sea, Jon Sanders performed a small ceremony from the cockpit of *Parry Endeavour*. He tossed a biscuit jar with a message inside it into the Indian Ocean. It was no ordinary biscuit jar. On the morning of his departure, the Federal Member of Parliament for Fremantle (and Minister for Trade) John Dawkins, handed Sanders a jar of biscuits on behalf of the Prime Minister, who had asked that when the lone sailor had eaten the biscuits, he cast the jar into the sea with a message in it. The Prime Ministerial comestibles having gone down well, Sanders sat at his chart table and pencilled the following message:

> To whoever recovers this letter in the Prime Minister's bottle: At the suggestion of the Prime Minister of Australia, the Hon. Robert Hawke, MP, this message was placed in this bottle given to me by one of Mr. Hawke's colleagues on behalf of Mr. Hawke and thrown into the Indian Ocean on June 7, 1986 at 19 deg. 59.6 south latitude and 89 deg. 46 min. east longitude, 1380 nautical miles west of Western Australia, from the yacht *Parry Endeavour*, being sailed by the signer single-handed (solo) by Jonathan Sanders three times round the world non-stop without taking provisions on board. The voyage began in a gale on Sunday, May 25 1986, from Fremantle Harbour, Western Australia, and is scheduled to finish in Sydney Harbour, Australia, April, 1988

(approx. one year and 11 months. 1988 is the year that Australia will celebrate 200 years of European settlement, known as the Bicentennial celebrations). This voyage is an official bicentenary activity. The voyage is sponsored (paid for) by Kevin Parry, through his company Parry Corporation. The voyage comes under the umbrella and management of the Centre for Marine Science and Technology at the West Australian Institute of Technology (which is being renamed the Curtin University of Technology). Dr. John Penrose is the director of the centre and Dr. Don Watts is the overall director of WAIT.

Signed—Jon Sanders.

At the time of publication the Prime Minister's bottle with the lone sailor's message had not been found—or reported found.

4

Oops, Wrong Way

Alone, alone, all, all alone,
Alone on a wide wide sea!
Samuel Taylor Coleridge,
The Ancient Mariner

AFTER two weeks at sea, during which the specially-strengthened *Parry Endeavour* made 1826 nautical miles, Jon Sanders had settled into a routine, though he was still finding things out about the boat and its supermarket-sized food inventory. He found himself thinking repeatedly about Dr. Jim Chute's proposal for a mail exchange off Cape Town. Finally, he sat at his chart table and composed the following telegram to Parry Corporation executive Laurie Humphry:

Please advise Kevin Parry worried about proposed exchange of letters off Cape

Town. I am familiar with the coast from Cape of Good Hope to and including Table Bay, but have no chart of the region. It is a lee shore. There are four times more gales in the area than off Cape Leeuwin [Western Australia] in winter. Very heavy shipping around Southern Africa. I find it fatiguing getting in and out of places without some sleep and avoid coast and shipping in thick weather. Moreover, a guarantee would be needed that South African Military, Customs and Immigration would not board the yacht in their waters.

Kind regards, Jon Sanders.

With that off his chest he felt in a happier mood and set about a routine gear check. He found that his mainsail was in need of repair. His log tells the story:

Sun, June 8, 1340: Tore luff of mainsail about top spreader, hatch slide jammed, silly me, but think I can repair strong. 1730: Repaired sail and hoisted. Laminates of sticky-back sail cloth over tear, sewn tape each side of sail cloth along torn luff. Unfortunately, luff cord came away at peak so loose at tear. Hope it survives. The shackles that attach the slides jam at the spreaders. Shame never picked that problem before leaving. I must always luff yacht [bring it head-to-wind] *before hoisting or lowering mainsail.*

Sanders, in fact, was very happy with the mainsail, which was built by Chris Sherlock (from the internationally known Rolly Tasker firm). Sanders knew and trusted Sherlock, who had often sailed in his crew. *Endeavour* carried that mainsail for the first year before the lone sailor decided to replace it with a new one from his comprehensive inventory. The original sail, however, is still serviceable, though a little frayed, after powering the sloop for more than 40,000 nautical miles.

His last entry for that day carried a touch of poignancy. He wrote: *Dad's funeral today. I should be there*. In a faint radio-telephone talk with his younger brother Colin a few days earlier, a decision was reached that Colsell Sanders' ashes should be scattered over the Swan River near the university campus where the gentle professor and his vital family spent so many happy days. Appropriately the ceremony was to be done from the cockpit of *Perie Banou*, which was so much a part of the family's lives. So the solo sailor was at least present in his thoughts and prayers. On the day of the funeral, he had received a radio telegram of condolences from the Commodore, flag officers and members of the Royal Perth Yacht Club.

The lone sailor had a great affinity with the Royal Perth club, which honoured him with life membership soon after his return from his epic voyage. Two other local clubs—Royal Freshwater Bay and Fremantle Sailing Club—also accorded him the same honour.

In melancholy mood that night, Sanders lay in his bunk and reflected on his thirty-five years of sailing, a chequered career that started when his mother bought him a fourteen-foot sailing dinghy for passing his first grade piano exams. He remembered the day he asked his sea cadet commander, Jock Anderson, whether he would allow him to sail his skiff from Garden Island (about eleven kilometres off the West Australian coast) to the coastal resort of Rockingham by himself—his first single-handed voyage! Commander

Anderson had qualms about it, but reluctantly agreed. Immediately the fifteen-year-old sailor set sail he climbed to the top of a gantry and watched the youth all the way to Rockingham.

Sanders could not resist a smile when he thought of his first ocean-going cruising yacht called *Sirius*, a twenty-one-foot open sloop with no cabin and a fixed keel. Sanders never missed a long weekend sailing to Rottnest Island. He badly wanted to enter *Sirius* in the Iberia Cup ocean race from Fremantle to Rottnest, but because it was an open boat and therefore deemed unsafe, he was ruled ineligible.

Young Jonathan approached Royal Perth rear commodore David Foulkes (chairman of the race committee) and begged to be allowed to race. Foulkes was sympathetic and suggested he fill in a race entry form. The following morning, the day of the race, Sanders sneaked into the club office for a look at the race programme. There at the bottom of the fleet list was the name *Sirius*. The race was sailed in a characteristically strong sou 'westerly and Sanders and his rag-tag drenched crew won the race and a handsome sterling silver trophy from the P & O shipping company.

Questions were asked about how *Sirius* got into the race and the tiny sloop was barred from future ocean races. So, when Sanders heard that prominent Perth yachtsman David Orr was selling his well-performed ocean yacht *Lyelta*, he approached his mother for finance and bought the racer. His mother helped him rename her—*Theodora*, after a character in her novel *Sixth for Heaven*. The budding wool expert entered Theodora in every race for which she was eligible and won his share, though he did not set the world on fire with the veteran yacht. He was still learning.

After six years and much fun, Sanders sold *Theodora* to buy a bigger yacht. His second *Theodora* (he liked the name) was a catastrophe, albeit a speedy one. He bought the thirteen-metre plywood yacht *Saga* from ace Perth yachtsman Frank Corser and changed her name, an action many sailors believe bodes ill luck. During the 1974 Fremantle-to-Geraldton ocean classic, bad luck struck *Theodora*. She sprang a leak during a gale on the way to Geraldton, where a boatbuilder tightened the keel bolts to stop the leak. On the return race to Fremantle, the keel broke away from the hull in a moderate sou'wester in the black of night.

Sanders squirmed in his bunk at the memory. Fortunately for him and his crew, the stately cutter *Ilena*—once owned by media magnate Rupert Murdoch—was not far from *Theodora* when water started gushing in, and skipper John Court and his crew quickly sighted *Theodora*'s distress flares and heard the mayday radio call. The deck of the yacht was already awash when *Ilena* came alongside to take off the crew, who were already in a life raft. *Theodora*, which was insured for only three-quarters of her value, sank without trace.

Jon Sanders remembered how devastated he was at losing his yacht, but now he told himself that he might never have crossed an ocean if that incident had not occurred. He promised his mother he would buy a Thunderbird 27, a cabin-class yacht designed for inland waterways and sheltered ocean. But one day soon after

Theodora was lost, a sailing colleague and boatbuilder, Tom Swarbrick, took him to lunch and told him he had a Sparkman & Stephens-design thirty-four-footer hull with cabin and deck for sale. If he bought it Swarbrick would supply a shipwright to fit it out and install an engine so that Sanders could use it as a power launch.

For weeks after signing the contract to buy the hull-cabin, Dorothy Lucy Sanders' son could not pluck up the courage to tell her what he had done. But, taking his brother Colin as a one-third partner, and with his family's support, the brothers had the yacht in ocean-going condition within a year. She was named *Perie Banou* and Jon Sanders sailed her into the record books in 1981–82. The yacht has since been bought by the West Australian Government to spend the rest of her days in the State Maritime Museum.

The vast reaches of the Indian Ocean continued to surrender gradually to *Endeavour* as she forged on towards the Cape of Good Hope, aptly named the Cape of Storms by early mariners. At 4.45 a.m. on the twenty-third day at sea, Sanders scribbled a routine log notation: *Wind, jib hoisted, nice quiet progress*. Five hours later he realised just how "quiet" his progress had been—he was actually sailing the wrong way! *Ugh! What a dumb fool!* he berated himself in a later entry. What had happened was that the yacht had put itself about with a wind shift while Sanders was sleeping. He woke up as usual in the early hours of the morning and, groggy with sleep, poked his head through the companionway hatch and read the cockpit compass backwards. He did not make the same mistake twice.

At noon he observed: *First time my daily run ever went backwards!* (His distance-made-good for that day was only sixty-seven nautical miles compared with 125 the previous day.)

His log around this time revealed a preoccupation with catching fresh drinking water via a canvas bucket under the boom and a hose feeding the main water tanks stored in the aft cabin. To avoid contamination, Sanders always waited for the initial burst of rain to wash away accumulated salt from the sails before setting up the bucket. Hence there was a certain jubilation on 22 June when he logged at 0245:

Wind north and increasing, barometer falling, time to reef mainsail—three (reefs), I think ahead of what I think may be a gale in the offing.

0530: Caught 18 litres of water. Jib down for catching water in mainsail. Another rain squall approaching. Using canvas bucket with hose.

By day thirty-five he had traversed 4289 nautical miles of Indian Ocean and he noted in his log: *Should begin to feel the effect of the South Equatorial Current from now, followed by Aghulas Current later. I remember its effect late in 1975 in* Perie Banou.

The following day, 29 June, he wrote at 4 p.m.: *Been attempting to raise Cape Town Radio on four, eight, 12 megs off and on today. No success.*

A few hours later he sighted the first sign of mortal life since leaving Fremantle. He logged: *Ship four points port bow. Fishing or restricted vessel, red lights fore and aft, approx two miles. Do not like hovering their proximity.* Four minutes later: *Perhaps two vessels, one mile, will alter course.* Six minutes later: *Gybed. Plain ship's riding lights, on reciprocal course*. A further ten minutes: *Gybed back. Wind gusting 28 knots ESE*. The ship apparently passed in the night, because this was the last mention of it.

At 11 a.m. next morning he wrote happily: *Despite strong following wind, hung out washing high enough, I hope, out of any spray. Washing rinsed in fresh water caught previously, but with a little too much salt for drinking.*

Parry Endeavour's passage so far had been relatively uneventful, and though weighed down with food and marine equipment, the sloop was sailing reasonably well. Sailing north from Fremantle to cross the tropic of Capricorn and get into the path of the South-East Trade winds had been a good tactic. But with the approach of landfall, the prospect of having to sail close to a lee shore in a busy shipping lane for a mail exchange still nagged at him, and he hoped to clarify the position in a call to Cape Town Radio.

On 2 July 1986, his thirty-ninth day at sea, he pencilled into his logbook at 11.40 a.m.: *Wind change to NW. Not much wind and rain coming, I hope*. His water tanks badly needed topping up before he headed northwards in the South Atlantic towards the Equator. Five minutes later he finally got through to Cape Town Radio, which promised him "sked" (radio schedule) at 2.30 p.m. next day. But this did not eventuate, to his chagrin.

The following day he noted at noon: *Surprising. A set against the yacht. Will soon get into Aghulas Current*. Fifty minutes later: *Time to reef mainsail*. Thirty-five minutes on: *Heavy rain and squall to 35 knots*.

Part of Jon Sanders' great success as a single-handed sailor is his ability to read weather conditions accurately—and take heed of them. When racing a yacht he will push it to its limits, but always with safety the prime factor. But sailing alone when no speed records are being attempted, he sails conservatively and carefully. He never ventures on deck without wearing his safety harness—"unless I know I can swim faster than the yacht is sailing." Throughout his triple circumnavigation Sanders was seldom caught napping by sudden squalls that could damage sails and rigging. On the rare occasions this did happen, he literally *was* napping—trying to snatch a precious few minutes' sleep in order to stave off fatigue.

This stormy July afternoon Sanders was glad he had put three reefs in the mainsail, because at 3.30 p.m. he noted in his log: *Proper gale at the moment, 49 knots SW*. At eleven-fifteen that night he logged: *Gale continues, wind west, 35–40 knots. Will heave-to*. Half an hour later he heaved a sigh of relief into his logbook: *Hove-to. Much better on me and the yacht. Wind over 40 at times*.

Still hove-to at 10.15 a.m. next day, Sanders huffed: *Cape Town Radio definitely avoid making radio-telephone contact with me and when they do they prevaricate. I'll try St. Helena*. Early that afternoon he logged triumphantly: *Got through to Cape Town Radio and they were very helpful—how strange! Spoke to Sheila Cheminais in Cape Town. Son Mark will be in helicopter as I sail past Cape and later on the boat for the mail drop*.

(Mark Cheminais is a close friend of Jon Sanders, having crewed on several ocean races with him on *Perie Banou*, races like the Cape Town to Rio de Janeiro (1976) and the Sydney-Hobart (1977).

In mid-afternoon that day he noted: *Wind west and rough. Oh dear, slow, bumpy progress*. Exhausted, he turned in, but awakened at 3.50 a.m. when he sensed in his sleep that the yacht had a different motion. The wind had dropped and swung, putting *Endeavour* eighty degrees off course per courtesy of the self-steering gear. After his usual breakfast of Weeties, milky coffee and eggs "fried" in tomato juice, he noted: *Not much wind. Sea quietening quickly, blue sky, bit of cloud and rain here and there on the horizon. I think it will be a quiet day*.

But by 8 July, day forty-five, the wind was up again and Sanders put three reefs in the main. At 9.15 a.m. he logged: *Cape Town Radio kept their sked, wow! 165 miles east of Port Elizabeth, 65 miles south-east of East London*. As he approached the South African coast he noticed unmistakable signs of civilisation —shipping. The wind moderated and out came the mainsail reefs, but after a few hours Sanders noticed the wind shifting to NNW and building up. At 9.48 p.m. he noted: *Three reefs in main, strobe light on* [to make his yacht visible to shipping]. *Methinks I will take the headsail down; going too fast into head sea.*

As he neared his rendezvous point with the Royal Cape Yacht Club for the mail exchange, Sanders saw more and more shipping and trawlers. This was a worry to him, because at night he slept only fitfully and got out of his warm bunk every half hour to look around the yacht. At 10.55 p.m. on day forty-six he noticed a ship on his port bow about two miles away. It looked like a trawler, but whatever it was, it respected *Endeavour*'s sailing rights and passed at right angles to Sanders' wake. "Good old strobe light and radar reflector," he told himself.

The solo sailor was worried about a big blister-like sore that had formed on his left eyelid. *Probably does not like salt water*, he wrote. *Have put antibiotic eye ointment on it*. The following morning the infection had worsened and he felt some stiffness in his left jaw. He put himself on a course of Amoxil from his well-stocked medical kit. He blamed the infection on constantly-wet hair rubbing against his eyelid and immediately lopped five centimetres from his forelock. It stayed short for the rest of the voyage. That afternoon he logged: *Eye quite a mess*.

Shipping was getting thicker and Sanders cursed the impending mail exchange. At 3.55 p.m. on day forty-eight the lone sailor wrote: *Land ho! South Africa*. Soon after dark he sighted the lights of a port and saw ship after ship, prompting him to log: *It is a very shippy place*. At 9.15 p.m. he started his motors for battery charging when a ship appeared to be on a collision course, but a few minutes later it changed direction.

The following night he noted with alarm: *Oh dear, my strobe light has stopped working*. After an interview with the Australian Broadcasting Corporation he noticed a ship approaching from astern and stood ready to take evasive action if necessary.

At 6.55 p.m. he logged: *Ship getting closer . . . passing close astern . . . can hear motor . . . wish strobe light was working . . . ship 100 yards away . . . another ship approaching from astern*.

And so the nervous circumnavigator

spent a restless night dodging shipping, though he never once had to engage his engine to escape danger. His nerves were a trifle frazzled when he made his last log entry for the night at 11.10 p.m.: *Very annoying. No wind and main slats (flaps) heavily*. About midnight he scribbled an addendum: *Watched some of Monty Python's* The Meaning of Life *on video. I found the humour boring and in very poor taste. I threw it overboard*.

Progress was painfully slow on day fifty (30 July), a Sunday, as *Parry Endeavour* drifted towards her rendezvous point for the mail exchange. At mid-morning he noted in his log: *Becalmed*. That afternoon when he decided to start his motors to recharge his batteries, he found them both difficult to turn over. This was to be the start of his engine problems, which saw him complete three-quarters of his voyage without engines, relying entirely on solar panels for recharging.

But now the Cape of Storms was starting to live up to its evil winter reputation. A strong wind had sprung up from the west and after Sanders had put his sloop about, he found he was sailing backwards for a while. When the wind reached thirty to forty knots in mid-morning, he decided it was time to reef the mainsail down. At midnight he logged: *Seas big, gale continues. Loom of Cape Aghulas light seen*.

After breakfast next morning he spoke with Mark Cheminais on radio-telephone and while they were talking, a South African Air Force DC3 circled his yacht. At 2.30 p.m. he noted that he had tacked under the lee of Cape Aghulas, the southernmost point of South Africa. *Can see town and lighthouse several miles away,* he wrote. *Helicopter due in one hour*.

The gale rose and fell and rose again. He took down his working jib and hoisted his trusty spitfire jib. Squalls of forty knots were hitting *Endeavour* head-on. At 3.40 a.m. on 17 July he wrote as he hunched over his chart table: *Would lay Cape Town region possibly now if one tacked. I will give it one more hour or so*. Three hours later: *Gale continues. Wind 35–40 knots NW. Time to go about*.

By noon the gale had abated and the reefs came out of the mainsail. At 3.50

p.m. he logged: *Land ho! Cape Peninsula*. He noted that the mail meeting was to be held the following day three nautical miles south-west of Green Point. Ships and trawlers seemed to be everywhere he looked. Just before dusk he started his forward motor to give his batteries a last boost before nightfall. *Must burn lights all night on mast to fend off ships*, he noted.

Three minutes after midnight on the day of the mail exchange, he logged: *Heavy wind, rough sea. Will gybe now and remain hove-to with fully-reefed main*. By 1 a.m. he had thirty-four miles left to the rendezvous, and shortly afterwards hoisted the storm jib in the face of rough seas and a gale blowing forty to forty-five knots. His log entry at 3.05 a.m. was cryptic: *Terrible night, rough as bags. Gale. Wish I could heave-to. Blow this rendezvous.*

Endeavour passed three more ships or trawlers in the early morning darkness, but as the first pale streaks of dawn appeared on the horizon astern of the sloop Sanders logged more cheerfully: *Sea conditions much improved nearer coast, but visibility very poor*.

Sanders constantly "spoke" to his

logbook—he was still using the first of five books—as if seeking reassurance that his tactics for the unwanted sea meeting were correct . . . *5.40 a.m.: Rain causing nil visibility. 6.05 a.m.: Gybed yacht and now sailing reciprocal course for 20 minutes because of poor visibility in case I am closer than I think. 6.25 a.m.: Gybed around, back on original course. 7 a.m.: Windy, bleak. 7.35 a.m.: Getting close to coast, a lee shore, very rough. 7.50 a.m.: I think I will put a tack in.*

These dramatic, almost minute-by-minute references show how a mail exchange at sea in winter is a far cry from sailing blithely up to a waiting launch on benign seas, shouting a few pleasantries and then sailing on.

The exchange eventually was made without too much trauma at 10.30 a.m. that day, and, as usual, Jon Sanders was right on time. The launch *Jacqueline* from the Royal Cape Yacht Club drew up alongside *Parry Endeavour* in rough and dangerous seas. As the lone sailor logged: *They threw waterproof container on yacht (first time went into ocean). I took mail out and put mine in and threw container into ocean. They picked up. Sea rough and dangerous*. Overall, he concluded, the manoeuvre to get near Cape Town was dangerous in winter weather, and unwise.

Under the *Guinness Book of Records* rules laid down by Squadron Leader D. H. (Nobby) Clarke, Sanders was allowed to take on board letters and newspapers, but nothing else. He could have had mail exchanges on his second and third roundings, but decided against it because of the obvious hazards.

Jon Sanders was too exhausted, mentally and physically, to open his mail straight away, though he had been away from his friends and loved ones for fifty-five days. He got *Parry Endeavour* sailing on course again, still in the shipping lane, and tried to grab twenty minute snatches of sleep during the afternoon, continually poking his head out of his companionway hatch to scour the horizon for ships. At 6 p.m. he logged: *Awoke from snooze to find* Parry Endeavour *ringed by trawlers*.

With the worry of the mail exchange behind him and his sloop now back on course—albeit slowly—for the South Atlantic, Sanders felt more relaxed next day. He cheerfully noted at 7.30 a.m.: *Nice small dolphins with yacht*. But early in the afternoon: *Large green supertanker going to pass close ahead of the yacht. I am becalmed and will start motors in case (and to charge batteries*). Only after his yacht crossed the tanker's propeller wash did the solo sailor open his mail and greedily devour the contents.

5

Crossing the Equator

"What's the good of Mercator's North
Poles and Equators,
Tropic zones and meridian lines?"
So the Bellman would cry: And the
crew would reply,
"They are merely conventional signs!"

Lewis Carroll,
The Hunting of the Snark

AFTER rounding the Cape of Good Hope, Jon Sanders set a north-westerly course that would take him past the islands of St. Helena and Ascension towards the Equator and north to the tiny rocks of St. Peter and St. Paul, which was to be his turning point before he headed south again for a rounding of Cape Horn. His original intention when he left Fremantle nearly two months earlier was to sail north of the Equator as far as the Cape Verde Islands. Under the rules laid down by the *Guinness Book of Records*, a true circumnavigation must take the sailor above the Equator for at least twenty-four hours, and Cape Verde was the original turning point chosen by Sanders. However, at the suggestion of his Perth radio contact, Jack Seabrook, the solo circumnavigator decided he could save himself about 10,000 nautical miles during his three globe-girdlings if he chose St. Paul's Island as his turning point.

Explained Seabrook, who monitored every mile of Sanders' double circumnavigation four years earlier: "It will take you twenty-four hours of sailing to get around the island, which is sixty nautical miles north of the Equator, and the Argos satellite can monitor and authenticate you as being north of the line for at least a day." Sanders agreed that it was a good idea and a note was sent to Nobby Clarke to see if he shared the same view. He did.

Jack Seabrook had known Jon Sanders since he was a kid sailing a trainer dinghy on the Swan River. "I knew his parents for many years and it impressed me the way Jon was always willing to help other sailors," the former rear-commodore of Royal Perth Yacht Club said. "It was an honour when Jon asked me to head his organising committee for his double circumnavigation in 1981–82, and monitor his progress by radio for his triple-rounding attempt."

A radio "ham" since his childhood, Jack Seabrook was born in the picturesque country town of York, about seventy kilometres inland from Perth. The silver-haired farmer-pastoralist and sea dog had walked with a limp from the time he suffered osteomyelitis in the hip when he was fourteen. But it never affected his mobility or his energy. Night after night he would travel the few kilometres from his home in suburban Nedlands to the Royal Perth Yacht Club to try to call Sanders from the radio room, one of the most sophisticated in the southern hemisphere. While monitoring Jon Sanders' five solo circumnavigations, Seabrook knew intimately the sea conditions he was encountering and all of the navigational problems that beset a circumnavigator. He became so engrossed in the remarkable voyage, he could tell what Sanders was thinking most of the time.

To the affable septuagenarian, Sanders is a superb yachtsman and a brilliant navigator, one who makes provision against heavy weather well in advance. "He respects the sea and I believe he can get out of almost any predicament." These words proved true, time and time again.

As if to celebrate his rounding of the Cape of Good Hope, Sanders gave himself a haircut after he had read his mail. He used his mother's old kitchen scissors which he had borrowed for the voyage. *It really does look as if the moths have been having a go at it—a close crewcut*, he told his log.

That night he spoke to Mark Cheminais, who told him that his mail exchange the previous day had made the front pages of the Cape Town newspapers. He mused in his log before climbing into his bunk: *Why do I not round a mark near New York, USA on my third circumnavigation? . . because I might prang a ship*.

As he sailed north-westwards in a mild sea, he noticed that a wind vane from his self-steering had fractured. In fitting one of George Montgomery's heavier-built vanes, he wrote in his log: *I fractured retaining jaws trying to make it fit with a cold chisel. Stupid Jonny!* Early in the afternoon he sighted a whale and quickly put his hydrophone over the side. But he heard nothing.

The infection in his left eyelid had been arrested by the antibiotics he had prescribed for himself, being reduced to a small, painless sore.

Soon after midnight on day fifty-nine he heard rain on the cabin roof and went on deck to rig up his canvas bucket and hose to the mainsail. By 8.30 a.m. he had caught about 130 litres of valuable water and celebrated with an all-over wash. By nine o'clock that night the going was anything but pleasant as he logged: *The waves are huge, insomuch one has to wait till yacht gets to top to look out. Full moon*.

Now that he was sailing well out of any shipping lanes, he turned his satellite navigation equipment on only once a day—to get a noon fix. This was to conserve his batteries, which were now being kept charged by his solar panels. He always checked his own sextant reading against the satellite fix, and invariably he was only a minute (one mile) or two out. His progress was good under a balmy sky and running before a twenty-five-knot warm breeze. He flippantly logged: *Jonny-wonny the Woo-Pooh has got the South Atlantic trade winds.*

His voyage now sixty-five days old, the former shearing team boss was surprised to see in the distance a white-painted ship—it looked like a trawler—heading towards him. As it got closer in mid-morning he saw it was a twin-funnelled ship of about 3000 tonnes with the name *Casablanca*, home port Rotterdam. He waved to the ship, but he saw no sign of life on the bridge. After the ship had passed on his port side he noticed a man standing on the stern. *I bet it was on auto pilot*, he told his log. *No lookout.*

With his engines becoming less reliable—he suspected water in the fuel—he relied more and more on the sun to recharge his batteries. On day sixty-eight he noted in the early afternoon: *Completely out of wind. It is all overcast, but cloud-cover thin—the sun shows through. Keeps the solar panels busy charging batteries. With sat-nav turned off except for a couple of hours to get one fix and no over-use of the two-way radio (cannot get through), but making use of the cabin lights at night and using TV-video for two hours, but no navigation lights, the solar panels are coping in this region. In other words this yacht would be able to cope and operate all electronics—with care—should the engines fail. Nav. lights would have to be used very sparingly in such conditions. I only burn nav. lights near coast and shipping lanes. For the main the yacht is isolated and the lights are always off.*

That evening he spoke to his brother and Dr. Jim Chute by radio-telephone and was told that Nobby Clarke had approved the new strategy of rounding Isle St. Paul instead of Cape Verde Islands and that he was free to sail his own course from now on. *Thank goodness*, he logged. *Now I am responsible for my own mistakes without their help*.

The lone sailor was not exempt from silly little mishaps that more often befall weekend sailors. For example, when tossing a bucket over in order to take the water he neglected to fasten it properly. Worse still, for Sanders, he had done it twice!

His general progress now was so good, he mused jokingly in his diary: *Four times!!?!—Why not? I'll be ahead of schedule if not.*

On day seventy-five as *Endeavour* reached or ran nicely before balmy breezes, he noted: *No sea birds of late. There are never many birds in deep ocean trade winds, unlike the Roaring Forties where they always accompany me or are about the yacht.*

The quietness and solitude of the sea seemed to be all-pervasive, and the following night Sanders was struck by how low in the west and how red Venus appeared—he even wondered if it was a ship.

As he neared the island of St. Helena he felt so bored one night he took out a bottle of port placed on board by his old friend and sailing adversary, Bill Fitzhardinge, a former vice-commodore of Royal Perth Yacht Club. After quaffing half of it, he tossed the remainder overboard. Jon

Sanders had always enjoyed a drink, usually beer, while ashore but is adamant that solo sailing and alcohol are bad mixers. A few days out from Fremantle he found no fewer than nine bottles of port on board *Endeavour*. Crewman Richard Stainton had planted them there well knowing his skipper would probably not accept them. Sadly—partly because they were from close friends, partly because it was a waste of fine port—he threw all but Fitzhardinge's overboard. "They take up weight and space," he explained on the radio-telephone, "and I don't really want to drink them—I hope nobody is offended."

As he sailed past St. Helena—the island on which Napoleon Bonaparte was exiled in October 1815 (and where he died on 5 May 1821)—Sanders watched the last of his videos, *Educating Rita*, rating it a "good movie". It was one of the more pleasant legs of his voyage, for he had always found the tropical Atlantic to be much more mild and pleasant than the tropical Indian Ocean.

On day eight, 12 August, Sanders eagerly opened a package that had been placed on board *Endeavour* the morning of his departure. The label read: *Not to be opened till Aug. 12*.

The circumnavigator had a fair idea what was in the parcel, for he read the handwriting of Hillary Sawyer, the shearers' cook who had worked with his shearing team for many years. Today was Sanders' forty-seventh birthday, and he was delighted to find inside the parcel some of the fruits of the shearers' cook's culinary art. Speaking through St. Helena radio-telephone that day, he divulged the contents—home-made biscuits, home-dried fruits, jams and a flask-sized bottle of home-made brandy. Said Sanders: "I'm about to celebrate my birthday by eating them and drinking some of the brandy." His final entry in his log for that day was: *End of birthday me, and all I am is older*.

Over the radio Sanders admitted being apprehensive about rounding Cape Horn in a westerly direction—always considered the "wrong way" by circumnavigators. "I've just been studying my admiralty charts," he said, "and I found a warning that to round the Horn from the east during August-September equinox is dangerous with heavy gales, snow and ice. But I've had it comparatively easy so far —except round the Cape of Good Hope— and I'm fit enough to tackle the Horn in any conditions." He ended on a cheerful note—"Tell everyone I'm fit and well and enjoying the voyage."

As *Endeavour* made good progess towards Ascension Island, Sanders noted at mid-afternoon on day eighty one: Do not feel 100 per cent today. He put it down to some purifying tablets he put in his starboard water tank. He logged: *Makes the water smell like a very over-chlorinated swimming pool and my lips and throat to burn*. That night he started watching his video library for the second time, screening *The Man Who Would Be King*.

The following day he complained of his first headache of the voyage and surmised it was eye strain from too much reading. But at 11.20 p.m. he logged: *Just brought my supper up. I think it is the water, but might be the tablets I put into the water. Shall drink juices out of cans tomorrow*. Sanders kept away from the water in his starboard tank the next day and drank only canned fruit juice. At ten o'clock that night he wrote: *Fit as a fiddle, but drank no water today, just juices. I'll try water tomorrow, but boil it first*. The following night he reported: *Bit of a stomach ache again—it's the water. Probably the purifying tablets I put in it*.

He was now in radio touch with Ascension Island as *Parry Endeavour* made good progress—between 130 and 135 nautical miles a day—in the path of the South Atlantic Trade winds. Always thinking of ways to make life easier, and safer, Sanders decided to rig travel lines from the cockpit, over the cabin roof to the inner and outer forestays. *I can now move from cockpit to bow and quickly transfer from one travel line to the next with my safety harness, and always be connected to the yacht—I hope*, he wrote in his log.

On Monday 18 August he logged his noon position as just over a degree (sixty miles) south of the Equator. That night as the lone sailor slept in his bunk, *Endeavour* sailed across the line into the tropical North Atlantic. At 10.15 a.m. the following day he hoisted his jib for the first time in many days as the wind was now on his stern quarter. He logged: *I am sailing more northwards to get into the Doldrums to catch rain, but this had made the cabin a bit warmer as breeze not blowing through the cabin, because of increase in boat speed and wind angle*. At 4 p.m. he sighted a ship off his starboard bow, the first such sighting in more than three weeks. He observed: *A cargo ship, about 10,000 tonnes, could do with a paint job. Could not make out name with binoculars*.

He was now heading toward St. Peter and St. Paul rocks, his scheduled turning point, but he had no intention of turning there. He needed to top up his water tanks and would sail on into the Doldrums to find rain. At 5.40 p.m. he tightened up his sheets and course. The Guinea Current was setting the yacht to the west and he did not want to run into the rocks, which jut out of the Atlantic about twelve metres. At 10.15 p.m. he logged: *Cleared St. Paul and Peter by lots*. The following afternoon he mused: *I must be the only yachtsman in the world looking for the Doldrums*.

Steamy day eighty-nine produced no

rain, but Sanders recorded it as the hottest day of the voyage thus far—31C. Just before dawn he sighted dolphins swimming with the yacht, and after lunch he put out a fishing line for the first time—no luck. The solo sailor is not a great fish-eater, but now he felt like a change of diet. On his 1981–82 double circumnavigation he had not taken fishing lines. (He bought some at a Fremantle ship chandlers, but left them on the counter.)

At 8.45 p.m. he was surprised to see a ship going by heading towards Brazil. *What's that ship doing in my ocean?* he asked his log.

On his ninetieth day at sea he was still searching for rain, and at noon he noticed, with great expectations, the sky becoming overcast. At 4 p.m. he logged: *Looks like rain in front. Hope so—and lots*. At dusk the first visitor he had received in three months—a small sea bird he could not identify—flew into his cabin. *Hope it stays*, he told his log. *Guess it won't*. His guess was correct.

At two-thirty the following morning *Parry Endeavour* sailed into pouring rain, accompanied by little wind. At dawn

Sanders triumphantly wrote in his log: *Water tanks, jerry cans, toilet, sink, kettles, jugs, cordial bottles, all full of water*. It was time to head south.

6

Mid-Ocean's City Block

Icebergs behoove the soul
(Both being self-made from elements
least visible)
To see them so: fleshed, fair, erected,
indivisible.

Elizabeth Bishop,
The Imaginary Iceberg

AS *Parry Endeavour* sailed southwards to recross the Equator and head for the Falkland Islands region and a later encounter with Cape Horn, Jon Sanders took advantage of full water tanks to do some washing. His clothes were stiff with salt, but soon they were hanging fresh and clean on a line stretched from the mast to a tensioned windward running back stay. As he finished hanging up his laundry, the lean, sunbronzed circumnavigator sighted a tanker approaching from astern. An hour later it passed his yacht on the port side and he identified it as a Polish ship, the *General Yaruski*, and he spoke to the radio operator on VHF Channel 16.

He had not been able to get through to his brother, Dr. Penrose, Jack Seabrook or the author for several days, but nobody was worried. Everybody knew exactly where *Endeavour* was in the North Atlantic—soon to be South Atlantic. Thanks to a sophisticated satellite system called Argos, the yacht's position could be pinpointed several times a day, even in the unlikely event that Sanders did not know where he was. This marvel of modern communications was worked with the help of a satellite called Noah 9 that was whizzing round the earth at a height of 850 kilometres in polar orbits that took only 101 minutes.

At the Centre for Marine Science and Technology in Perth, the genial Dr. Penrose explained how science could be applied to help mariners. "On the stern of *Endeavour* is a platform transmitter that radiates out in all directions a special code signal at sixty-second intervals. It's a low-powered signal with a code identifying

Jon's platform. There are hundreds of code signals throughout the world. Noah is carrying a whole lot of packages and one is a receiver for the Argos system."

As Noah approached *Endeavour* it received a reading from its platform, and it took another one when it was receding. The signals give a high-low combination depending on the Doppler effect (which can be likened to the way an approaching car makes a higher-pitched noise to the one when it is retreating). The signal data was stored on board the satellite until it was downloaded to a computer on Wallops Island in Virginia, USA, every few orbits. A computer on the island sent the data to a world clearing house in Toulouse, southern France, which sent it on to Dr. Penrose's centre.

"We believe the system is accurate to within three kilometres, usually to within a hundred metres, and Jon's manual sightings have always been quite close to the computer's," said the scientist.

If Sanders had to abandon ship, he would first activate an alarm button on his transmitter platform. This automatically would alert the French scientists at

Toulouse, who would notify the French Coast Guard, which, in turn, would notify the Perth centre and the Sea Safety and Surveillance Centre in Canberra. If, for some reason, the transmitter ceased to send out a proper signal (as it did later in the voyage), a similar process would start. The last thing Sanders would do before climbing into his inflatable liferaft would be to grab the platform with its transmitter (it had a special release lanyard). The platform, which could run on its own batteries for sixty days, would continue to emit signals and his exact position could be plotted and radioed to searching aircraft or ships.

The circumnavigator had two other safety allies on board *Endeavour*—his radio (later to fail) and his EPIRB, an acronym for Emergency Position Indicating Radio Beacon. Radio beacons from this device, which floats, could be picked up by overflying aircraft, though most of Sanders' voyage traversed remote stretches of ocean where few aircraft are seen. The Toulouse boffins sent up to seven position reports a day for the lone sailor and they followed his voyage closely, taking a personal interest in a man they had never met—or were likely to meet. Their position reports were logged daily on a big map at the Perth centre.

As *Endeavour* plugged away to windward towards the Equator, Sanders reported in his log that conditions were humid and he cursed himself on day ninety-five for missing a radio sked with St. Helena Radio. At 12.45 a.m. the following day he again chastised himself, this time for forgetting to turn his distance log back on after turning it off four hours earlier while he tried to make radio contact with Miami Radio. *Silly me*, he logged.

On the morning of 29 August he wrote in his logbook: *Yacht on course, sailing south, blue sky and sea. Batteries charged only by solar panels now for many weeks*. His custom was to rest one bank for about a week every third week, thus always maintaining a bank in reserve. There was also a fourth bank of two batteries for the 24–volt Argos system, which had its own two solar panels and was not connected to the rest of the yacht's 12–volt system, solar panels or engines. (The Argos system uses very little power.)

The solar panels and regulators were manufactured by Solarex and installed by Tim Pauley, a WAIT masters student.

That evening Jon Sanders made contact with his home city by radio-telephone through Miami Radio. The operator's voice from Miami—about as far as you can get from Perth—came through loud and clear: "I have a call for Mr. Schmitt from the yacht *Parry Endeavour*." A second later a very Australian voice said "wow" from a position about sixty nautical miles south of the Equator. Sanders was amazed at how quickly he got through from his splendid isolation.

"I just picked up the radio phone, called Miami Radio—Whisky, Oscar, Mike—told them your number and I was through in seconds," the impressed circumnavigator said. Giving his position as 360 nautical miles north-east of the "corner" of Brazil, he spoke about catching rainwater in the Doldrums and an unsuccessful fishing foray that day. "I wasn't surprised at not getting any bites," he said, "because you have to be within a hundred miles of land or an island to catch fish."

He said he was feeling well, despite a considerable loss of weight and was looking forward to the challenge of Cape Horn, which he expected to reach before the end of September.

Having imparted his own news, the lone sailor was eager to hear about events "back home", in particular the America's Cup, then about to start off Fremantle. His sponsor, Kevin Parry, headed the Kookaburra syndicate which was to win the right to defend (but then lose) the cup Alan Bond won in Newport, Rhode Island, in September, 1983.

As he sailed under sunny skies on day ninety-nine (Sunday 31 August), he logged *Should pass the island of Fernando de Noronha* [off the shoulder of South America, north-east of Recife] *in about six hours. The last time I passed close to Fernando de Noronha was while sailing* Perie Banou *single handed from Rio de Janeiro to Barbados in 1976.*

After spending a quiet "centenary", Sanders sailed into a gale with heavy rain the next day, but at least this enabled him to top up all water tanks and containers.

Day 105 saw kindlier weather, and from a satellite navigation "fix" Sanders ascertained his yacht to be much farther south than he thought, probably because of the south-flowing Brazil Current which could run up to two knots.

As he headed down the Brazilian coast towards the Falkland Islands, the weather moderated and progress was good under sunny skies. He logged just before noon on day 108: *Man has been about. I have just passed a plastic bucket floating in the sea*.

The following day he had his last sked with St. Helena Radio, by now at the limit of its range. At about this time he also experimented with his log entries, noting *I WONDER IF MY LOUSY PRINTING WOULD BE EASIER TO READ THAN MY WRITING*. But after one more entry in his lousy printing, he went back to his tiny scrawl.

While most of his friends back in Perth were watching their favourite football team in action, Jon Sanders spent the afternoon of Saturday 13 September servicing his mainsail for his impending rounding of Cape Horn. He sailed under jib alone for five hours as he worked on his main, repairing chafing. That night he listened to the final night of the "Proms" concert from Royal Albert Hall, London, by courtesy of the BBC

The following day he got through to Rio Radio and spoke for twenty minutes on the radio-telephone to Perth. He sounded apprehensive about reported weather conditions around Cape Horn where for three successive days winds had been sixty-five knots and the temperature minus 18 degrees. "I've also heard reports of pack ice about a hundred miles south of the Falklands, so it's going to be a bit chilly down there," Sanders added. He had decided to set a course to take him between the Falklands and Patagonia, though he believed he would not sight the Falklands, because he intended to sail closer to the Argentine coast in deference to westerly gales often encountered in the region.

When asked about his daily menu, he responded: "I drink coffee and Milo off and on all day, made with hot, full-cream powdered milk. For breakfast I had muesli and milk, lunch, freeze-dried savoury mince and rice, supper, freeze-dried lamb and peas with corn and canned tomatoes. I try to mix up the meals as much as possible. Tomorrow's supper will probably be tinned Hawaii chicken and macaroni and tinned tomatoes."

The day after this chat, Sanders logged at 10 a.m.: *How annoying. While outside discovered yacht sailing wrong way. Put about and now going to windward, bumpy and rough, with two reefs in mainsail and jib—on course. This is the second time ever—the first time June 17, 1986—I have gone backwards*. He explained that earlier that morning when he was only half awake, he had read his cockpit compass from inside the cabin, which meant that he had read it backwards. He had done this hundreds of times, but this time, with sleep in his eyes, he had failed to realise he was sailing a 180–degrees opposite course.

His noon log entry read: *All last night and today grey and damp. Suspect I am now into the Falkland (cold) Current. Saw first albatross in a lot of weeks this morning*. That night after supper he logged: *Black, raining, windy. Nearly on course. It's winter!*

His pronouncement was backed up the following day by a force eight gale which moderated at lunch time. But he wrote: *Nothing's worse than a full-blown gale to stop suddenly and leave the yacht to roll terribly everywhere in a big, rough sea, which is what it is now*. Minutes after he wrote that a line squall came through and he was forced to put three reefs in the mainsail. His last entry for the day was to report a forty to forty-five-knot gale from the south.

The farther south he went the colder it got. *Nip in the air*, he told his log on 19 September, *and likely to get nippier. Nice breeze, on course, about 300 miles east of the Uruguay coast*. The sloop was now being visited by several species of birds. He wrote: *Got pigeon-sized brown sea birds with varied white markings flying around the yacht. Pretty bird, called Cape Pigeons, I think*. That afternoon: *A grey bird like a dove with pointed wings and dark markings, always found by me in the southern oceans, is flying about with the pigeons and albatrosses*. Just before dusk he added: *Just sighted the tiny black and white bird that flies about in the southern oceans.*

Soon after noon on day 121 he sighted a pod of five whales only about fifty metres from his sloop. He put about to avoid them, realising that one whack from a big bull could end his voyage suddenly. By the time he got his hydrophone out of the stern cabin the whales had disappeared and he heard nothing but sea sounds from his headphones.

His cabin stove was again proving to be a headache and he logged on 24 September: *I sometimes leave one burner of stove on to warm cabin with a small metal sheet on legs above the burner. In the last month or so I have used only one burner for cooking, because of pressure gauge leaking near right tap of stove burner, also less methylated spirits for priming needed. It seems I have plenty of kerosene for voyage, but not enough methylated spirits. I feel a pressure liquid stove for a voyage such as this is not a good idea. But that is what I have got.*

When he woke up from a short nap at eight-thirty the next morning, *Endeavour* was sailing slowly northwards instead of south-westwards, but he soon corrected this. That evening he got through on a radio sked with Argentine Radio, only to be frustrated: *They do not understand my international radio code. They do not understand English nor me Spanish.*

Day 125 found him becalmed. Although it was sunny the cabin temperature was only 9.5C. *The sea is the murky, dirty colour that is found in this part of the South Atlantic*, he wrote. It was getting colder by the day. The following morning he logged: *It is tracksuit pants, fleecy-lined shirt and yachting jumper, because of the nip, but it is a beautiful day. Just passed a seal.*

As he sailed inside the Falkland Islands he saw more shipping and trawlers, including a big Japanese mother ship. At mid-afternoon on 3 October he estimated *Endeavour* to be sixty nautical miles west of Jason Island in the Falklands group, and at 7 p.m. he was seventy-seven miles west of West Falkland Island. An hour later he complained: *Another bloody trawler*. At 8 p.m. he was buzzed by a Royal Navy helicopter and had a radio conversation with a navy ship. *Nice to have the Royal Navy about*, he wrote in his log.

Next day—day 133—was to prove an interesting one for the lone sailor. In pitch darkness at 2 a.m. he noticed the lights of a ship approaching from astern. *Methinks, perhaps Royal Navy*, he told his logbook. Forty minutes later he could not contain his curiosity and called the ship on his VHF radio and confirmed it was the Royal Navy. *Wow*, he wrote, *I've got an escort!* But the ship peeled off after a while and disappeared.

At 10 a.m. he logged: *Wind south (not much). 6.5C outside. I'm leaving the reefs in because it is so cold on hands reefing and unreefing*. Same afternoon: *Out of wind. Using special scrubber on long handle, I cleaned side of yacht. Turned into cold, but nice fine day with little progress. Lots of albatrosses sitting in ocean looking like ungainly ducks. I always get becalmed for a while in this region*. At 9.15 p.m.: *No wind and Falkland Current taking yacht north*.

After breakfast the following morning an Argentine Coast Guard vessel came alongside *Endeavour* and Sanders' heart sank. He feared that an officer might try to board the yacht, which might have disqualified him under the rules of single-handed sailing—though it would scarcely constitute "outside assistance". But a genial officer politely suggested that Sanders should fly his national flag and he quickly dragged the flag from its locker and ran it up his backstay. The coast guard men waved and headed off in a north-westerly direction. The wind was starting to pick up and Sanders hoisted a full main and working jib. But by noon the wind was building quickly and he was forced to reef down. He logged: *Three good and tidy reefs in mainsail. I suspect wind will increase, so I've put them in before it does. The sea is covered with icy spray and so making my hands very sore.*

Big dolphins—the biggest he had seen—played around his yacht in the early hours of day 135 and Sanders put over his hydrophone and recorded a loud "human-type" whistle. The temperature in his cockpit was down to 3.7C and inside the cabin with the stove going for an hour it was 13C.

At 10.30 a.m. he logged: *Isla de los Estados ahead of yacht—Tierra del Fuego!* His navigation was spot on. He had intended to pass through the Straits of le Maire, which are south-east of Grande Island, part of Tierra del Fuego, but he noted a day earlier that the wind was too much on his bow to go through the straits and he opted to sail east of Estados. By noon he could see Estados plainly. *Some snow on mountainsides*, he noted. *Must clear Estados by more than six miles to the east because of dangerous overfalls in the area*. At 2.06 p.m.: *Rather confused sea at moment. Swells from Drake Passage mixing and I suspect tidal currents affecting things. Crazy sea*. At 4.30 p.m.: *Yacht is now due east of Estados and being set to the east (unfortunately). Also close-hauled cannot lay course*. An hour later: *Getting very bumpy again, squall coming up*. At 7.10 p.m. he had a radio sked with Argentine Radio, who asked him when he would be rounding Cape Horn. He responded: "In two days, I hope."

The temperature inside his cabin next morning had dropped to a shivering 5.7C. He had known for weeks that there was a danger he would have an encounter with an iceberg in this region. But he leapt to his feet in the cockpit at mid-morning when he saw an iceberg about a hundred metres high and as big as two city blocks a few hundred metres to the north of his yacht. "Yikes!" he expostulated, and grabbed his video camera to start filming the mass of ice—from a respectful distance. But as the iceberg receded in the distance, Sanders was worrying about his yacht's progress in the confused sea and wind.

7

Round the Horn

Familiarity with danger makes a brave man braver, but less daring. Thus with seamen, he who goes the oftennest round Cape Horn goes the most circumspectly.

Herman Melville, White Jacket

WITH the iceberg behind *Parry Endeavour*, and hopefully no more ahead, Jon Sanders had another worry—adverse winds and currents. At mid-afternoon on day 136 (7 October) he logged: *Getting nowhere. Made SSE with SW wind and current last night. Went about to make westing this morning and wind veered to west, so I am back-tracking almost. But if the wind goes to NW, it is better to be north (of here), so that one can make west (or SW with current), then when wind veers SW, make NW, hopefully past Cape Horn by then. I can well understand Captain Bligh's problem. It is not just the wind against (but worse when the wind veers against your next tack) and the current against. I will go back north. Hope for north component in wind. After Cape Horn, hope for south component. SW usually follows NW wind.*

At 4 p.m. he wrote: *The satellite navigator makes me wonder. Between 1403 and 1516 I did terrible. Between 1516 and 1553 much better. Wind and steering the same. With west wind the port and northern tack takes me into stronger adverse current, the starboard tack and southern tack presumably increases the ice risk for night sailing.*

Fifteen minutes later, after checking his position again, he logged more cheerfully: *Since noon I've made some westing. Better than nothing*. At 4.25 p.m. *Wind change to SW. Now making west, nearly*. At 7 p.m. he logged: *From 1900 yesterday to 1900 today I have sailed 113 miles, but only made good towards Cape Horn 20 miles*. At 10.15 p.m.: *Wind has been very light but now seems to be filling in from the NW. (If it will only last 24 hours or more and not get too strong.)*

While Sanders slept on his problem, the wind picked up to thirty knots from the north-west and *Endeavour* was once more on course. At 8.40 a.m. with this reasonably favourable breeze still blowing, and 105 miles to go to Cape Horn, the lone sailor confided his strategy for rounding the Horn in his logbook, as if seeking reassurance: *Now if the wind goes SW it would be better to err course to south (it will eventually go SW), but if it goes west, a northern err would not matter and the sea would be flatter because of Tierra del Fuego. I think I will steer direct course 254 deg. true for Cape Horn. But as my self-steerer never can steer exactly, I will err north side.* Almost in the same breath he added: *These days I have the stove going for an hour to two hours two or three times a day to warm cabin, which it does very well. Blue sky, very windy sea. Keeping an eye out for icebergs.*

These were busy and anxious hours for the solo circumnavigator, who was about to make his third (two in 1981–82) lone rounding of Cape Horn, the world's most notorious cape, one that has been the watery graveyard of many a mariner. He noted that an average 1.4–knot current had been against his yacht for five hours. He observed that the wind was only moderate —twenty to twenty-five knots—probably because he was in the lee of del Fuego. *It is a good breeze* he confided at 6 p.m. on day 137 (8 October). Now the gap had been closed to fifty-two miles.

A little after his final radio sked with the Argentine Coast Guard he logged: *Wind slacking off. Perhaps because of land to north*. His last entry for the day was at 10 p.m.: *Not much wind, but barometer still falling. Will keep all three reefs in mainsail*. Sanders well knew it paid to be conservative.

As a cold dawn broke the following day he could see Cabo de Hornas, as South Americans called it, ahead of his starboard bow. Tierra del Fuego was clearer than he had seen it before and he noticed snow on some mountains. He decided that rounding the horn without music in these conditions would be a travesty, so he climbed down into his cabin and put on a tape of Gilbert & Sullivan's HMS Pinafore.

It promised to be a rarely benign rounding, he told himself. By mid-morning the wind had moderated to twenty knots. For a man so long at sea he could not fail to be impressed by the spectacular scenery to the north. *Endeavour* was plugging away against the strong Cape Horn Current, but getting there.

Not long after noon Sanders logged: *See buildings on Horn Island, pebble beach for landing for lighthouse. I am close to breaking reef not far away*. At 1.40 p.m.: *Quarter of a mile off Cape Horn, can hear the waves breaking. The wind is light, the sea is flat and the yacht is slowly and gracefully sailing past the Greatest Cape—with Beethoven's Pastoral Symphony No. 6 on the cassette player. Dark in the south-west, could be south-west change. Hope not*.

At 1.58 p.m. he logged: *Due south of Cape Horn, 56 deg. S, 67 deg. 17.6 W. Light wind change pushed yacht slowly a little farther away. View is excellent. Some mountains have snow on top. Couple of teeny pockets on Cape Horn. One mountain is very snow-topped.* At 3 p.m.: *Cape Horn region nice view and very quiet sea. Like a small inland lake for calmness. Not like the last time I passed the Horn in* Perie Banou *April 13, 1982 in a frightful gale.*

At 4.27 p.m. a seal swam up to the yacht and seemed to want to play. Sanders grabbed a tin of sardines and fed his new companion.

As darkness pulled a black silken mantle over a tranquil Cape Horn the lone sailor logged with some relief: *It was a nice pleasant quiet day close to and off Cabo de Hornos.* Quiet indeed it was—he was even becalmed for an hour. But this was to prove deceptive; at around eight o'clock he took the reefs out of the mainsail in the hope of catching some water, then, with the barometer still dropping, decided to reef down again. Half an hour later his stratagem proved correct. He logged: *Wind 25 knots, came quickly. Fully reefed, expect gale.* At 8.50 p.m., as the glow from the lighthouse on Cape Horn started to fade, he logged: *Visibility now poor. Nice day today, but what about the icebergs tonight . . . I'm tired.*

By midnight the Horn was at last living up to its time-worn reputation. A gale from the WNW was blowing at thirty-five to forty knots. At 1 a.m. Sanders noted: *I will heave to. Just wait till this squall goes. Glad I had pre-reefed main. Becalmed off Cape Horn and now hove-to in gale off Cape Horn!* He had been trying all evening to contact his friends in Perth to tell them about the day's benign rounding, but Argentina's Ushuaia Radio, located on Beagle Island in the Cape Horn area, had not answered. It was not till 2 p.m. the following day, with a gale continuing to blow, that he was able to get through with the details.

"I'm having a real stormy ride now," he said. "For the past twelve hours it has been blowing between forty and sixty knots. The waves are about sixty feet." He had made good only eighty nautical miles in four days. "At this rate it will take me another week to get round the Horn," he added. "The boat is falling heavily off waves, but it is handling it well. The barometer is rising and it's 3C outside."

Lost at the southernmost tip of South America, Tierra del Fuego was once a dark and forbidding outpost. Its name, meaning "Land of Fire", was given by the Spanish explorer Magellan, who saw mysterious flames on the island's unknown shores.

For centuries afterwards, Tierra del Fuego was feared by sailors for the icy winds that blew their ships on to jagged rocks—and the Horn won its infamy. The only refuge from the storms was Ushuaia, a primitive whaling station that doubled as a prison.

Today this land at the end of the world is a strange combination of modern tourist centre, Klondike-style boom town and gateway to one of the world's last great wilderness areas. It was the radio station in this growing town, approached through snow-capped claws of granite, that Jon Sanders relied on for his radio contact with the rest of the world—while his radios were working.

At 1 a.m. on day 140, (11 October) *Endeavour* was still hove-to in the gale, but by 7.30 a.m. it had moderated to twenty to twenty-five knots. "It's from the north-west (where I want to go)," Sanders muttered to himself. "I really don't want to go any farther south on starboard tack. I will wait for the sea to die down a little and put the jib up."

At 8.50 a.m. he logged: *Jib up, going directly into a big sea, but sailing preferred course. Must be careful of Ramirez Island*. Later that morning he sailed the farthest south he had ever been—57 deg. 16.5 S, or seventy-eight nautical miles south of Cape Horn's latitude. He was in iceberg country. At 11 a.m. he scribbled: *Just fell very heavily off head sea. Wind just veered north-east, on course, but barometer going down fast—all the signs of a pending heavy gale*. But by 3 p.m. the seas had abated and Sanders took advantage of the lull to do some spring cleaning in his cabin.

This proved, ominously, to be the lull before the storm.

By 1 a.m. on day 141 it was blowing a full gale, and in winds of up to fifty knots, the lone sailor fought his way for'ard in giant seas to drop the jib and secure it to the foredeck. When he returned half-frozen to the comparative warmth of his cabin, he wrote in his log: *Somewhere south of Tierra del Fuego, Jonny's in a fierce gale*. At noon that day he tried to take video footage of the seas, but a big "greenie" swamped the camera.

The gale lasted all day and *Endeavour* made little progress. In fact he noted at 4.43 p.m.: *I'm in the same position as I was at 0923, seven hours back*. Just before midnight he had to again clip his safety harness to the travel line and venture up to the foredeck to resecure the jib he had lowered hours earlier. Back in the cabin, he wrote: *Job done. Gale continues. Go away gale!*

The storm heeded his bidding, and by dawn it had dropped. Sanders rehoisted his jib and tidied the reefs in the mainsail. *Endeavour* was making little progress in a big head sea and swell. At 11.30 a.m. he logged: *Not much wind, not much progress. Barometer falling. Weather brewing itself up for another diabolical gale*.

For his icy trip around the Horn, the solo circumnavigator had rugged himself up like a sea-going eskimo with the following apparel: long woollen socks, deck shoes, track suit pants, thermal long johns, jockey underpants, fleecy-cotton shirt, thermal sleeveless waterproof vest and his old school football jumper. On some days he swapped this for a thermal zip-front cardigan.

When he ventured on deck it was in foul-weather gear but without shoes or gloves. His bare feet get a better grip on the wet deck and his hands can work the sheets easier without gloves, but they quickly get sore with the cold.

On his bunk which is to port in the cabin, he slept with a sleeping bag opened out like a doona or quilt and a rug over him. He slept with another sleeping bag folded under his bunk, because he found the bunk cushion was not thick enough. Stored under his bunk are his charts and spare wind vanes for his self-steering, all of which are on top of his port water tank.

Just before dusk he noted that the wind had backed towards the south-west. *I am in a good location for a south-west wind*, he wrote. *Looking for a change. Some blue sky*. An hour later: *Quiet sailing on course—just a little more wind needed—not too much, mind you*.

Squalls sprang up again the following

day, but *Endeavour* made some westing. Sanders had a rough ride for two more days in bitterly cold weather. The temperature was only 6.5C in his stove-warmed cabin on day 145 as his sloop bounced over steep seas. At mid-afternoon he logged: *Got myself a gale. Think I will drop the jib and go quiet for a while*. At 10 p.m.: *Oh dear, it is awfully rough again*. By 11 p.m. he was hove-to with a fully-reefed mainsail and no jib.

He was still hove-to at sun-up, but soon after the icy dawn, the gale had moderated and Sanders thought it was time to get going again. After breakfast and two cups of coffee, he rehoisted the jib and *Parry Endeavour* tacked into a twenty to twenty-five-knot westerly in a big sea. That afternoon the lone sailor gave himself his second haircut for the voyage. "A bit cold for a crewcut," he told himself as he donned a woollen beanie.

The wind rose again the following day and Sanders was beginning to get accustomed to a rough ride. At 3.30 a.m. he hauled himself out of a warm bunk to drop the jib. By mid-morning it was time to rehoist the jib. *Jib up*, he reported, *and off, bashing to windward*. At 1.40 p.m. he logged: *Wind coming from exactly where I want to go (NW). Tomorrow if same (usually is) I will sail north, even if the yacht makes easting doing so. Like in* Perie Banou *in this region 1982, nightly gales. I suppose tonight's one is coming up, barometer is falling*.

His words were again prophetic. At 9.50 p.m. he scribbled: *It is rough tonight going to windward, a lot of cross swell and sea*. Two hours later: *Oh dear, time to take the jib down again*. Midnight: *Jib down, hove to*. At 8.30 a.m. the following morning he was still hove-to, and he logged: *The yacht throws itself about too much, but more worrying is the green water over the foredeck in continuously sailing boat to windward over 30 knots. Hove-to is boring, but safer*. At mid-morning he decided to tack the yacht to see if he could make some northing, but five minutes later told his log: *Tacked around, now going back from whence I came. Perhaps the wind will back more*. In the middle of the afternoon he was still hove-to ("what a waste of time"), but at 5.30 p.m. he hoisted the jib again. At 5.45

p.m.: *Going north, but east, too. This rotten weather cannot last forever.* He logged at dusk: *If the wind does not moderate in the next two hours will drop jib again—too rough. Too much heavy water over the yacht.*

His penultimate entry for Sunday 19 October (day 148) was: *Rough going. Sailing northwards, some easting. Weather usually moderates when the barometer reaches 1006. It is now 1006, wish weather would moderate. It is supposed to!*

Day 150 (21 October) started badly. At 1.15 a.m. Sanders wrote in his log: *Oh dear, the wind has headed the yacht and so prevented me sailing true north, now north-east. Will continue on this tack a while longer to get as much north as possible, and then tack and make west.* At 2.45 a.m. he tacked and noted: *Gale on way.* Just before dawn: *Gale time! Better drop jib, rather than risk busting something.* By breakfast time a full-blown gale of forty-five to fifty knots was tearing at *Endeavour*'s stout rigging and rain was lashing the sloop, but it was too rough to catch any water in the mainsail.

During these post-Horn days Jon

Sanders was constantly hoisting or lowering the jib, reefing and unreefing the mainsail, as his yacht bumped her way northwards and sometimes eastwards as well.

He had a long haul across the Pacific Ocean ahead of him, but at least Cape Horn was behind, with all its attendant dangers, and he could ease just a fraction the tight reins he was holding on himself.

8

A Scientific Diversion

Sweet and low, sweet and low,
Wind of the western sea,
Low, low, breathe and blow,
Wind of the western sea!

Alfred, Lord Tennyson,
Sweet and Low

AFTER 155 days at sea, during which *Parry Endeavour* had logged 17,030 nautical miles (but actually made good 16,231 miles), Jon Sanders sat down at his chart table in his comparatively warm cabin and worked out a course that would take him across the Pacific back into Australian waters.

After studying the manual *US Ocean Pilot Chart of the South Pacific* he expected that nice weather and suitable breezes should be found by sailing along approximately 26 deg. S latitude. *Ocean Passages for the World* suggested 12 deg.

S. He planned to continue from here to sail north-west to 38 deg. S, then continue westward if the wind proved favourable, or north-west towards 26 deg. S if not. *I suspect I will make west from 38 deg. onwards*, he wrote in his log. *Going north when breeze unfavourable. From my other voyages across the southern South Pacific I have found more easterly component winds than the* Pilot *atlas suggests. Also southerlies, south-westerlies and northerlies can also prevail—we will see. There might be more chance of catching rain at 38 deg. S at the early stages of a "low" without the wind being too strong—perhaps! In other words, I'm half expecting now to make good westing from 38 deg. S, may never get to 26 deg. S—we will see.*

Having got that off his chest, he took advantage of the smooth sailing conditions to do his (almost) daily exercises. Although the constant motion of the yacht—especially the wild gyrations in a storm—keep a sailor's muscles working all of the time, Sanders often went even further by completing an exercise regimen mapped out for him before his departure. Most of the exercises could be done in the sitting position like raising legs one at a time, then both, stretching the toes, or raising each knee against chest, then both together, or jog-sitting using arms and legs, or bending elbow to opposite knee fifteen or twenty times. While standing he would draw in his stomach for seven seconds ten times and on the eleventh hold it in for fifty seconds. With no room for jogging, he would run on the spot to the count of one hundred.

When the lone sailor completed his double circumnavigation of 1981–82, physiologists declared that he would not be able to walk properly for several days after being cooped up in a ten-metre yacht for fourteen months. Sanders confounded them all by leaping ashore at Royal Perth Yacht Club and bounding up three flights of stairs to the locker room for a shower before lunch. Psychologists opined that he would need considerable "debriefing" before again being able to mix with the outside world. Sanders laughed at the suggestion and mixed gregariously with his clubmates and friends.

His formula for keeping in good mental

balance, even though alone for many months on end, is a healthy one. "I read a lot on long voyages and I tune into every BBC, Radio Australia or Voice of America broadcast I can get on my shortwave radio," he explained. "I speak to my friends or radio monitors as often as possible, and when I'm not talking to them, I talk to myself, aloud much of the time."

When the Duke of Edinburgh invested him with the Chichester Award at Cowes in 1982, he asked the lone sailor if he talked to himself at sea. The response: "One would have a big voice problem if one didn't." He elaborated: "You've got to talk aloud to yourself. If you go for hundreds of days without speaking, your voice muscles clam up and if that isn't enough of a problem, you'd probably risk infection too. If you're not very good at talking to yourself, and you want to do some long-distance single-handed sailing, then you'd better practise."

But now as he headed north-west towards a favourable latitude, the solo sailor was having difficulty getting into a radio conversation. At 8.30 p.m. on

Monday 27 October he logged: *I was trying to raise a coast radio station—Pacheco, Ushuaia or Rio (believe Valparaiso speak only Spanish)—to no avail. But the electrical interference from the radio on 12 megs turned the log back to zero and the boat speed seems stuck. And the wind speed (indicator) is way out.*

But Sanders had no gripe with his sails, his sloop's trusty "engines". As he sailed before an eighteen-knot SSE wind, he observed in his log: *So far in 158 days the only sails used have been the mainsail I departed Fremantle with—built by Tasker's Chris Sherlock—the heavy-duty working jib, also Sherlock's, and a storm jib.*

On Saturday 1 November Sanders spent the afternoon servicing his mainsail, putting laminates of adhesive tape where chafes were beginning to appear and greasing the sail slides with vaseline. He also serviced the jib, which had become chafed while lashed to the foredeck in gales. He then stripped, greased and cleaned the main halyard winch. The whole chore took him four hours, but he was in no hurry on this cold, overcast day, sailing through quiet seas. His position was 1597 nautical miles north-west of the Horn and he had averaged only 69.4 miles a day since rounding the cape.

Sanders used the next two days of quiet weather, during which he was often becalmed, in stripping and servicing his three deck winches. At dawn on day 163, he logged: *Calmer than Lake Monger* (a lake near his suburban Perth home). After breakfast he complained to his log: *Much ringing in my ears when I wake of late. I wonder if it is the high pressure?*

At noon he wrote: *Overcast, but not heavy, flat, clear ocean and horizon. No sea birds, nothing. Just me and a quiet ocean*. But by ten o'clock *Endeavour* was joggling along in a light southerly, which came and went all night and the next day. Before supper on day 164 he logged: *In for my nightly calm. The sea is like oil*. Overnight it picked up and Sanders quickly hoisted his No. 1 genoa and full main and *Endeavour* was off, tacking nicely in a NNW wind of twelve knots. By 2 a.m. the following morning he was out of his bunk reefing the mainsail as the breeze filled in to thirty knots from the north. But it was shortlived, and out came the reefs.

Light drizzle began to fall; never one to miss an opportunity to top up his fresh-water tanks, Sanders rigged his canvas bucket under the main. The result was hardly stunning—eight litres in seven hours, or in his words, "Catching rain, dribble by dribble." He kept the rain bucket out for the rest of the day and night with better results—135 litres, enough to last forty-five days.

The wind was now coming from the direction in which he wanted to sail—west—and progress was slow. It prompted the lone sailor to confide to his log: *To arrive in Fremantle January 26 (Australia Day), 1987, must average 96 miles a day for 7500 miles, allowing for zig-zags, capes and tacks. Tactic now to sail due west when possible and choose the northern (port) tack for time being in west winds*. He had hardly finished writing this when he recorded: *Oh dear, the wind has further headed yacht on this tack*. And at 10 p.m.: *The wind is all coming from the wrong way—bit of NW in W wind*.

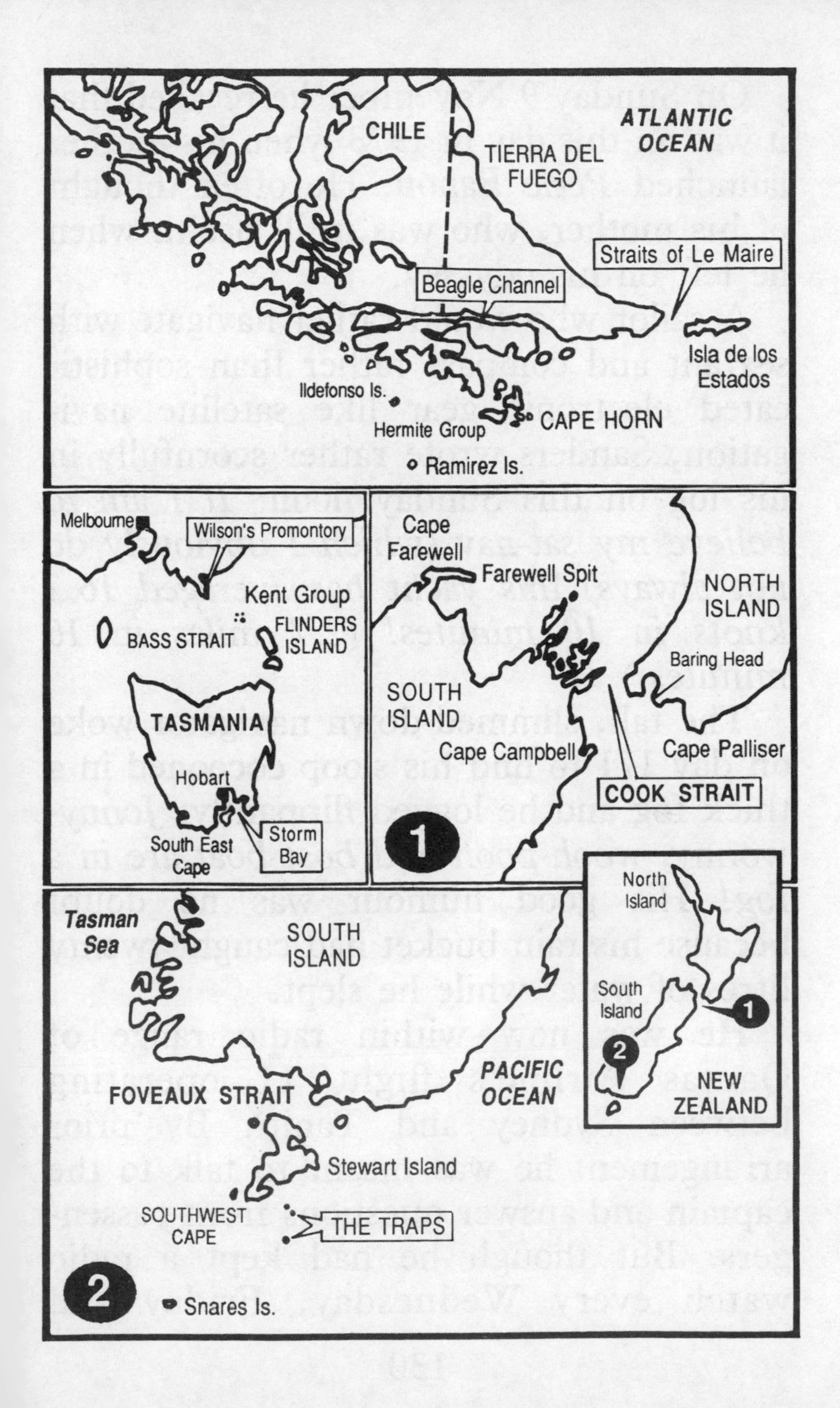
CHILE
ATLANTIC OCEAN
TIERRA DEL FUEGO
Straits of Le Maire
Beagle Channel
Isla de los Estados
Ildefonso Is.
CAPE HORN
Hermite Group
Ramirez Is.
Melbourne
Wilson's Promontory
Kent Group
BASS STRAIT
FLINDERS ISLAND
TASMANIA
Hobart
South East Cape
Storm Bay
Cape Farewell
Farewell Spit
NORTH ISLAND
Baring Head
SOUTH ISLAND
Cape Campbell
Cape Palliser
COOK STRAIT
1
Tasman Sea
SOUTH ISLAND
North Island
South Island
1
2
PACIFIC OCEAN
NEW ZEALAND
FOVEAUX STRAIT
Stewart Island
SOUTHWEST CAPE
THE TRAPS
2
Snares Is.

On Sunday 9 November he recalled that it was on this day in 1973 when his mother launched *Perie Banou*. He often thought of his mother, who was in ill health when he left on his odyssey.

A sailor who would rather navigate with sextant and compass rather than sophisticated electronic gear like satellite navigation, Sanders wrote rather scornfully in his log on this Sunday noon: *If I am to believe my sat-nav (which I obviously do not always) this yacht has averaged 16.2 knots in 10 minutes! (2.7 miles in 10 minutes.)*

The tall, slimmed-down navigator woke on day 171 to find his sloop cocooned in a thick fog and he logged flippantly: *Jonny-wonny, wooh-pooh and boat-boat are in a fog!* His good humour was no doubt because his rain bucket had caught twenty litres of water while he slept.

He was now within radio range of Qantas Airline's flight 11 operating between Sydney and Tahiti. By prior arrangement he was meant to talk to the captain and answer questions from passengers. But though he had kept a radio watch every Wednesday, Friday and

Sunday between 6.30 a.m. and 7.30 a.m. he had failed to make radio contact.

Now in that empty region known as the Variables, far south of Easter Island and "civilisation", Sanders began to understand why it was so-called. The breeze dropped, veered, built up, dropped and filled in, banks of fog rolled over the yacht and rain, heavy at times, fell. As a consequence, when he attended to his log at 4.10 p.m. on 13 November (day 173) Sanders noted that his water tanks were full to the brim.

A particular source of annoyance to the lone sailor at this point was that the boat speed log was malfunctioning. The log and boat speed ceased to register correctly on the B & G monitor. As a result, miles run had to be estimated by hours sailed by Sanders' own assessment of speed. Unfortunately it was the high power put out by the Codan 4000 radio transmitter that had damaged some of the functions on this sailing monitor.

As *Parry Endeavour* plugged westward, the lone sailor wondered if he would have time to explore the seabed of a patch of ocean 220 nautical miles to the north with his echo sounder—as requested by Dr. John Penrose. He decided against making the detour—there was a risk of losing time for Kevin Parry's America's Cup rendezvous off Fremantle. He had promised his sponsor that no matter which twelve-metre yacht defended the cup for Royal Perth Yacht Club, he would try to sail past the cup course off Fremantle a few days before the final match started on 31 January 1987. He would have to make his landfall on the day chosen by his sponsor and sail past his starting point without stopping at a given hour. Quite a logistical exercise, he told himself. Would he be on time? Only the winds over the next two months would tell.

On the afternoon of day 176, a Sunday, Sanders decided to tackle a big pile of washing which had been building up for the past two months because of the weather and lack of fresh water. His rather curious technique might raise a few eyebrows among the experts, but it evidently got the right result. As Sanders explains, he soaks the lot in a mixture of salt water, detergent and shampoo for twenty-four hours, washes the clothes in the same mixture and follows this up with a salt water and shampoo rinse. Then comes a second rinse, this time in fresh water, to allow for proper drying rather than remaining always damp and attracting mould. Wrote Sanders in his log: *At the moment hanging out to dry are 10 pairs jocks, two pairs socks, four pillow slips, two cotton-flannel shirts, one windcheater, one T-shirt. Soaking for tomorrow to wash are one bath towel, one beach towel, two flannel sheets, three cotton-flannel shirts and in wash bag are one windcheater, two tracksuit pants and two pairs of socks.*

It was a good day for drying washing but bad for sailing. He logged at 2 p.m.: *Sunny, 14–knot west wind (trying to go west!)* He again tried to radio Qantas flight 11, but without success. Later he was to find out why he could not make radio contact with the flight. At 7.05 p.m. with the wind rising and falling and veering constantly, he had trouble steering a proper course. His slow progress, he noted, reflected the fact that from Cape Horn to around New Zealand the current was against the yacht.

He was picking up Radio Australia by

now and catching up on whatever news not conveyed to him separately by his friends on private radio. He also managed to contact Wellington Radio staff and asked them to pass on a message to Royal Perth Yacht Club that all was well on board *Parry Endeavour* and the voyage was on schedule.

On 19 November he entered a slight grouch in his logbook: *I find the US Pilot Charts not very accurate. Rarely does one ever get a proper south-west wind. Lots of westerlies and north-westerlies and northerlies. To the west of Cape Horn the US atlas also suggests a reasonable percentage of south-west, but not so. WSW, but not often SW. To the east of Cape Horn, yes, SW there.* After his noonday position fix he logged gloomily: *A bad day's run, only 54 miles made good.*

He cheered up that evening when he managed to get through to his friends in Perth by courtesy of Wellington Radio.

The westerlies persisted the following day and *Endeavour* made little progress. "I wish the wind was SW or NW or any direction except west," he muttered. "South-west proper is very rare." If he was sailing round the world from west to east, it would be different. And his next two circumnavigations were east-about. At 5 p.m. he wrote: *Oh dear, I'm getting nowhere*.

His spirits soared on day 181 when he logged at 2.30 a.m.: *Wow, wind change to south, but not a lot of it*. But two hours later: *Running out of wind. If it is not all the wrong way, it is not at all*. He surmised some unwelcome passengers in the shape of gooseneck barnacles were slowing his yacht.

After logging 18,500 nautical miles on his epic voyage, he had some pertinent observations to make about *Parry Endeavour*. Although easy to handle, he found she did not perform well to windward as might be expected, but was "good and comfortable" off the wind. Sanders noted: *This yacht has a nice wide beam and after sections, not a lot of freeboard and fine pointed or wedge bow. For a yacht of this type the peculiar thing is that the keel and mast are well forward; that weight, together with the water tank, which should have been built into the aft cabin instead of the forward section of the saloon, and the forward reinforcement, takes the yacht bow down—a design fault. She digs her nose frighteningly into rough seas if going too fast and when the wind is forward of abeam. It is necessary to heave-to to slow her down in rough seas going to windward.*

Despite all this, he concluded, *Endeavour* had an easy and comfortable motion.

That night he again mulled over his slow progress in his log: *If I head north I gain no westing—lose if I keep tacking the making board as I am. I get farther and farther south and more undesirable westerlies. Never proper south-west which would help. Nor, of late, NW or N. It is my expected* [America's Cup] *schedule I worry about, otherwise it would not matter.*

The following morning he realised why he had been unable to contact Qantas flight 11 by radio. He had been trying to raise them at 0630 plus eight hours instead of minus eight hours. "No wonder they never answer," he told himself. "They're probably tucked safely away in the hangar." A few days later, however,

Sanders kept his radio sked with the pilot-captain, talking for more than ten minutes with him and his co-pilot with the conversation being relayed to the main cabin for passengers to hear.

Soon after midnight on Saturday 22 November he logged: *Yacht on course. That's nice. Wind is up a bit, 20–25 NW, that's okay, but better change jib now . . . oh dear, here goes*. It took him less than five minutes to replace the number one jib with a working jib and three hours later *Endeavour* was tacking westward—slowly. Sanders had a bucket under the mainsail and collected some brackish water. At noon that day he logged: *Yacht still sailing due west in 25–knot NW wind. Cross my fingers and toes it will continue to do so for a while*.

His dissatisfaction at his rate of progress was leavened by the fact he could now call English-speaking radio-operators, report his position and find out what was happening in the world. At 2 a.m. on Sunday 2 November he spoke with the Royal Yacht Club of Tasmania and told them all was well on *Parry Endeavour*. At 10.45 a.m. a gale-force north wind of forty knots caused Sanders to scamper on deck, clip on his safety harness and put a reef in his mainsail. The storm jib was already on the forestay. At 11 a.m. he again made the uncomfortable sortie on deck to put two more reefs in the main. At 1.45 p.m. he logged: *Sea becoming very rough*. Later in the afternoon the wind veered north-west and dropped to twenty knots. He logged: *Yacht a little sluggish . . . I could take two reefs out now, but barometer is so low.*

The wind went around to the south and it started raining in the early hours of the following morning—out went the canvas rain bucket. After breakfast he logged: *Not so much progress as yacht was over-reefed overnight. But at least I'm as gentle with the yacht as possible. After all, it is the longest non-stop voyage in history I am attempting*. The barometer was low—998 millibars. Cryptic log entries for the rest of the day convey the vicissitudes of the wind and weather.

1.59 p.m.: *Wind has shifted west. Oh dear*.

2.05 p.m.: *Wind getting up, 25 knots west*.

3 p.m.: *Put three reefs in mainsail; now wind's dropped.*

3.30 p.m.: *Two reefs out with work jib. Got the rig right for now! Close-hauled. Not quite on course.*

5.05 p.m.: *Squall 30 knots.*

5.40 p.m.: *Rain, bumpy, damp. Not getting far into westerly.*

5.55 p.m.: *Will put all reefs back in mainsail.*

6.30 p.m.: *Gale at moment, 35 knots.*

7.05 p.m.: *Change to storm jib after cup of coffee.*

8.05 p.m.: *Gale now 40 knots.*

8.20 p.m.: *Tacked. Windy and wet.*

8.45 p.m.: *Bleak.*

9.25 p.m.: *Wind west, yacht off course and I'm not tacking again. It is too rough and it's raining continuously.*

After a few hours' sleep he logged at 1.25 a.m. the following morning: *Onwards into a rough night. Every reef in mainsail and spitfire jib*. At breakfast time he noted that the wind was moderating but the sea was still rough. "Too rough to increase sail area and go faster and submarine into it," he told himself. The wind gradually moderated, but the sea was still rough. At

6 p.m. he took two of the reefs out of the main. His last entry for the day was on a despondent note: *Wind shifted west again —yuk*.

And so the lone sailor drove his sloop across the unpredictable southern South Pacific towards New Zealand. He would soon be in the region where scientists believed a huge submarine land mass might rear out of the ocean floor—and he was looking forward to his scientific work on behalf of Curtin University at home.

The only diversion on day 187, as November drew to a close, was another whale sighting. It had a very high dorsal fin and Sanders drew his impression of the finny appendage in his logbook.

Next day he recharged his batteries by starting, with great difficulty, one of his two small diesel motors. He needed topped-up batteries to operate the sophisticated echo-sounding equipment on board *Parry Endeavour*. After breakfast he tried a test probe of the Pacific depths and reported: *Getting good echo in very deep water, 3000 fathoms*. At 8 p.m. the following day as the sloop ghosted along almost becalmed, Sanders again turned on his echo sounder. He was surprised at what he saw on the monitor. He logged: *Found shallow water, shame I missed the incline*.

After breakfast on Sunday 30 November he was again probing the depths and reported: *We are sailing over a plateau. Yesterday the bottom went from 3800 fathoms to 4000 fathoms. Now 280 fathoms*. Soon after noon he logged: *Water getting shallower, 150 fathoms*. (He was not to realise that the echo-sounder was misreading.) At 6.35 p.m.: *Echo sounder lost bottom. Suggested shallower than 100 fathoms. Lat. 38 deg. 50.3, Long. 155 deg. 24.1 W. Penrose Sea Mount (35 fathoms approx.)*. At 7.55 p.m. he wrote facetiously: *Would not want to be driving Queen Elizabeth around here, but it is getting shallow! I think an echo rebound*. At 11 p.m. he logged: *Getting windy. Water deep. Did some searching on echo sounder—910 fathoms*.

Throughout the early morning of the following day he probed the South Pacific and at 4.40 a.m. he reported to his log: *Possible volcano. 60 deg. shape per echo sounder*. It soon became too rough to continue his scientific work and by 10 p.m. he was in a forty to forty-five-knot NNW gale. An hour later he decided it was too rough for safety and he dropped his storm jib and hove-to into a screaming fifty-knot wind. But Sanders was delighted to get through to Dr. Penrose by radio and tell him about the ocean-bed protuberances he had plotted over the previous two days.

A stormy dawn on 3 December saw *Endeavour* heeling in a forty to forty-five-knot westerly squall and throughout the morning the sturdy sloop was battered by big seas. Sanders logged at noon: *It is a very rough sea, but the yacht with its little sails is slowly going into it and not being knocked about*. At 10 a.m. the following day he wrote: *West wind, yacht 50 deg. off course. Huge swell. There must be a bit of a storm in the sun. My shortwave radios are not picking up programmes. Should be loud and clear*.

Early that afternoon, back in his office at *The West Australian*, the author received a radio-telephone call from the solo circumnavigator bursting to tell someone else the news of his plotting of

It's a spirited departure for Sanders as he sets out in stormy weather and big swells off Fremantle. Far more ferocious gales lay ahead.

Kevin Parry congratulates Jon Sanders at the relaunching of *Parry Endeavour.*

Special fibreglass reinforcing was used to strengthen *Endeavour's* hull. Here Sanders looks on as boatbuilder Des Piesse sets to work.

Proud parents and affectionate son in happy mood together.

A reassuring contact . . . radio 'minder' Jack Seabrook at the controls.

Before departure Sanders gets briefed by John Penrose, of the Curtin University's Centre for Marine Science. Below Dr. Penrose evaluates data recorded by *Endeavour's* echo-sounder in the South Pacific.

Amid a maze of rigging, the lone sailor waves on the approach to Fremantle near the end of his first rounding.

Local people had their own way of congratulating Sanders.

The communications area, and chart table, on *Parry Endeavour*.

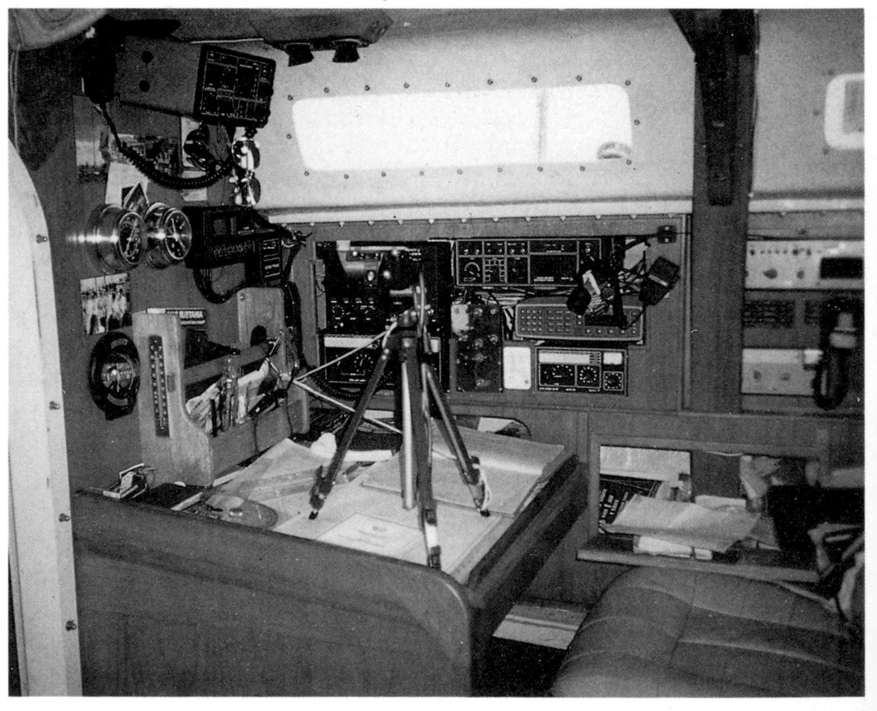

A welcome, though infrequent, addition to the menu . . .

. . . cooked here in the galley, on a troublesome stove.

A flotilla of boats greet Sanders, whose arrival during an America's Cup training run created extra confusion. Behind *Parry Endeavour* (KA 1988) is Sanders' former sloop *Perie Banou.*

submarine protuberances on the South Pacific ocean floor. From a position 1820 kilometres east of New Zealand's Cook Strait he said with some excitement: "The bottom rose dramatically from 400 fathoms [about 730 metres] to 100 fathoms [180 metres] and I have no doubt it was a volcano on the ocean bed. Later, I got distinct echoes from a series of mountain peaks in between deep gullies. It was fascinating because I was probing ocean beds that have never been charted."

He said he would transfer the depth-sounding plottings from *Endeavour* to a waiting boat from Curtin University when he sailed past Fremantle at the end of his first circumnavigation.

Asked if he was feeling fit, he responded: "I'm getting a bit tired of the same old food, but then most people have muesli for breakfast these days, don't they? I'll be glad to get to the Great Australian Bight where I usually catch some tuna. It would be a welcome change of diet to have some fresh fish."

Already apprehensive about the planned welcome off Fremantle as he passed through without stopping just before the

America's Cup final match in late January, 1987, he put forward a request. "Would you please ask Kevin Parry if *Kookaburra*'s chaseboats will escort me across the Cup course?" He was worried that some over-exuberant boatsman might try to board his sloop—which would disqualify him as a single-handed circumnavigator.

Day 195 (5 December) was notable—almost typical—for its lack of wind and Jon Sanders was wondering if he would be able to make his 26 January deadline. At 2.30 a.m. he logged: *Not a lot of wind coming from the wrong way—west 10 knots*. At breakfast time: *Out of wind, sails flapping*. At 4.30 p.m.: *The gooseneck barnacles have slowed this yacht to slow, slow!* 8.20 p.m.: *Sailing the yacht 30 deg. off course because the wind is so light sails will not set by pulling away to correct course*.

But Sanders got his breeze early the next morning when he logged exuberantly: *Wow, yacht is scooting along, nice breeze. Full main and No. 1 genoa*. Ever looking ahead to possible trouble, Sanders told his log at 10.20 a.m.: *All overcast, barometer falling. In for the usual north, northwesterly (probably a gale). Then yukky west, then WSW and fading wind at SW—I suppose*. No sailor had taken a yacht single-handedly as far as Jon Sanders and few could match him for predicting the vagaries of the weather and sea.

At 10.45 a.m. he wrote: *Horrible sloppy sea, must have been some stronger wind in the region before I got here*. Trying to get every fraction of a knot of speed out of his yacht, Sanders poled out his working jib and got instant reward. *Just zooming along*, he told his log at mid-afternoon. *Nearly time to drop the pole and jib, getting windier. Will run under full main until wind lessens or backs*. Just before his supper of beef curry, rice and fruit and custard, he logged: *Full main with storm jib, wind on stern quarter 25 knots. Comfortable rig and progress. Very overcast, barometer down*.

His exhilaration was short-lived. He awoke on day 197 at 2 a.m. and found *Endeavour* enveloped in fog and almost out of wind. After breakfast he logged despondently: *Dear me, becalmed*. He complained all day about the lack of a breeze. Some typical log entries: 6.30 p.m.: *I wish there was some wind*. 8.20 p.m.: *Absolutely no wind at all. Sails slatting*. 9 p.m.: *Why does not the wind come?* 9.25 p.m.: *Hey, got a light NW breeze*. 9.40 p.m.: *Not a lot of wind. My sat-nav. says I went backwards. Not fair*. Midnight: *Sails flapping around annoyingly*. And so ended another day of frustration.

The disheartenment continued to breakfast time the following day when *Endeavour* was still lying dead in the water, her sails flapping like the wings of a dying seabird. But as he finished a cup of milky coffee at his chart table, Sanders felt the sloop tighten up and heel slightly. *Hello*, he logged, *got a nice, quiet SSW—hope it holds. Blue sky and sunny. 10 miles since noon yesterday*. At 9.10 a.m. he exulted: *Yipes, doing about five and a half knots (did not even get whiplash!)*. But just as quickly as the wind and his hopes rose, they both fell about noon. Sanders took advantage of the quiet conditions to do some more washing, which he had to take into his cabin to dry when light rain fell. And, with typical duplicity, the breeze picked up again from the south-east and *Endeavour* was again forging westward.

The following day, 9 December, he made good progress, and just before supper he received a radio-telephone from Dr. Jim Chute, Parry Corporation's technology division manager, telling him of arrangements for his scheduled sailpast. It had been set for Thursday 29 January, two days before the America's Cup final match was to start (neither the defender nor the challenger had been decided). He was to sail through South Passage between Rottnest and Garden Islands, north of rocks known as the Stragglers, past the North Mole of Fremantle Harbour, along the nearby white sandy beach of Leighton and then round a buoy to head north of Rottnest and back eastwards on his second "lap". He was to have a brief (shouted) chat at sea with Royal Perth Yacht Club Commodore Alan Crewe and a group of his mentors and Parry officials before heading back to his lonely existence.

On 10 December he noted that he had 415 nautical miles to go to Cook Strait, named after his idol. He was only 230 miles east of New Zealand. The following day he noticed that the colour of the sea had changed to a darker shade of blue and was flecked by scraps of seaweed.

The next page of Sanders' logbook is almost blank. The only entry: *180 deg. W, 180 deg. E. Today is cancelled! Because it is tomorrow! PTO*. He had sailed across the international date line and "lost" a day.

Saturday 13 December saw *Parry Endeavour* joggling along in a quiet north-east breeze. Sanders was interviewed by radio-telephone by the Australian Broadcasting Corporation's John Bell and later that day picked up the broadcast on Radio Australia. He was pleased with the interview. Sanders was now burning his navigation lights because of the danger of shipping close to the New Zealand coast.

The lone sailor could not decide whether to pass below the South Island of New Zealand or go round the north of the North Island, so he decided on a compromise. He would go through the middle—Cook Strait. He was apprehensive about doing this, not having a chart of the strait, but he did have an admiralty list of lighthouses for all of Australia and New Zealand with their latitude and longitude.

At 3 a.m. on the Sunday he awoke to a rare sensation—the first smell of land since he left Fremantle 205 days earlier. And to him after all that time, it was "beautifully sweet". At 7.35 a.m. the smells took tangible shape—Cape Palliser, New Zealand was looming up.

Snub-nosed dolphins accompanied his yacht as *Endeavour* alternately surged or drifted towards Cook Strait according to the rise or fall of the flukey wind. At nine o'clock that night he noted that the sea was confused, indicating a strong current or tide. An hour later, when the wind approached thirty-five knots, Sanders went on deck to put three reefs in the main. While on deck he spied a ship astern, the first sighted since the Falklands region two months earlier. In typical thorough fashion, he listed the lighthouses or promontories he had to keep watch out for and their bearings from his yacht—Cape Palliser, Cape Campbell, Boring Head, Point Curran Head, The Brothers, Stephens Island, Cape Farewell Spit and Cape Farewell itself.

"Only eight shopping days to Christmas," he mused jokingly the following morning, 16 December, as he sailed down towards Cook Strait with Cape Palliser north of his yacht. "I wonder what Santa will bring me." He had taken the reefs out of his mainsail because the wind had dropped. At 1.45 p.m. he logged: *Ship ahead*, Sydney Express, *going other way, passed close*. At 4 p.m. he was abeam of Boring Head and forty-five minutes later he had to gybe the yacht to avoid a ferry crossing the strait. Visibility was poor, but he could pick out suburban homes of Wellington on the hillsides. Just before dusk he cleared Carrow Head and at 7.05 p.m. he reported: *Temporarily becalmed under headland. Can see rocks before The Brothers across strait. Dolphins about.* 7.30 p.m.: *Wind all over the place and huge current overfalls. Noisy, too.*

That evening he sent twelve Christmas telegrams to his family, friends and his voyage officials. Each read simply: *Happy Christmas and New Year, warmest wishes, Jon Sanders*, Parry Endeavour.

The solo sailor spent a restless night and morning watching out for ships, ferries and fishing vessels which he spotted every ten or twenty minutes.

At 5 a.m., as the first streaks of dawn caressed the calm waters of Cook Strait, Sanders wrote: *Not much wind, "parked"*. Twenty minutes later: *Not much progress, abeam Stephens Island*. After breakfast: *Calm. View through binoculars is stark and beautiful*. 11.25 a.m.: *Nice quiet north wind on flat, flat blue sea. I have been walking around without holding on everywhere, so flat is the sea*. Twenty-five minutes later: *Light WNW wind, yacht not on course, but nice sailing, best since departure. Blue sky and sea and nice scenery.*

Endeavour zig-zagged her way through Cook Strait in the early hours of 18 December avoiding shipping. Sanders tacked to clear Farewell Spit and sighted the light of Farewell Cape on his port side. As these manoeuvres unfolded, so did the spirit of Christmas, for on the same day he received festive telgrams by radio from Commodore Crewe and his flag officers at Royal Perth Yacht Club and the club's office girls.

At 1.30 p.m. he cleared Cook Strait but

maintained vigilance throughout the evening because of the presence of fishing boats.

Into the Tasman Sea, *Parry Endeavour* picked up a good sailing breeze and Sanders' hopes of keeping his 29 January rendezvous off Fremantle soared.

With three days to Christmas it was anything but smooth sailing as Sanders had to contend with a confused, mixed-up sea, and a radical squall accompanied by rain which necessitated raising the storm jib. He sailed slowly into a diabolical cross sea.

On Christmas Eve there was not a great deal of festive spirit on board the sea-stained yacht as it slogged to windward in thirty-knot WSW winds. *Rough and lousy day*, Sanders told his log at noon. At 5 p.m. he logged: *Golly, wish the wind would moderate. I wish it would back south, anywhere away from west—rough!* To cheer himself up he played a tape of some Christmas carols given to him by his staunch friend, Noel Semmens, a former Royal Perth commodore. His thoughts turned to his family and close friends and he wondered what they were doing this

Christmas Eve. He well knew his own plans.

His first log entry on Christmas day—at 3 a.m.—was: *Happy Xmas me and the birds. 20–knot WSW wind, big sloppy sea*.

After eating his usual breakfast he kept a radio sked with Wellington Radio and heard Parry executive Laurie Humphry read him a Christmas message from Kevin Parry and his executive staff and John Penrose. He was touched and immediately put on the Christmas cassette tape again. By dusk on Christmas day the wind had dropped and his last entry was: *Out of wind, sails flapping, yuk*.

That was the lonely Christmas Day for Jon Sanders, who felt in a melancholy mood as he turned into his bunk that night.

9

One Down, Two to Go

The white sails still fly seaward,
  seaward flying.
Unbroken wings

And the lost heart stiffens and rejoices
In the lost lilac and the lost sea voices
T. S. Eliot, Ash-Wednesday, 1930

THE loneliness of a long-distance solo sailor did not get to Jon Sanders' psyche. True, he missed his family and close mates at Christmas time, but he knew when he set out on that stormy May day that year that he would have to spend two Christmasses alone at sea. He accepted it, and now he cheered up by reminding himself that he would soon be seeing all his relatives and friends at the end of his first "lap" off Fremantle in about one month.

Now, as his sloop *Parry Endeavour*

danced across the sparkling Tasman Sea towards Tasmania on Boxing Day, Sanders busied himself sandpapering the woodwork on the topsides of the yacht and listening to the start of the Sydney-to-Hobart bluewater racing classic, a soul-stirring race that had a special affection for him. His mind snapped back to the race of 1984 when, in *Perie Banou*, he and his young crew had finished third in the roughest "Hobart" in history. Of the fleet of 152 yachts that left Sydney on Boxing Day that year, 105 retired, some with gear failure, some through seasickness, but most because of the toughness of the race in those conditions. One man had been lost overboard and never seen again.

Perie Banou was one of the smallest yachts in the race, and few gave her much chance of winning. Sanders knew when he heard the pre-race forecast of strong headwinds that many yachts would pull out. The veteran yachtsman had faced much worse conditions alone on his single-handed double globe-girdling of 1981–82. And now, he reflected, so far on this voyage he had suffered worse conditions than he had faced in the 1984 Hobart race.

At mid-morning, he telephoned to wish me a Happy Christmas (he had tried unsuccessfully the day before) and a few minutes later received a call from Sydney Radio with a telegram from the West Australian Premier, Brian Burke. It promised a warm welcome when he completed his first leg off Rottnest in a month's time. "We are proud a great adventurer from our State is doing so well in his attempt of achieving something which no other human has ever before accomplished," Burke added. "God bless and good luck."

By supper time the wind was strong enough to warrant three reefs in the mainsail. But when Sanders woke up the following morning, his yacht was enveloped in fog and the wind had dropped right away. After breakfast he logged: *Out of wind and foggy, going nowhere*. He did not go anywhere all day. His last entry for the day at 11 p.m. was: *Oh dear, less wind and a bit more west*.

The Pacific weather pattern, if you could call it that, was reminding Sanders of the old New England saying: "If you don't like the weather, then wait awhile". By 2.45 a.m. there was so much wind he had to leave his cosy bunk and put two reefs in the main. But the wind was almost on the sloop's nose and progress was slow and bumpy. It prompted Sanders to radio-telephone Squadron Leader Nobby Clarke in Sussex, England, to check on the *Guinness Book of Records* rules for single-handed, non-stop sailing. Was it permissible for the sailor to use mechanical power along with his sails? He was still worrying about whether he would need the motor if becalmed off Fremantle during the welcome now being planned for him on completion of his first circumnavigation. He wanted his generous sponsor Kevin Parry to get maximum exposure, because Fremantle and Perth were full to the brim with America's Cup visitors. Having made eleven previous crossings of the Great Australian Bight—most of them alone—Sanders knew that he was now ahead of schedule.

Clarke ruled that motor-sailing would not disqualify him, but as Sanders told his log: *I do not really want to. Besides, very limited fuel.*

As it happened the propriety of motor-sailing was to become purely academic, because before the yacht arrived off Fremantle both of his motors had failed, and his banks of batteries had to be recharged only by solar panels.

At noon on day 218 (28 December) Sanders wrote: *Progress over 24 hours disappointing. It is the constant head-winds.* At 1.30 p.m.: *Yacht got the wind bang on the nose. I wish I could get a couple of good days to build up a bigger reserve. Tacked, may have to tack again, so far off course both ways.* 4.05 p.m.: *I am tired of slow progress in westerlies. I could increase headsail but pushing this yacht is not a good idea on the world's longest voyage.* Late in the afternoon he reported his slow progress to Penta Constat Radio, a marine radio safety network for small craft manned by Derek and Jeanine Barnard, and gave his position as forty miles east of Flinders Island and thirty-five miles off Wilson's Promontory. The wind rose again and by midnight he was forced to reef down again. "West wind with a vengeance," he muttered gloomily as he climbed into his bunk.

After an hour's fitful sleep he rose and noted sardonically that the wind was from "exactly where I want to go." But at 2.20 p.m. that day his spirits soared when the wind backed to south. His elation was brief—by five o'clock *Endeavour*'s sails were flapping again.

His hopes of making the 29 January deadline off Fremantle now seemed assured when a fresh north-easterly found *Endeavour* on 30 December. At 7.30 a.m. he heard the weather forecast and noted: *SW change now late tomorrow—goodie, hope I can get round the promontory in time. Nice sunny, blue sky, dry, strong following wind, mainsail only, good progress, okay*. In mid afternoon a BP tanker, the *Goliath*, passed so close to him travelling in the opposite direction that he was forced to change course to avoid a potential mishap. He sighted nobody on the bridge and received no answer to his VHF radio call.

Ninety minutes into the last day of 1986 he saw three more ships passing close by and logged: *I am in the wrong lane*. Just before breakfast Deal Island in the Kent group came in view, and at 6.40 a.m.

Sanders logged exultantly: *Land ho! Wilson's Promontory—Australia again*. Minutes later he got the adrenalin flowing when a vessel at Deal Island reported to Lochsport Radio that a line squall had hit the island. "I observed a squall approaching," he recounted, "and just got my number one jib down and working jib up and trimmed when the squall hit with a bang—forty-five knots."

Lochsport is the call sign for Bass Strait Radio, operating through Western Port Safety Council. The solo sailor had made many friends from Lochsport, including a delightful septuagenarian named Alwyn Tamo, who in 1987 was named Ampol Boat Person-of-the-Year for the years she had manned her radio on a voluntary basis. She also received the Order of Australia.

Early that afternoon Sanders reported a stowaway on board the sloop. *Been invaded, there is a fly on board*, he noted.

The frustration showed in the lone sailor's log that afternoon in successive entries: *Out of wind, most disappointing*, and later, *No calms forecast this region, but I am 100 per cent becalmed*. He wondered what his family and friends were doing on New Year's Eve. As far as he knew, he had no liquor with which to usher in the New Year.

His first log entry for 1 January was *0000 Happy New Year 1987—me*. He was happy too because he was sailing along in a fresh SW wind. From his radio came the strains of Auld Lang Syne.

In a shipping lane Jon Sanders sleeps only lightly and often pokes his head and shoulders out of his cabin companionway to scan the horizon for shipping. In the English Channel during his double-circumnavigation he set his alarm clock to go off every twenty minutes. After the first two awakenings he no longer needed the alarm, waking automatically to look for ships. "I reckon it would take a ship at least twenty minutes to reach my yacht from the horizon," he explained, "so I chose that as my sleeping pattern."

Just after 3 a.m., still groggy through lack of sleep, he saw a yacht on port tack approaching. Sanders was on starboard tack and he knew he had the right-of-way under the rules of the sea, but he had to take last-minute evasive action as the other yacht failed to yield. The same yacht then passed dangerously close to a ship. Was the crew asleep? he wondered.

It was not surprising that at 4.15 a.m. when he entered a tack in his logbook, he added: *I'm sleepy*. The wind was again dropping and veering and at 9.20 a.m. he wrote: *Wind shift making yacht go back from where it came*. Soon after noon: *Completely out of wind, becalmed, oh dear . . . such poor progress is alarming*. But he cheered up at sundown when he picked up a breeze as he sighted East Moncoeur Island and Rodondo Island.

At 11.10 a.m. the following day he heard the forecast for Bass Strait between Tasmania and mainland Victoria—strong west to south-west winds. At noon it was warm and sunny and *Endeavour* was making fair progress. But by mid-afternoon he was out of wind again. The vagaries of the sea were driven home again the next morning when Sanders found himself rushing on deck to reef down in a howling gale with rain. By mid-morning the wind was pushing the yacht too fast, so he changed to a storm jib. At 4.30 p.m. he logged: *Very windy and rough as bags*.

But his yacht logged 141 miles—a good run—and he added 117 miles the following day when the wind moderated.

On his stop-start leg across the Great Australian Bight, Sanders monitored the Hobart-Adelaide yacht race fleet positions. He knew most of the yachts in the race, which was part of a Hobart-to-Fremantle race to coincide with the America's Cup. On Tuesday 6 January 1987 he logged: *Got front motor started, but kept stopping. Now won't start*. At 6 p.m.: *Oh dear, out of wind and what little wind there is is coming from the wrong way*.

The following day he turned his satellite navigation equipment on only for a few hours to conserve his batteries, knowing that from now on they might have to rely on solar power for recharging. He spent the day reefing and unreefing his mainsail as the breeze rose and fell. Next day he discovered his port fuel tank was empty, so he vented the fuel and motors and got the front motor going, only to stop each time. *After zillions of starter motor cranking got rear motor going and running like a clock*, he wrote.

On Saturday 18 January—day 231—he

caught some much-needed rain and was in high spirits in a radio-telephone message to Perth. "I believe I'll be able to make it off Fremantle by the twenty-ninth," he said, "but I can't promise. At the moment I'm becalmed."

But at mid-afternoon he logged: *Busy, busy. This morning wind was north, then north-west, then west, then south-west (now). Rain now gone. South-westerly came with squalls 30 knots, put three reefs in and tied. No sooner did that and time to take out two reefs, storm jib on, going slow*. By 3 a.m. the next day the gale had blown itself out and at noon he logged cheerfully: *Only 43 miles a day to average to sail past Fremantle by January 29 on schedule. Almost an impossibility to be late*.

He had previously caught small tuna in the Bight, so on the afternoon of day 233 he got out his line and tried to catch a fish for his supper—a welcome change, he thought, from the drab food he had been eating for more than seven months. But he lost the lure from the line and caught no fish. He rigged the line again with an ingenious fish-alarm system—a rubberised shock cord and empty coffee tin with a shackle inside to rattle when a fish was hooked. That was the theory, anyway, but by midnight, the score was Sanders 0, Fish 0.

The following day as *Endeavour* bumped into a strong headwind with three reefs in the mainsail, Sanders listened to a description of the America's Cup challenger final between *Stars and Stripes* and *Kiwi Magic* on ABC radio. By midnight the wind had died, and so rarely did it appear the following day that Sanders busied himself with bleeding both motors, putting special additive in the fuel to fend off fungi. He got the front motor to start, but it ran "like a chaffcutter". That afternoon he relaxed by the radio again and heard *Stars and Stripes* defeat *Kiwi Magic*, and *Kookaburra III* beat *Australia IV* in a defenders' semi-final. *Hope Kook wins*, he noted.

Day 236 (15 January) saw *Endeavour* hove-to in a howling gale from the southwest with winds up to fifty knots. The yacht was knocked down seventy degrees. *Huge seas "grow" in this region*, he wrote. But by the end of the following day he was lamenting: *I wish I could find a decent breeze and sail on course*. At 1.25 a.m. the next day he sighted lights on the south coast of his home State, a coast he had not seen for nearly eight months. He tried fishing again, but lost another lure. Just before sunset he sighted the Stirling Range on his starboard beam.

By mid-afternoon on 18 January he could see to the north Bald Head and Eclipse Island, both near Albany. Now he even had an added "luxury"—he was able to get a television reception from Albany, and watched *Rocky II*.

Dawn on 19 January saw *Endeavour* surrounded by playful dolphins and Sanders stood on his foredeck and admired their grace.

Favourable breezes drove the sloop northwards the following morning, but by mid-afternoon it was a full gale and Sanders had to reef down. At 4.40 p.m. he logged: *Not forecast but blowing 35 knots. Put all three reefs in*. An hour later: *Golly it is rough*. The gale had not abated late that night when he sighted the familiar blink of the Cape Leeuwin light and the Hamelin light.

But by mid-morning the next day Sanders was again sailing in light southerly winds. Now it was a question of killing time, because although his rendezous was still eight days away, in real terms Fremantle was just a day's sail. Within twenty-four hours the lone sailor had a further reminder of the trappings of civilisation—a news helicopter from Perth's Channel Seven television station buzzed his sloop. *That was fun*, he told his log. *They dropped a newspaper*. Ever cautious, he made a quick telephone call to the UK to ask Squadron Leader Nobby Clarke whether it was permissible for him to accept the newspaper (that morning's *The West Australian*, with generous coverage of his voyage). Permission granted.

He was becalmed off his home coast, but he was in no hurry. At 6 p.m. he logged triumphantly: *Caught a fish, caught a fish!—Yum, think it is a tailer*. The following lunch time as *Endeavour* idled around, Sanders salivated when he smelled the fish baking in his oven in tomato sauce. *Tasted yummy too*, he wrote an hour later. That night he was able to pick up Perth television and he could see the loom of the Rottnest lighthouse ahead. He was back in the home waters he knew so well.

His second circumnavigation (and third) was to be east-about and he could not get it out of his mind that if the sail-past had not been scheduled, he could be halfway back across the Great Australian Bight by now. But he was looking forward—albeit apprehensively—to seeing his loved ones and friends again.

On Sunday 25 January, with four days to go, he tried in vain to get his engines to work. They started but would not run for more than a few seconds. Late that night he gybed around to avoid yachts returning to Fremantle in the annual Fremantle to Bunbury and return ocean yacht race.

Early the following morning a photographer and I left Fremantle in Perth builder Bob Williams' luxury 14–metre power cruiser *Contessa* for a secret rendezvous (to which Sanders had agreed) forty kilometres out to sea beyond Garden Island. At the helm was one of Sanders' best friends, Murray Smith, who had sailed in his crew several times. After two hours of searching a lumpy sea whipped up by a strong south-easterly we could find no sign of the yacht. But persistence paid off and finally we sighted a tiny triangle of grey sail on the western horizon. By this time the photographer and a Channel Nine reporter were suffering badly from seasickness, but, to their credit, they did their jobs well.

Sanders, who had not spoken directly to any human since his mail drop off Cape Town five months earlier, waved cheerfully and yelled, "Sorry I'm late. This breeze blew up this morning." He looked lean, suntanned and fit, but his yacht was stained badly by the sea. "I could go a good feed of steak, onions and eggs and a cold can of someone's beer," he called. "But I'm not going to break any of the rules. I'll stick to my mundane diet for another fifteen months."

Recounting highlights of his voyage to date, he gave the most frightening award to when he saw a huge iceberg off Cape Horn. "Ginormous" was Sanders' particular superlative for the scary floating mass. "It was a few hundred feet high and as big as two city blocks. I must have sailed right past it while asleep." He said he felt more confident than ever of completing his triple circumnavigation. "The boat is in fine shape even though it looks a bit grotty." His main worry about sailing past Fremantle Harbour's North Mole on 29 January was that elderly people might injure themselves clambering over the rocks with the crowds. "My Aunt Paddy will be there," he called. And he was looking forward to seeing the faces of his brother and sister and their families and his old sailing cronies, though he would be glad to be on his way again. As we pulled away from *Parry Endeavour* he yelled, "See you on Thursday."

The following morning his Aunt Sheila (Kenworthy) telephoned him with details of the morning newspaper coverage of his delayed arrival. That afternoon he logged: *Running on solar panels only for power. Motors will not start, but all okay*. He spent the next day dodging shipping and unsuccessfully fishing. Early in the evening, at news time, he saw himself on Channel Seven's State Affair programme —a strange sensation after so long a time with no company but his own.

As he sailed towards his home port early next morning, he got through on radio-telephone and expressed extreme nervousness about the coming day's proceedings. But by day's end he was elated and he happily entered in his log: *A magnificent refreshing day—out of this world*.

He had ended his first circumnavigation at precisely 1.16 p.m. that day. And as he swung the tiller of *Parry Endeavour* to round an orange marker buoy off Leighton Beach, he made the classic quote: "Here we go again."

10

Stormy Seas

That dolphin-torn, that gong-
tormented sea.
W. B. Yeats, Byzantium

WRITING of the tumultuous welcome given to Jon Sanders on that sunny late-January day, I paused at my typewriter to call him by radio-telephone as he navigated *Parry Endeavour* round Rottnest Island's North Point on his second circumnavigation. I wanted to hear his thoughts. "It was a wonderful day," he said, "better than the last time." He was referring to his arrival back in Fremantle in May, 1982, after his double rounding. "But it's a relief to be out here alone again," he added. "I was a bit nervous back there with all those boats, but seeing my old friends again brought a lump to my throat." This was typical of the man. After eight months alone at sea he was happy to be alone again, courting his fickle mistress.

That night he entered his cryptic, but accurate, version of the day's proceedings: *Approx. 8.30 a.m. two Parry chaseboats were alongside, then Sutherland* [Kevin Parry's power yacht] *with media. By 1330 sailing under new working jib for first time, joined by massive range of spectacular Swan yachts and some huge spectator craft, including Royal Perth Yacht Club's Parts VI and John Curtin with Premier Brian Burke and Dr. Watts, vice-chancellor of Curtin University. But specially* Perie Banou, *skippered by* [brother] *Colin and my crew, all dressed in yellow rugby pullovers with Parry Endeavour printed on the pockets. Thousands of people were on North Mole, but I was directed to a rounding buoy too far away and I was most disappointed. Rounded buoy off Fremantle at 32 deg. 03 S, 115 deg. 43.5 E.*

On the facing page of his log, he wrote: *Congratulations, Jonny. So far, so good—onwards still.*

Among the estimated crowd of three thousand well-wishers who went out to greet the lone sailor was uniformed Fremantle postman Frank Reid, who swapped his bicycle for a sleek, jet-powered chaseboat to deliver three bags of mail to Sanders. The mail had been closely vetted by Australia Post, Curtin University, Parry Corporation staff and Colin Sanders to make sure it did not contain food or equipment likely to assist him on his voyage—a no-no under the rules of solo sailing. Although Nobby Clarke's rules allowed letters and newspapers to go on board *Parry Endeavour*, Sanders decided there would be no more mail drops for the second or third circumnavigations.

I had jumped at an invitation from Colin Sanders to join the crew of *Perie Benou*, which would be allowed to take up station immediately behind *Parry Endeavour* during the sailpast. As *Endeavour* and her accompanying welcome flotilla of about two hundred craft of all shape, size and seaworthiness reached Gage Roads, a cacophony of sirens, hooters, whistles and bugles assailed the lone sailor's unaccustomed ears. On North Mole some two thousand well-wishers waved flags and cheered their hero on. As *Endeavour* approached the harbour she had left the previous 25 May, the two San Diego twelve metre yachts, *Stars and Stripes '85* and *'86* emerged from the Fremantle Fishing Boat Harbour where they were docked and made a spectacular sight as they sailed under red, white and blue spinnakers before a brisk south-easterly. Then came skipper Dennis Conner's unmistakable voice over *Perie Banou*'s VHF radio: "What's this armada doing cutting across my course? Are they going into the harbour, or what?"

A few seconds later the spinnakers on the two yachts were dropped as the San Diegans slammed on the brakes. From *Perie Banou*, Sanders' exuberant crew shouted jocularly, "Call 'starboard' on him, Jonny," or "Ram him, Jon." (A yacht on starboard tack has the right-of-way over a yacht on port tack in normal circumstances.) After altering course to avoid the bedraggled yacht and her escort, Conner ordered spinnakers up again and the American twelve-metres sailed northwards. "He doesn't look too unfriendly," called Jon Sanders. I was able to interview him by perching precariously on the pulpit of *Perie Banou*. Yawning frequently—he had got little sleep the previous night—he said he was disappointed to learn that his sponsor, Kevin Parry, whose *Kookaburra III* had won the right to defend the America's Cup, had not been able to get there in time from an overseas business trip. But later, as *Endeavour* left behind her escorting armada, a chaseboat carried Parry, tired from a long flight from Beijing, out to wish Sanders godspeed.

Sanders said he would give anything for a feed of prime West Australian beef, smothered in onions and served with chips, or a home-cooked roast mutton dinner. But if so much as a potato crisp had gone on board *Endeavour*, his record-shattering voyage would have been aborted.

As on all of his landfalls and departures, the Sanders yacht was flying a football jumper from his alma mater, Christ Church Grammar School, alongside the Australian flag, Bicentennial flag and Royal Perth Yacht Club burgee.

As a light aircraft circled overhead,

playing second fiddle to several media helicopters buzzing lower down like angry hornets, Premier Brian Burke called to the solo circumnavigator from the government-chartered power boat *John Curtin*: "We're all proud of you, Jon . . . and we're all following your voyage with interest . . . God bless you!" Dozens of boatloads of well-wishers took turns at skirting the wedge of protective craft to give Sanders three cheers and an emotional sailor waved till his arms ached. I was within five metres of *Endeavour*'s transom as Sanders swung the tiller to round the marker buoy off Leighton Beach and yelled, "Here we go again."

When *Endeavour* got into more open water the two Parry twelves, *Kookaburra II* and *Kookaburra III* weaved their way through the protective shield with white gennakers flying to salute the lone sailor. The crews gave him three lusty cheers and Sanders waved both arms.

After the last boatload of friends turned back to Fremantle, leaving him once again alone with his thoughts, Sanders cooked a goulash of baked beans, chicken and tomatoes (all canned) and wolfed it down.

He had not had time for lunch because of the reception. He set a course for well out to sea, away from shipping lanes, to allow himself a good night's sleep.

At 8 a.m. on 30 January, the day after his tumultuous welcome, he logged soberly: *Took reef out of mainsail* [put in the day before to keep *Endeavour*'s speed down]. *Fine, mild wind and day. Ship went by*. He telephoned his Aunt Sheila who had not been well enough to come out to see him the previous day. The lone sailor was back in the business of safely navigating his rugged sloop twice more round the world, this time the "easy" way —west to east.

As he sailed in fresh ESE breezes towards Cape Leeuwin, which he had rounded ten days earlier, he tuned his radio into the lead-up and start of the America's Cup final match between *Kookaburra III*, skippered by Iain Murray, and *Stars and Stripes '87* (Dennis Conner). He was disappointed to hear the San Diego yacht win the first match race of the best-of-seven final.

He anticipated, and got, strong breezes as he headed towards Leeuwin, one of the world's great capes. After supper on Sunday 1 February, with the wind hitting thirty knots, he decided it was time for a third reef in the mainsail.

With *Endeavour* being buffeted by rough seas and winds up to fifty knots, Sanders sat down at his chart table and wrote some telegrams. To the Commissioner of Police, manager of the Marine and Harbours Department and the vice-chancellor of Curtin University, he wrote: *My most sincere thoughts and thanks for the considerable efforts in protecting* Parry Endeavour *and adding to the magnificent spectacle on the occasion that I rounded the mark off Fremantle at the end of my first circumnavigation of the world and the beginning of the second. Kindest regards, Jon Sanders*. To Commodore Malcolm Baird, Naval Officer-in-Charge, Western Australia: *I wonder if you would accept and convey my warmest thoughts and thanks to the Naval Reserve Cadets and the NRC crew of* Dampier *for their support and kindness during my long voyage. Yours sincerely, Jon Sanders*.

Endeavour's power supply was now relying on the solar panels fitted to the yacht, because Sanders could no longer start his small diesel motors, suspecting water in the fuel. It would be a handicap, because he would be able to use his satellite navigation equipment sparingly and navigation lights only when necessary. Radio use would also have to be kept to a minimum. But the solo circumnavigator was not overly worried. He was more concerned with the fate of *Kookaburra III*, which was being severely mauled by *Stars and Stripes*. After listening to the American yacht wrap up the series on the afternoon of 4 February, he logged at 3.15 p.m.: *Sunny and mild, SSW breeze 14 knots. Listening to America's Cup—it seems last race. Looks like back to USA the cup goes, this time the west coast.*

The following day—his 257th day at sea—he received a telegram from Commodore Malcolm Baird: *Thank you very much for your kind message which has been passed to the Naval Reserve Cadet movement in WA and to the NRC crew* Dampier. *Your voyage, accompanied as it is with discipline and professional seamanship and navigation, is inspiring all Naval Reserve Cadets who join me in saluting you. We all send our very best wishes. You are never far from our thoughts.*

As *Endeavour* sailed into a boisterous Southern Ocean and headed towards the Great Australian Bight—notorious for its rough seas—he noted at 3 p.m. on Friday 6 February: *South-west wind 30–35 knots. Rough, sun out, blue sky and sea, lots of white caps. Going with it okay, one reef, no jib*. Before dawn that day it had started to rain lightly and Sanders hoped (in vain) that there would be a fall heavy enough to catch. His one water tank was empty and he fed some into it by gravity from the number two tank, which was full. His yacht's battery systems had been fully charged by the West Australian sun pouring energy into the solar panels.

The following day as *Endeavour* rolled sickeningly in heavy swells left over from the previous day's gale, Sanders heard the America's Cup handing-over ceremony on radio. He told his log: *Done with great dignity, Kookaburra looking great*.

Although very much a casual fisherman, Sanders decided to try his luck on day 260 (a Sunday) and was quickly rewarded; his catch was a fish such as he had never seen before. He logged: *Don't know what sort—not a tuna. A wide, shortish fish, tough skin, but can be cut with a sharp knife, white meat*. He sketched the fish in his logbook, then filleted it for his supper the following night.

His Monday menu: Breakfast—three cups of coffee made with hot milk; lunch—muesli and hot milk; supper—fish. He tossed the fish fillets in flour, put them in a baking dish with tinned tomato juice and pepper, added boiled rice and baked the lot. It was delicious, but he still mourned the absence of oil or butter for frying (both commodities having been left off the boat in the initial packing).

That evening he sent the following telegrams: *To Jim Chute, Parry Corporation: I wish to most sincerely convey to you and Graeme Henry and your assistants my deepest gratitude for the delightful afternoon and nautical spectacular of* Parry Endeavour*'s end of her first circumnavigation and the beginning of the second*. To Royal Perth Yacht Club Commodore Alan Crewe: *May I congratulate yourself and all the fellow club members for the superb conduct of the America's Cup that*

I concluded from many radio broadcasts. Furthermore, I wish to convey my deepest gratitude for the delightful afternoon and nautical spectacular when Parry Endeavour *completed the end of her first circumnavigation and began the second.*

Sanders had a small oven in his galley, but so far had not been too ambitious with it. Now, for the first time, he tried his hand at some scones, and the results were a pleasant surprise. He ate them with jam and tinned cream, and before long had an expectant audience of dozens of seabirds outside. There was even a big speckled wandering albatross following *Endeavour* in the cold, bleak Southern Ocean.

He liked the scones so much he made a second batch the following day as he trolled a fishing line behind his sea-stained sloop.

In a radio-telephone conversation that afternoon, Sanders enthused about his fan mail from "lots of wonderful people in this world." There had been dozens of letters from elderly people, he said, including a nonagenarian at a retirement home, and from schoolchildren. "They are all following my voyage and to hear from them is really heartwarming. Many of the children are doing projects on my triple circumnavigation attempt."

Sanders still had two mailbags to open and was intent on savouring the contents for as long as possible, opening only half a dozen letters each day. He was mindful that the Fremantle mail exchange would be his last for the voyage.

At 3 a.m. on 12 February his ingenious fish alarm wakened him with a clattering of shackle in coffee tin. He had hooked an identical fish to the one he had most recently caught. The line had tangled, so he waited till after breakfast to untangle it and fillet his fish. For lunch he had hot scones—yes, a third batch—even trying vegemite on some, washed them down with hot, milky coffee. For supper that night he cooked the fish fillets on a dry tray in his oven, covering them with canned mushrooms before adding heated baked beans and cold potato salad, also from a can. More scones and coffee. He was eating well, though his diet was monotonous—except when he caught a fish. Every morning the lone sailor swallowed a multi-vitamin tablet and an extra-strength vitamin C pill with his muesli and hot milk breakfast.

At 3 p.m. on Black Friday (13 February) he logged: *Fine rain—oh, I hope I get lots for drinking water*. But the weather cleared. He was not overly worried about his water supply, knowing that it often rained in Tasmanian waters and he was only just leaving the Bight, south of Adelaide. *Endeavour* was becalmed on the forty-first parallel of latitude, but the following day she was plugging into a headwind. On 17 February her skipper kept a radio sked with Western Port (Victoria) Safety Council and with *Endeavour*'s sister ship *Parmelia*, which was on a passage between Fremantle and Hobart after the America's Cup.

At 6.10 p.m. on 19 February, due south of Mt. Gambier, South Australia, he logged: *Thunderstorms about. Turned most electrics off, put rain bucket out, perhaps I shall catch some rain, put one reef in mainsail in case of severe squall. Thunder and lightning about. Disconnected two-way radio earth wires to ring frame as that is also earth from mast to keel bolts*. (These precautions were taken in case a lightning strike damaged the sloop's electrical system. The mast was earthed.) Half an hour later: *Raining, I hope I get lots, been on number two tank for 15 days and I need to catch rain*. After supper (freeze-dried lamb and peas, baked beans and potato salad) he exulted: *Caught first run-off water 15 litres for rinsing, washing. Now running hose into number one tank. Steady rain, not heavy*. At 10 p.m. he added: *Raining steadily—goodie*. Midnight: *Caught approx. 30–40 litres drinking water*.

At 4 a.m. on Saturday 21 February he woke up to find *Endeavour* in a gale. He quickly went on deck to put three reefs in the main and secure the jib to the foredeck. *I suspect this lot is going to be a real blast*, he told his logbook. Again he was correct. At 7.45 a.m. the wind was squalling to more than fifty knots. For safety he hand-steered his sloop through the squalls. The gale, with frequent squalls between forty and fifty-five knots, swept the yacht all day. At 11 p.m. when he kept his radio sked with Jack Seabrook at Royal Perth Yacht Club, he reported: *Sea now very rough and at this moment heavy rain and hail*. He noted in his log that he had heard on radio that two men in a kayak had left Tasmania that day for New Zealand. *I hope they are okay*, he logged. *I am much farther south, but conditions here are not good, full gale*.

When the barometer plummeted to 998 millibars and the wind started gusting between fifty and sixty knots, it was time to take safety precautions. Sanders donned foul-weather gear, clipped his safety harness to the travel line and dropped the mainsail altogether. He was now under bare pole and the yacht was still going too fast. He put out both sea brakes over the transom. At 2.30 a.m. he logged: *Anenometer goes only to 50 knots and much of the time is over that. Thank goodness for Des Piesse* [the veteran shipwright who strengthened *Endeavour* for the voyage].

In raging seas at 3.15 a.m. the yacht suffered a jarring knockdown—the mast tipping over 100 degrees—ten degrees below the horizontal. As a bleak dawn cast its pale light over a sea of galloping white horses, Sanders heard a storm warning from Hobart Radio. He had been enduring the storm for seven hours. At 11.20 a.m.

he logged: *Severe gale and enormous sea continue*. Late that afternoon, however, still under bare pole, *Endeavour* was riding safely enough for Sanders to haul in one of the sea brakes. That evening on a radio sked he heard that a wave had filled *Parmelia*'s cockpit to the brim the previous evening and the yacht *Balandra* had torn its mainsail. He was pleased to learn that the kayak men had been picked up by a fishing boat. By 10.10 p.m. he noticed the gale moderating—down to thirty knots—but he did not venture on deck to rehoist the mainsail. He was now due south of Tasmania in a still-angry sea.

Soon after midnight he managed to get the remaining sea brake in. He unwrapped a messy mainsail and rehoisted it in the darkness with three reefs. It was not an easy task in a huge sea with a thirty-knot gale lashing him and his sloop. The gale gradually abated and that afternoon he started tidying up the cockpit. He was glad that a few days earlier, when he was almost becalmed, he had replaced the seals on his stern lazaret lockers. They had taken little water during the storm.

Two days later, having cleared the south

coast of Tasmania by more than two hundred miles, he took stock of his yacht as it sailed before a strong nor'wester towards the South Pacific with two reefs in the mainsail and a storm.

He had consumed a considerable amount of food since the voyage began, and hence felt that the yacht was floating and handling the seas better. *It has not been sailed fast because of gooseneck barnacles*, wrote Sanders. *I also keep the sails small—self-steering requires short sails in heavy winds, anyway—and as I have a long way to go, gently, gently has been and still is my long-established formula*.

11

Squidly-didly, Snares and Traps

Sunset and evening star,
And one clear call for me!
And may there be no moaning of the bar,
When I put out to sea.

Alfred, Lord Tennyson,
Crossing the Bar

HAVING cleared South-West Cape, Tasmania, Jon Sanders sailed the 14.5–metre sloop *Parry Endeavour* into the Tasman Sea again, this time setting a course for New Zealand's South Cape (also called South-West Cape). So far all of the capes he had crossed—Good Hope, the Horn, Leeuwin and now South-West Cape—had lived up to their reputation of being gale-swept and treacherous most of the time. He hoped that New Zealand's southernmost promontory would be kinder.

Now on Wednesday 25 February 1987 —day 277 at sea—*Parry Endeavour* was making steady progress in a brisk twenty to twenty-five-knot sou'westerly breeze on a bleak, sloppy Tasman Sea. At 11 a.m. he made his third cup of milky coffee for the day and wondered (in the absence on board of alcohol) whether he was becoming a "coffeeholic". He was drinking up to ten cups a day, always made with hot milk.

The former shearing contractor was confident at this stage that his food supply would last him for the full twenty-three-month voyage. That night he mixed himself another of his goulashes—macaroni with Californian chicken, beef burgundy and tinned tomatoes.

Considering it had been in continuous use for 277 days, *Parry Endeavour*'s mainsail was standing up to the voyage exceptionally well. Sanders' only problem had been with the slides sticking because they were shackled on (his idea). To overcome this, he had removed some of the shackles and taped the slides instead. Showing more wear, but still going strong was the working jib (one of two on board) which had done most of the headsail work. The extra wear here was evident because the jib was sometimes lashed to the foredeck in heavy weather. Sanders was full of admiration for these sails, and the storm jib and lightweight number one jib which were all made, without computer help, by Chris Sherlock of the Tasker company. They bore all the hallmarks of durability that the solo circumnavigator admired—all seams lacquered, four or more rows of stitching, many chafe patches and two leach cords for each sail.

The next afternoon Sanders put out his fishing line and, somewhat begrudgingly, did some housekeeping, mainly in the galley, navigation area and his own berth section. He also attacked the little-used forepeak section to keep out mould.

The early hours of Friday 27 February found *Endeavour* becalmed in the cold ocean wastes east of Tasmania, but by 8 a.m. a light NNE wind had sprung up and the sloop was sailing comfortably. A little while later he had a radio telephone call from his number one crewman back home, Richard Stainton, who was keen to impart a bit of nautical gossip. It concerned

Endeavour's predecessor, *Perie Banou*, whose mast, Stainton now divulged, had been found to be shorter than the measurement which appeared on her IOR (International Offshore Rule) certificate. The discrepancy had come to light when it was found the sloop's new tape-drive mainsail, designed by computer, was too big. Later Sanders mulled over the news—galling, because it meant that *Perie Banou* had been over-handicapped for years. He reflected in his log: *Would that have changed my third in the Sydney-Hobart race to a better place? It certainly would have affected other races, including the Parmelia race (I was second overall) . . . oh dear, never mind.*

On the Saturday afternoon just after he had put three reefs in the mainsail (the wind was rising), he tuned in to Radio Australia and heard a familiar voice—his own. It was an interview done while he was sailing around off Fremantle a month earlier.

He was pleased to hear from his brother Colin the next day that *Perie Banou* had finished first and fifth in the first two races of the State S & S 34 championships. At

10.35 a.m. he observed to his log: *It is amazing that after weeks or months at sea how strong and clear I can smell land. I smell New Zealand—nice, too, sweet in smell*. He noted, too, that he was 250 nautical miles away from the South Island.

He saw signs of rain and quickly rigged up his canvas rain bucket. But an hour later he reported only a sea mist. Just before supper he logged: *Oh dear, number one water tank empty and number two just over half full—five weeks' supply. I need more rain*.

By 2 March he was in the southern New Zealand region and had put his clock on to Kiwi time. With his batteries on full charge through his solar panels, he now kept his satellite navigation equipment switched on. He also listened to New Zealand Radio as *Endeavour* sailed into thirty-five knot winds that had Sanders putting three reefs into the mainsail.

The following morning he was in a gale. He logged at 6.40 a.m.: *Wind 35 to 45 knots SE. Oh dear, just where I do not need it. Three reefs in, storm jib, going to windward, heavy cloud, no rain*. Two hours later: *Trust me to get this lousy weather from the wrong way in this neck of the woods*. A few minutes later: *Sea very steep and close. Nasty. Suspect current. Think I shall heave-to. Annoying, but best be cautious*. He decided against heaving-to, however, and *Endeavour* plugged on into the teeth of the gale. At 12.35 a.m. he logged: *Land ho ahead of yacht—Stewart Island*. An hour later as his sturdy yacht slogged to windward in big, steep seas off South Cape, he tacked to avoid Stewart Island, which put him on course for the notorious Snares.

Sanders was constantly alert in this, one of the world's most treacherous regions for sailors. At 7.15 p.m., with *Endeavour* still under storm rig, he logged: *Think the wind is moderating a little—hooray*. Half an hour later he added: *Tacked. Maintaining wide danger circles from Snares, South Cape and the Traps*.

Now south of Stewart Island, Sanders awoke at 12.15 a.m. and was surprised to see a ship passing a quarter of a mile astern of him. He logged through sleepy eyes: *Lot of light glow to east, would be fishing boats, squid boats, I think*. Fifteen minutes later after tacking, he observed:

Not a lot of progress tonight, sea rough, sails at storm rig. Will leave be till morning, no need to go too fast. Navig. lights on. At dawn he sighted land ahead of the yacht and assumed it was Stewart Island—South Cape is the southernmost tip of the island. The treacherous, well-named Traps were a series of low rocks and reefs a few miles further on. With a fresh east wind right on the bow of *Endeavour* he was making little progress and he tacked back and forth around the cape.

At mid-afternoon he grouched to his log: *My recent bad weather has caused lots of rain and mild flooding on South Island, NZ, and closed Wellington Airport and harbour today, but no rain here!*

At 4.15 p.m. he noted: *Twenty miles to the Traps. Now due south of Stewart Island, going to windward, wind still bang on the nose*. Just before sunset he sailed close enough to get a fine view of South Cape and the surrounding rugged coast-line. At 10.15 p.m. that night he logged: *Oodles of bright lights ahead and SE of yacht. Fishing boats in long illuminated line similar to as seen on departure from*

Cook Strait. I do not know how they work, but I suppose into the wind. If so, I am following them, if not . . . we will see. Won't be good for sleep. Later that night in his radio sked with Geoff Boyes of the Royal Yacht Club of Tasmania he inquired about the fishing habits of New Zealand squid boats, the lights of which he could see plainly. An operator from Western Port Safety Council overheard the conversation and called *Endeavour* to tell Sanders that the boats he could see were operating in similar fashion to squid boats in Bass Strait—side-on.

Endeavour officially cleared South Cape at 5.55 p.m. on Thursday 5 March—day 285—but Sanders still had plenty of hazards to occupy his mind . . . trawlers, squid boats and natural pitfalls like the Snares and the Traps. He was also worrying about his schedule and told his logbook: *Schedule running late? So far the speed of this yacht is less than anticipated from Fremantle. I hope I begin to slide faster or it will cost me an extra month or so to my schedule.*

At three o'clock next morning he wrote: *Not much wind. Cannot go to sleep because of proximity of squid boats*. At 3.25 a.m.: *Tacked, Snares clearly seen jutting over western horizon, flat top big rock (black) and small rock to south of it —from my viewpoint*. He was now closing on the squid boats and at 8.45 p.m. he could see the bright glow of the boats strung across the horizon like fairy lights at Christmas. "Ruin my sleep again," he muttered. At 11.35 p.m. he logged: *Squid boats galore*.

Just before midnight he tacked to avoid the conglomeration, which he referred to light-heartedly as "squidly-didly boats" circling the eastern horizon. He wondered if some were Japanese chased out of the Falklands by "Mother Thatcher". In bitter cold at two o'clock he tacked again to keep clear of the fishermen, and half an hour later was pleased to see the nearest squid boat move off. *That's good—now I can hold course for time being*, he wrote in his log.

By noon that day in fine and mild conditions he was enjoying Dunedin (South Island) Radio and had his fishing line out. The wind had changed from ENE (on his bow) to NNE, which enabled him to bring the yacht on to its proper course. He promptly turned off his satellite navigation, which had been consuming battery power for five days. His navigation lights had been burning for the past few nights and he had watched a video—for the third time—two nights earlier. His batteries were coping, just, and it was time to bring them back to full charge with his solar panels.

That following day, on an impulse, he decided on a drastic means to reduce his heavy coffee intake. The lone sailor grabbed several tins of coffee and hurled them overboard, leaving only a few tins. *So in a few months' time*, he told his log, *it will be tea. I'll become a "teaholic". Better that, I think*.

On Sunday 8 March, day 288, I had a long conversation with the solo circumnavigator, telling him about my Continental Airlines flight back to San Diego, Washington, DC, and New York with Dennis Conner and his crew and the America's Cup. I was fortunate to be one of only two journalists on board and Sanders was fascinated to hear of my visit to the White House, where President

Reagan honoured the crew, and the ticker-tape parade down New York's Fifth Avenue and a reception by Mayor Ed Koch.

In mid-afternoon he logged: *Wind has increased and is giving me a rough ride. Lots of water over the foredeck—always wet, and green weed slime is growing on the deck. Will scrub off when weather abates*. After supper that night he wrote: *Glow high in the sky SW. Squid boats, I suppose, eerie. Not the moon. Half of that is hanging low in the north*.

As *Endeavour* crashed her way through abysmal seas south of New Zealand, Sanders told himself that this was no new experience for him. In February-March 1982—in *Perie Banou*—he had experienced similar strong winds with an easterly component for twenty-one uncomfortable days. Now at 2.15 a.m. on 9 March he logged: *Oooh, wind 30–35 knots going to windward in aquatic earthquake conditions. Time to change down to storm jib. Rough as hessian bags—no, rougher*.

By mid-afternoon, however, the wind had moderated and the lone sailor pulled on his foulweather gear and went on deck to take two reefs out of the main. *About to give myself my four-monthly skinhead haircut*, he told his log. Fifteen minutes later he added: *Now I look like a crew-cut Yank—and I wonder where my beanie is.*

The following day he gravitated some fresh water from his number two tank to the less-than-half-empty number one tank. He was worried about his water supply. As *Endeavour* bashed her way into a persistent nor'easter he logged: *No rain here*. And he was using his cabin lights as little as possible—no navigation lights—to try to conserve battery power.

On day 291 (1 March) he observed that the weather was "persistently damp, boring and gloomy", and that *Endeavour* was going nowhere. Static from distant, unseen electrical storms was causing annoying interference on the radio.

That night he did not feel like a big meal, so he made a batch of scones and ate them hot with Vegemite, peanut butter, honey, jam and cream, followed by hot milky coffee. The following evening he made up with a big supper—macaroni, beef burgundy, Hawaiian chicken and half a tin of baked beans, all blended into an unappetising-looking goulash.

With the wind against him, and progress consequently poor, Sanders had decided not to head for his first echo-sounding patch, *because I will lose so much time, but will shape a course towards 177 deg. W, 43 deg. S—another patch. I could not possibly do them all anyway, too spread out. I must be able to fetch right conditions somewhere. Meanwhile I am conserving power and building up the batteries with the solar panels, specially for the high-voltage echo-sounder.*

He was also growing concerned about eventually running out of methylated spirits to prime the galley stove. Experiments with using kerosene as a primer were not a great success—black smoke filled the cabin, and he had to wipe the roof clean of stains each time.

Light rain fell the following day as *Endeavour* still plugged into an easterly. But the rain did little more than wash the salt off the mainsail and Sanders collected no water. In the afternoon he put out his fishing line, but failed to catch a fish. So the evening meal became another variation on a predictable theme of freeze-dried provisions.

The wind veered to the north on 14 March and Jon Sanders was able to steer a better course. At mid-morning he put out his canvas rain bucket when rain threatened, but the precipitation was tantalisingly close to the yacht without yielding a drop on *Endeavour*.

Clipping on his safety harness, he went to the foredeck with a scrubbing brush and removed some of the green slime growing on the deck. While on the forepeak, he leant over the side and found out why his sloop had sailed sluggishly in recent months. The whole forepeak topsides were thick with green weed and slime. There was also a sprinkling of thick gooseneck barnacles on the anti-fouling; certainly it was not over-infested or on the increase. The bottom anti-fouling, except for the gooseneck barnacles, was blue and generally clean.

A second inspection of the stern revealed bad gooseneck infestation, and Sanders realised he would have to go over the side when in South Atlantic sub-tropical waters and remove as many unwanted "passengers" as possible.

Light rain was falling as he watched a pod of dolphins with creamy white markings frolicking below *Endeavour*'s bow. But before the rain went away, he caught only two litres of brackish water.

12

Easter Near the Horn

Who hath desired the Sea?—the sight
of salt water unbounded—
The heave and the halt and the hurl
and the crash of the comber wind-
hounded?

Rudyard Kipling,
The Sea and the Hills

JUST as he had lost a day three months earlier—on Friday 12 December 1986 —when he crossed the International Date Line heading westward, Sanders now gained it back on 14 March 1987 as *Parry Endeavour* plied eastward across the South Pacific towards a second encounter with Cape Horn. He crossed the 180 deg. longitude line on day 295 at sea.

"Zooming along," as he put it, in a thirty to thirty-five-knot southerly, Sanders sighted Chatham Island on the port horizon and a big conical rock, which he supposed was Pitt Island. Later, Wellington Radio told him that mariners called the island "the Pitts".

In mid-afternoon, he was "guest speaker" at a Rotary dinner being held at Western Australia's Rottnest Island, answering questions through Wellington Radio from Dr. John Penrose, his brother Colin and others before a receptive audience of 700 Rotarians. It was a unique experience for the group to hear a guest speaker from the middle of the South Pacific.

Sanders was now starting the third of his five logbooks and took the opportunity to enter some salient notes on navigation: *All dead reckonings in the previous two logbooks have been done manually with my NC77 calculator. Needless to say, self-steering device zig-zags and wind variations cause other zig-zags, and while I'm asleep the yacht zig-zags—whenever. So course steered is my estimate, as is also the speed and distance run (the B and G speed and distance-run log is malfunctioning). From today, I will dead reckon with NC77 as above when satellite navigator is switched off, and let the satellite navigator do a constant dead reckoning between fixes by programming the estimated course being steered and the estimated speed—correcting from time to time as course and speed changes. And if ever all should break down, it will be back to sextant, tables etc. that have served me so well in all my other voyages.*

About five weeks after he logged this, his satellite navigation equipment failed through condensation in his cabin, necessitating a return to "seat-of-the-pants" navigation for the solo sailor.

On Sunday 15 March (day 296) he had high hopes of replenishing his dwindling water supplies when light showers started to fall mid-afternoon. The rain did little but wash the salt from his mainsail, but he stuck to his task and by supper time had caught about six litres of potable rainwater.

The favourable southerly wind continued blowing beam-on and *Endeavour* was making good progress—120 nautical miles a day—eastward. Short, sharp showers were helping his water supply position.

To conserve his food supplies, Sanders

stopped eating lunch every day, contenting himself with a cup of milky tea.

At 4 p.m. on day 300 he switched on his echo-sounder for a test pattern and to experiment in finding the bottom, which he did successfully on range 400. He promptly switched it off to conserve power for a thirty-mile probe of the ocean depths that night over 42 deg. 04 S and 162 deg. 55 W. At nine o'clock that night he logged: *Good echo on chart, perfect recording 1000 fathoms to 800 fathoms, but hopeless under 800. Don't know why. I've certainly searched the controls . . . it seems to only work on Phase 3.*

In some frustration he added before retiring to his bunk: *I have established poor to nil readout on Phase 2. But good read on Phase 3. Thus I lose bottom between 800 fathoms and 650 fathoms and under 400 fathoms. I have tested all functions and do not know why.* (Jon did not know then that the sounder was misreading. When he later consulted the service manual he found the fault, which made him a happy man, because the scientific input into this voyage was important to him.)

On Monday 27 March, after a quiet weekend, Jon Sanders again tried to probe the ocean depths with his highly sophisticated echo sounder. He got a recording on the ocean floor at depths of between 970 and 1040 fathoms, but the yacht was almost becalmed and he did not cover the area he wanted to. He was also limited by the amount of power in his batteries. The sounder needed a lot of power and he could not afford to have it turned on when he was almost stationary.

The lack of wind—only fifty-four miles covered in twenty-four hours—hampered the sloop the following day, so Sanders heaved to and did some work on his self-steering apparatus. He installed a new Servo rudder shaft and bearing unit (new cogs) because the bearing showed slackness from wear and tear. At 12.45 p.m. he noted: *Self-steering now okay, fully serviced. (This dummy also dropped two knives overboard.)*

Practising his camera work occupied much of a quiet day 306 at sea. At 6.15 p.m. he told his logbook: *Completed filming inside cabin but camera not functioning properly because of sticking (got wet off Cape Horn in October*).

Jon Sanders was determined to continue his search for a submerged south land mass, so he altered course the following day to follow a line drawn on his chart for him by Perth marine scientist Dr. John Penrose before he left on his voyage. Soon after midnight, following a night of probing, he logged: *Getting definite results on echo sounder.* He also logged his hourly readings during the night.

At 9.30 a.m. that day he got a good true echo at 411 fathoms, which indicated he was sailing over a submarine mountain or plateau. A NNE wind was pushing *Endeavour* along at a brisk rate in sunny weather, and the sun helped prevent the yacht's batteries losing too much power. That afternoon he put a reef in the mainsail as the wind got stronger, then found that the bottom was getting dramatically deeper and that the mountain peak he had sailed over that morning was right on the line Dr. Penrose had marked on his chart.

He radio-telephoned Penrose the following night through Wellington Radio, and both men were elated at the preliminary results.

On April Fool's Day—day 312—he logged as he sailed with a single-reefed main over a grey and bleak-looking sea: *Sewed some flaps on to my water-catching canvas bucket to help catch some of the outside splashes. I need to catch rain, but none about. Drought!*

Through Penta Constat radio he heard a tragic real-life drama of the sea being enacted. A French aircraft had dropped a liferaft to a sinking yacht in the two-handed Melbourne-to-Osaka ocean race and one person was seen to have swum to it. An RAAF Orion was flying to the area.

At noon the following day, Sanders was confiding his own small problems to his log: *Would like to steer 142 deg. or 118 deg. to pass over 45 deg. 47 S and 134.4 W, but cannot lift to that course. I crossed the South Pacific October-November against westerlies and now I'm going t'other way against easterlies—poor me.*

Sanders took advantage of a mild, gloomy day on 3 April to "make and mend". He scrubbed off the green slime growing on the foredeck and replaced

Endeavour's starboard genoa jib halyard. On his sked with Penta Constat that night he heard more of the drama in the Melbourne-Osaka race. A position was given for the yacht *Castaway Fiji*, which had lost her keel and capsized, throwing both crewmen into the sea. The yacht did not right itself till the mast snapped underwater. One crewman was lost and the other was crouched in the liferaft dropped by the French aircraft. His heart went out to his fellow yachtsmen, and it was difficult not to dwell on the potential hazards in his own journey. However, he was confident, barring a terrible accident, his sturdy yacht would stand up to anything the sea could hurl at it. Well, almost anything.

Still seeking rain, he put out his canvas bucket the following morning after breakfast and at 9.10 a.m. he logged: *The sweetest sound on* Parry Endeavour *is fresh water dribbling into the water tank as is now, sometimes at a rate of a fast dribble*. He noted two hours later: *Batteries' charges are just holding. I will not switch satellite navigation on today for first time this voyage in the hope the batteries will begin to pick up soon*. Later: *Suspect I may have caught 20 litres of drinking water. Sky now breaking up*.

He was now about halfway across the South Pacific and on a gloomy and sometimes foggy Sunday 5 April, he chased rain clouds again, observing that the gloom and fog were not helping his solar panels recharge his batteries, depleted because of the echo-sounding. But it rained late in the afternoon and he logged enthusiastically: *Hooray, it is raining and I am catching it*. Five minutes later: *Oh dear, it has stopped, perhaps more showers will come*. That night the barometer plummeted and *Parry Endeavour* sailed into a thirty to forty-knot gale, which rose to forty-five knots by dawn the next day. By breakfast, the yacht was running under fully-reefed mainsail and no jib. The gale moderated in the afternoon and backed to the west and the sun made the rough sea sparkle as the clouds cleared. *Endeavour* made 145 miles.

A superb navigator by any standard, Jon Sanders was having fair success with his sextant and dead reckoning as *Endeavour* surged towards Cape Horn. He logged at

2.20 p.m. on 7 April—day 318: *Took morning sight, then transferred that position line to noon when I took a meridian sight, dead-reckoned to 1407 hours. Got first satellite navigation fix for today. I have a 2.9 min. (nearly three miles) error from my fixes and dead-reckoning. Considering the very big swell and no (speed) log, that's okay. I also experimented with some other sights*.

That afternoon he serviced the main-sheet winch, but found he had run out of winch grease. He substituted a mixture of engine oil and vaseline and that appeared to work equally well.

At breakfast the following day he logged: *Jellyfish about with small sail on top, also a different sea bird soaring from the usual six one finds in the southern oceans*.

Cold, grey, damp and bleak weather continued. On his third successive foggy day he was unable to get a sun sight to fix his position. However, this did not worry him because he was still 1300 miles north-west of Cape Horn and steering a correct course.

At 1 a.m. on Sunday 12 April, just after

he kept a radio sked with Penta Constat, he noted that the nor'wester had piped up to thirty-five knots, and by breakfast time it was blowing force nine gale—forty knots-plus. *Dear me*, he logged, *it's awful windy. Time for third reef in mainsail*. After reefing the main he took down the jib and *Endeavour* was running downward at a brisk rate of knots.

Sanders became apprehensive when the gale strengthened to force ten—forty to sixty knots. The yacht was surfing too fast under her fully-reefed mainsail, so he tried putting out a sea brake. But he found the sloop tended to come side-on to the rough sea and decided to haul the sea brake back on board. *Hove-to*, he reported to his log at 9.15 p.m. as the wind tore at his yacht's rigging. But when he returned to his cabin after an hour on deck retrieving the sea brake and squaring things away, he found he had left his galley sink tap on. *Flooded jolly floor*, he wrote. *Very annoying as saloon area of the yacht is normally dry*. At one o'clock the following morning he logged: *Heavy gale continues, 45–60 knots SW. Some nasty waves pranging the yacht. Poor waves!*

A few minutes later he kept his sked with Penta Constat and told them his position and the weather he was encountering. The gale moderated slightly at mid-morning, so *Endeavour* was helmed around to run downward in a frightful sea. At 4.30 p.m. he logged: *Hoisted working jib. Waves left from gale huge, 60 ft., maybe more. Wind 25 knots SW, bleak.*

At dusk he noticed the forestays were clashing, so he climbed back into his foul-weather gear and edged his way to the foredeck. Clipped securely by his safety harness to his runner line and barefooted, he switched the jib from the starboard outer forestay to the port outer forestay. *Managed also to further tighten port fore-stay, but starboard ditto gummed up, so sprayed with CRC and will try another day*, he wrote. *Cold and bleak.*

To his relief the gale moderated overnight and though the South Pacific swell was still huge, at least the wind had abated. After a light lunch he decided to shape a direct course to 56 deg. S, 71 deg. W—the Cape Horn region.

Sanders spent five hours the next day servicing the mainsail, preparing it for the sort of gales he would expect around the Horn. Later in the afternoon he wrote: *Now shaping course in light breeze to 46 deg. S, 99 deg. 7 W to echo sound another region*. But his battery power was too low for echo-sounding—weeks of overcast and foggy days had seen to that. So by 4 p.m. he had decided against any sounding and altered course for Cape Horn.

Predictably another gale sprang up from the north-north-west overnight and by 2 a.m. Sanders had storm-reefed his mainsail again. But the gale abated during the afternoon and light rain began falling—sufficient for him to catch a few litres of rainwater, perhaps a day's supply, in his canvas bucket.

At 1 a.m. on Good Friday, 17 April, he logged: *Cold, sky clearing, 15 knots NNW wind, barometer low and falling. Caught a little rain, need lots more*. Radio reception for his sked with Penta Constat was excellent that morning. By breakfast time the wind had backed to south-west and was blowing at gale-force. Quickly he brought in his rain bucket and storm-reefed the main. When he noticed a lull around lunch time, he hoisted a working jib and logged a few minutes later: *Still very rough. I should have made it a storm jib*. Five minutes later: *Too rough. Oh dear, better change to storm jib, self-steerer not coping*. The gale continued at night, increasing to forty knots. The lone sailor realised his batteries were running low on voltage when Penta Costa could not read him the following morning.

The weather was still squally at dawn, but he kept his rain bucket out and was rewarded with five litres of fresh water. After his usual breakfast of muesli and hot milk and Milo, he logged: *Satellite navigation switch on. Lots of condensation about. Hope it does not interfere with my electrics*. The gale continued all day and at dusk he reported: *Yacht rolls muchly in a very big sea*. The Cape Horn region was living up to its evil reputation.

The gale persisted most of the next day, Easter Sunday, but moderated late in the afternoon. At 5.10 p.m. he logged: *It is dark in the cabin. Wind NW 20 knots, barometer falling. Put rain bucket out as NW usually brings rain—but keeping all reefs in*.

The following morning as he wondered

what his friends were doing back home on this Easter Monday holiday, he noted that he had caught about twenty litres of precious rainwater. The wind dropped right away to a few knots, but the yacht rolled in a sea that Sanders aptly labelled "yukky".

After breakfast next morning he saw the first Cape Pigeons he had seen for several months, testimony that the world's most notorious cape was looming up in this lonely corner of the world. He noted in his log: *Not getting much useful shortwave radio in this region. The BBC in* Perie Banou *was loud and clear, so that frequency must now be off the air. I get it on 12 megs later in the day—clear for a while*.

By mid-morning the wind was squalling at forty-five to fifty knots NNW and the barometer was low—998 millibars. He was catching nothing but sea spray in his rain bucket, so he brought it in. At noon *Endeavour* was sailing fully reefed in a howling gale, and two hours later Sanders logged: *Barometer reads 977, the lowest yet. The record low on* Perie Banou *was 977 in the same region*. At 3.45 p.m.:

Barometer 968! That breaks Perie Banou*'s lowest*.

The gale increased and at 6.15 a.m. he wrote: *Gale now most severe. Gybed yacht, which was hairy-scary and now hove to, winds 50 knots west. I guess it is what you get near Cape Horn, but I don't like it*.

Next morning he put his yacht's clock on two hours to Cape Horn time. He was unable to give his position to Penta Constat, because they could not read him. At noon *Endeavour* was rolling along on a cold, wintry, rough ocean, and while her skipper was trying to get a satellite navigation fix, the milk for his Milo boiled over. But that was the least of his worries. At 12.50 p.m. he logged: *Satellite navigator cold and cannot reinitiate it*. He badly needed the sophisticated aid in the rough seas he expected around the Horn. At 1.15 p.m. he wrote: *Oh dear, sat nav. will not initiate*. He lit his oven and one burner of his stove to warm up the cabin. He tried all afternoon to restart the equipment, but without success. Mid-afternoon saw *Parry Endeavour* surfing before a forty-knot gale. At 4.40 p.m. he logged:

Yacht gybed, got it back on course. The sea is so rough it is a sight to behold . . . very stormy. An hour later: *Hove-to 50 deg. into wind port tack. Wind to 50 knots NW. Very, very rough.*

Jon Sanders' wind speed estimates have always been conservative, as have his wave height reckonings. He is noted among his sailing colleagues to be a master of understatement.

When the gale moderated that night, Sanders climbed into his cockpit to square the mainsail and *Endeavour* leapt forward again. For his troubles the solo sailor was drenched by a big "greenie" that half-filled his spacious cockpit. *Bitter cold*, he noted.

Worried about the malfunction in his satellite navigator, Sanders installed a new display board and display panel into it, but it brought no improvement. But later that day he tried it again and it worked. He surmised that the cold was affecting it, or his batteries were a trifle low. The overcast skies were not helping his solar panels do their job, and Sanders' last entry for day 334 was: *20 knots NW wind, 5.6C outside, 11C inside. Batteries are low, writing this with torch to conserve power.*

The following noon he got a sun sight with his sextant and his fix and his dead reckoning tallied exactly, well, to a decimal point, with the latitude found. That afternoon he wrote: *Sun is out, but it is cold. I am living in a frigid world.*

As *Parry Endeavour* neared the Horn on Saturday 25 April—Anzac Day in Australia—Sanders "slept in"—instead of climbing out of his bunk at 3 a.m. for his radio sked with Penta, he arose at six o'clock. The yacht was in the middle of a thirty to forty-five-knot gale. At mid-morning she broached on a big wave, but slowly recovered by herself. Squalls up to fifty knots were lashing the sloop. It rained several times during the day, but the wind strength made it impossible for Sanders to catch any. That night he ate by torchlight to conserve his batteries.

But when the wind moderated next morning and rain was still falling, Sanders grabbed for his rain-catching bucket. At 9.45 a.m. he logged: *Light, steady rain continues. The drought on drinking water is broken. No. 1 tank now two-thirds full.* His fresh water worries were over for months now, because he knew he would catch lots later in the equatorial trough. The wind backed to a freezing southerly —"straight off Antarctica," he told himself as he shivered on the foredeck hoisting a storm jib.

Although it was freezing the next day, *Endeavour* was sailing comfortably in a twenty-five-knot sou'wester. He had made good 125 bleak miles in twenty-four hours. At midnight he recorded: *Gybed the yacht. Sea is crazy around here. Turned sat-nav. on as getting closer to Tierra del Fuego. I should see in morning*.

At 2.25 a.m. in pitch darkness Sanders logged with the aid of a torch: *Sat-nav. is rejecting fixes. Hope it comes up with one soon because of battery power. It is windy —35 with squalls to 40 and very cold*. The thermometer in his cabin read 6.8C. Two hours later he logged with some relief: *Sat. fix came up at last and all well. Need not have bothered to put it on. Never mind, we know where we are for sure*. (The fix when it finally came up, was close to his dead reckoning.)

His log entries just before noon on that day (28 April) read: *Hoisted storm jib. Conditions moderate, big swell, very cold.*

It is best to keep the sails small and tidy in the bitter cold conditions. Gales quickly rise in this region. In mid-afternoon he noted somewhat apprehensively that the barometer was falling.

At 4.20 p.m. he sighted the first land he had seen for weeks and logged: *Land ho! Tierra del Fuego to the north on the horizon. Sat-nav. on.* Twenty minutes later he wrote: *Isla Ildefonso three points port side.*

The following day, Wednesday 29 April, Jon Sanders sailed round Cape Horn for the second time on his epic voyage, his total non-stop voyage now 340 days old and 33,105 nautical miles long.

By way of pleasant contrast, his first log entry for the day, an hour after midnight, referred to mild sailing even though it was cold. Then he gybed the yacht as a navigation precaution (he was in the vicinity of the Hermite Group). *Maintaining 20–mile danger circles on all hazards because of black night and possible effect of currents*, he logged. *This is one area where I would specially like to have sat-nav. working.*

At breakfast time he gybed again and set a course to pass south of the east end of

Isla de Los Estados. After his muesli and hot milk, he sighted more land to the north and at ten o'clock he had a clear view of the famous Cape but it was too cloudy to get a sextant sight of the sun. Just after three he established radio contact with the Argentine Ushuaia base on the Beagle Channel, and through radio-telephone was able to get through loud and clear to his brother Colin.

With his satellite navigator out of commission and no break in the clouds through which to get a sun sight with his sextant, Sanders could only surmise exactly where he was. He wrote in mid-afternoon: *Suspect Cape Horn bears 293 deg. through Commander binoculars*. [He had focussed his binoculars, which has a built-in compass, on a land mass he could see through the haze.] *It is obvious I am much farther south, but will use my 1500 dead reckoning as that is closer to all hazards. Perhaps tomorrow I will get good fixes*. He tried to work out his position on his calculator, but he concluded that he couldn't be where he reckoned he was. *I am not there*, he wrote, *as Cape Horn would be jumping down my throat. Suspect at 56 deg. 11 min.*

At 7 p.m. he noted: *Stars are out and it is very cold, not much wind*. Two hours later: *Nearly out of wind—better that than a storm*.

After a quiet, cold night he logged at breakfast time: *Sea conditions and wind mild, hoisted working jib. Mt. Compana unmistakably clear. I've not made much progress*. At 10.10 a.m. he wrote: *Weather is as mild as it can be with seven-eighths sun in blue sky and quiet blue sea—how about that! It won't last for long in this region*. He was able to get a good sun sight and worked out his noon position—55 deg. 30.4 S, 64 deg. 41.5 E. *It seems*, he wrote, *I was close to where I thought I was yesterday, but I had doubts*.

At 2.50 p.m. he sighted Isla de Los Estados clearly. He noted that the Cape Horn Current was setting his yacht to the east—as expected. Just before dusk he could smell Estados—a sweet land smell to one whose olfactory nerves were so attuned to the sea.

Next morning *Parry Endeavour* tacked quietly northwards in a light northerly.

Sanders would have liked the breeze in any other direction—and the barometer was falling. Early in the afternoon he discovered that his Servo self-steering rudder had disappeared. It had either worked its bolt undone or snapped it. He fitted a new rudder and told himself he would replace the steering chain on the tiller as soon as he got into warmer waters. He noticed a lot of kelp in the sea that afternoon and theorised that heavy kelp could have snapped the self-steerer bolt.

On Saturday 2 May he noted over breakfast that the weather on the east side of Tierra del Fuego was definitely much better than on the other side. And he was able to get Falklands Radio on his set. Dozens of albatrosses wheeled around *Endeavour*, and early in the afternoon he sighted about twenty melon-headed whales around the sloop. On the radio he heard the minimum temperature forecast for Stanley the following day—4C. He logged at 4.25 p.m.: *If it was not so cold, it is beautiful sailing, but would like to get more west into my course*.

Of his four lonely passages around Cape Horn, this had been one of the less traumatic, he told himself. He was well pleased that it was uneventful and he looked forward to passing by the Falkland Islands shortly, then into warmer waters.

13

Collision!

Like a red morn, that ever yet
betokened
Wrack to the seaman, tempest to the
field

William Shakespeare,
Venus and Adonis

ON Sunday 3 May 1987, having cleared Cape Horn, Jon Sanders was sailing north-westwards to pass to the west of the Falkland Islands. Overnight he took four sights with his sextant on two stars to practise his celestial navigation. *Lovely day*, he told his log-book at dawn. *Cold, but clear*.

At 10.30 a.m. he logged: *Land ho! Falkland Islands. Very low, two points starboard bow*. By early afternoon the islands of West Falkland and Weddell were clearly visible abeam the starboard side of *Parry Endeavour*. At five o'clock he tacked so as not to get too close to the Falklands that night. At 10 p.m. he pithily referred to the "glow of squid boats to the north—many of them." That seemingly innocent little entry contained no hint of events that would threaten an abrupt and senseless end to his epic voyage.

It was Sanders' mother's birthday the following day, and he recorded it on top of his logbook page for his 345th day at sea: *My Mum's birthday today*. His dear mother, the guiding light in his unorthodox yet colourful life. He could still hear her words when he opted out of school team sports . . . "Son, who wants to be ordinary? Why don't you be original?" Being where he was on his mother's eightieth birthday, Jonathan Sanders was heeding his mother's advice. He thought of her a great deal that day and wondered what she would be doing. She had not been well when he left nearly a year ago on his triple-circumnavigation attempt, but he had sailed with her blessing—and his also-frail father's. Now he had lost his father and the lone sailor wondered if his mother would last till his return.

At 4 a.m. on his mother's birthday he

noted in his log: *Overcast. Squid boat glow seems farther away*. At dawn he tacked and logged: *Ship lights about two miles, two points starboard bow. Misty*.

By breakfast time *Endeavour* was shrouded by fog as Sanders tuned into the British Forces Broadcasting Service on Falklands Radio. He heard the radio's weather forecast—mild now, but an intense low pressure system moving into Drake Passage, its approach to be headed by northerly winds. At mid-morning he wrote: *Can make out the Falklands on the horizon. Expect to see Jason Island group clearly by dusk.*

Endeavour sailed on through patches of fog all morning and late in the afternoon Sanders put a reef in the mainsail, heedful of the low pressure weather warning. At 5.05 p.m. he logged: *Squid boats ahead, will tack soon*.

Half an hour later he told his log that he could see eight, possibly more, squid boats around him. They were well spread out, unlike those he crossed south of New Zealand. He put a second reef into the mainsail.

At 6.30 p.m. he sighted yet another squid boat's lights. It was going to be a sleepless night, he told himself. He could not afford to sleep for long periods in this crowded ocean. But he felt comfortable about setting a course in steadily-rising seas that would take him well away from the nearest fishing boats and allow him to rest after supper.

For a split second Jon Sanders thought he was having a nightmare. He heard a crash up for'ard followed by the agonised shriek of tortured steel. Leaping from his bunk, he reached the cockpit companionway in two giant strides.

He thrust his head and shoulders from the hatch entrance in time to hear excited oriental voices from above and see several wide-eyed brown faces as *Parry Endeavour* bounced off a squid trawler.

The trawler's arc lights bathed the unhappy scene and Sanders saw his jib ballooning away from the yacht and his mast had a strange lean. The bow rail was a tangled mess.

Traumatic thoughts of voyage's end flooded Sanders' mind as he clipped on his safety harness and almost ran forward along the pitching deck of his sloop to see if the collision bulkhead had helped *Endeavour* to survive the impact. The South Atlantic had been whipped up by a twenty-five knot NNW wind and the temperature was a frigid 5C.

Cursing himself, he was nevertheless relieved to find that below his mangled pulpit—the stainless steel frame around the bow—there were no apparent holes in the fibreglass hull. The starboard forestay had been snapped and was now gyrating wildly and clashing with the other rigging. Other mast rigging was loose.

His quick assessment was that he would be able to sail on, and though he was angry with himself, he knew this potential disaster was not going to stop his attempt to be the first sailor to circumnavigate the world three times alone and non-stop.

His logbook records it thus: *2035—AWFUL! Collided with foreign squid boat, about 4000 tons. Broke forestay (starboard), but port forestay appears to be okay. Smashed pulpit. Yacht seems okay. No holes that I can detect. Lucky the rigging is so strong. Most upsetting. Wind 20–25 knots NNW—a wind change.*

Twenty minutes later he added: *Yacht appears okay. Balance of broken forestay swinging around from top of mast, will recover in smoother waters. Centre back stay is now loose, must have helped take the shock. Lucky the bow is reinforced etc. Pulpit a tangled mess.*

And so ended his mother's birthday. He hoped that she had enjoyed her birthday more than he had.

Just after midnight he logged: *The broken forestay is flying around and making an unpleasant din on the other rigging. Wind 25–35, barometer falling.* Still shaken by the collision, Sanders got little sleep for the rest of the night. At 5.50 a.m.—before dawn—he logged: *Many squid ships about.*

Around dawn he spoke to the British fisheries patrol vessel *Falklands Desire* on his VHF radio and told them about the previous night's mishap.

The consummate sailor set about righting things as best possible given the conditions—a thirty to thirty-five-knot north-west wind. Let his logbook tell the story: *1020: Got yacht sailing again. Two reefs and storm jib. Got sights on sun through cloud. The starboard outer forestay broke about 10 feet above deck and it wrapped around and through everything. It took about two hours and climbing the mast to the first spreaders three times to free. I attached a rope to the stay with a bulldog clip—that was clever. The forestay remaining was looser and so were two of the three backstays. I adjusted them. The pulpit is a tangled mess. Nothing I can do, but on a quiet day will relocate the now-loose lifelines to the messy tangle.*

Just before noon he noted that the sun was shining through the clouds. Its brightness was cheering, and good for sights.

That afternoon he radio-telephoned Dr. John Penrose and his brother Colin to tell them of the previous night's collision, playing down the damage. As the afternoon wore on the wind dropped and Sanders was able to take the one remaining reef out of the main. At 6.10 p.m. he noted: *Squid boats all around but over horizon thus far.*

It was a sleepless night for the solo circumnavigator who did not want a repetition of the previous night's near disaster. At 9.30 p.m. he logged: *Light three points starboard bow, two or three miles. Out of wind*. Even though *Endeavour* was not going anywhere much, he could not afford to relax. At 3.10 a.m. he noted: *Still out of wind, squid vessels all around horizon*. When light rain started falling an hour later he put out his rain bucket. At breakfast time he logged: *Cold and quiet. Bow looks strange because pulpit is all smashed up*. But he continually told himself how much worse it could have been.

He made only thirty-four nautical miles for the twenty-four hours, and at sunset he logged gloomily: *Squid vessels all about again. Oh dear*.

Heavy hail lashed *Parry Endeavour* in the early hours of the following morning, Thursday, 7 May, and by breakfast time the begrimed sloop was running before a twenty-five-knot sou'wester, which squalled up to forty knots and over by the time Sanders had downed his second cup of hot-milk Milo. At mid-morning he was forced to brave the chill outside—it was 5C with a wind chill factor dragging it below zero—to put two reefs in the mainsail, because the wind was now a cold, southerly gale hitting forty-five knots.

Just after midday Sanders had to alter course to avoid a big red-painted trawler, possibly East European, which passed close by. Far out to sea he could make out a huge tanker.

The wind howled around *Endeavour* for most of the day. Later in the afternoon the yacht gybed and Sanders got it back on course and put a third reef into the mainsail. It then broached and partly filled the cockpit with water, so he gybed it to the other tack. The broach sent unsecured things flying everywhere in the cabin and saloon.

Towards sundown the gale abated, though Sanders could see plenty of squalls around his yacht. The wind had moderated enough by 5 a.m. next day for two of the three reefs to be taken out, and *Endeavour* was running downwind before a chilly south breeze. At 9.35 a.m. he logged: *Seem to have lost Seiko yacht timer, possibly came off my wrist and went splash. I only wear it part of the day, but might have lost it in yesterday's gale.*

But his next log notation recorded having found it under his chart table.

He was still in a busy shipping lane and had to be constantly on the alert. Just after noon he reported: *Ship out to starboard, perhaps fishing, and a seal nearby*. Two oil tankers passed him during the afternoon.

Endeavour sailed slowly in a light northwest wind through patches of fog, which lifted to enable the navigator to take a sun sight. At mid-morning on day 350 he logged with some relief: *It is definitely getting warmer, day by day, thank goodness*. After lunch he tensioned the lifelines that were loosened by the collision five days earlier, and the next day, as pleasant conditions continued, he spent a couple of hours resecuring lee cloths on the port quarter berth, restowing gear and generally cleaning up. Condensation was everywhere and so, inevitably, was mould.

Sanders was still navigating with sextant, taking running fixes of the sun in the morning on line-of-position and carrying them through to noon to get his latitude and then work out his fix. He noted: *I am navigating without a distance-run or speed log working. But I am used to that. I estimate the speed and multiply by time. I will monkey around with my satellite navigator when batteries build up again. I have a spare power supply for it and alternative aerial.*

After breakfast on day 353, though the wind was near gale force at thirty to thirty-five-knots, the sea water was warm, indicating the proximity of the Brazil Current. *No more shivering. Hooray*, Sanders logged. At nine that night all was peaceful, with *"a ribbon of moonlight across the sea".*

And so *Parry Endeavour* sailed north-eastwards towards the Equator and another rounding of the rocks of St. Peter and St. Paul. Sanders was enjoying the balmy sailing breeze and days of a hundred miles or more made good were aplenty. But soon after he crossed latitude 40 deg. he struck squalls up to fifty knots and frequent winds between thirty and thirty-five knots. They pushed his yacht along and on day 355, *Endeavour* made good 138 miles. As if to frustrate his expectations of plain and pleasant sailing for a while, the squalls now were accompanied by heavy gales and rain. Just before noon on 16 May he logged: *Gale persists, 35 to 40. I thought I left the gales behind, thought wrong*. But the temperature inside the cabin was a pleasant 20C, and the sun had come out.

At one minute past midnight the following day, he confided: *Would like this gale to die down. Think I will drop the jib and slow the yacht. There are some bad waves, perhaps caused by the Brazil Current*. Ten minutes later: *Jib down. Wind stronger than 35 knots. Bad sea*. It remained rough with persistent squalls till mid-morning when conditions moderated. After lunch he took out two of the reefs and left one in just in case the squalls returned. They did.

But by the following morning the weather was again mild and *Endeavour* was running downwind with a full main and no jib—it was secured to the foredeck ready to be raised. The wind faded right out and at 10.45 p.m. the lone sailor wrote: *Not enough wind for the yacht to steer properly. The yacht does not steer very well on the starboard gybe. I shall have to alter the cog setting on the self-steerer one calm day*.

For a man who tended to live by the clock at sea—to help him maintain radio skeds, and not oversleep in tight navigational situations—Sanders suddenly found himself in a predicament. Both his VDO ship's alarm clocks were out of action. The one over his chart table had simply stopped altogether, and had been replaced with an older model (normally positioned over the bunk) which was first prize in a yachting event. Its sweeping second hand had fallen off, and while trying to fix it back on, Sanders had damaged the alarm.

On day 360 he worked out his first navigational fix in four days and was gratified to find it was only 0.4 of a mile away from dead reckoning longitude and 0.8 of a mile out in latitude. That afternoon he worked on installing a new power supply to his satellite navigational equipment.

The solo circumnavigator got a big fright four days from the first anniversary of his departure. He was rudely awakened at 2.15 a.m. by the sound of a ship's siren and the glare of a spotlight on his yacht. "Don't need this," he grumbled as he climbed through the companionway into the cockpit. The ship, bigger than a trawler, cruised around the yacht, and Sanders wondered if it was a Brazilian navy vessel. He tried calling it on his VHF radio, but there was no answer. He wrote in his logbook: *It was approaching the yacht from the SE, rounded the yacht 50 metres away and sailed off to the east. Perhaps picked me up by radar*. He thought it might have been a survey vessel out of Mar del Plata, Argentina, more than a thousand miles away, or even the Argentine Coast Guard, possibly alerted by the Australian Department of Foreign Affairs.

After breakfast, with a pleasant, mild breeze evident from the south, Sanders hoisted the full main and working jib. By noon he realised that he had found the South-East Trade winds, which would speed him on his way north to the Equator. That evening he noted that his yacht's batteries still had not recovered from the leaden skies of the previous cold, stormy months.

When the lone sailor attempted to call Itajai and Santos Radio after lunch the following day, he was perturbed to get no sound at all, not even static. And the channel display had stopped functioning. *Perhaps radio out of action*, he told his log. Three hours later he tried again, without success. He logged pessimistically: *It seems the Codan 4000 is out of action. This will henceforth make it difficult to make contact as I am now very limited in frequencies. Though channel 404 is used by Brazil, and I have that left. May be able to make contact by sea on my other smaller sets in this region*.

Endeavour had been sailing well before the South-East Trades, but late in the afternoon the breeze moderated and swung, heading the yacht in a sloppy sea. The barometer was falling, so he left two reefs in the mainsail for the present. It was a prudent decision. He awoke from a short nap fifteen minutes after midnight to find *Endeavour* in a typical—for this region—north-east squall of about thirty-five knots. Sheet lightning was illuminating the white-caps round his yacht. By 1.40 a.m. it was a full gale and Sanders put a third reef in the main and hoisted a storm jib. The gale was still tearing at the sturdy sloop's patched-up rigging at noon when he logged: *Very rough. 35–40 knots*.

By early afternoon the gale had increased to forty to forty-five knots, and there was heavy rain. The bad weather continued all afternoon, but just before sundown it backed to the west and started to moderate. Sanders dropped the storm jib and *Endeavour* was running downwind at a good rate of knots at nine o'clock.

In the small hours of the following morning, Saturday 23 May, the gale died right out, but left an ugly swell. Sanders unreefed the mainsail and let the yacht have her head downwind.

It was turning out to be a mild, sunny day, so he busied himself with chores. He found to his consternation that both his old and new Codan 6801 radios were not receiving properly. Believing it could be the speakers, he sprayed them with electric cleaning solvent.

In the afternoon he spent several hours working on the rigging that was damaged by his Falklands collision. He had to climb halfway up the mast to effect some of the repairs. He hacksawed and tidied up the end of the broken forestay and attached a new kevlar rope to it with two bulldog clips, then moved the damaged wire-to-rope forestay out to the forepeak and fastened the rope with the bulldog clips to a turnbuckle and tightened it. He now had a "saver" forestay. It was for strength only —he could not hank a jib on to it, because of the bulldog clips.

He also decided to change sextants, putting away his old, trusty Saura that had seen him safely the equivalent of about four times round the world, and switching to a Tamaya. He logged the reason: *The Saura has a plus 8.2–minute index error and the Tamaya 2.4–minute index error. I adjust with calculations (prefer not to attempt to correct the sextants).*

Next morning *Endeavour* was becalmed. After breakfast Sanders tried his high-frequency radios again. He logged with some concern: *All three main HF radios playing up. Condensation must have got at the lot.*

He boasted to his logbook half an hour later: *My two sights this morning were within 12 nautical miles of each other and 0.6 of a mile away from my dead reckoning. How about that.* As his sloop sailed quietly in a light north-easterly, the lone sailor spent two hours servicing his self-steering gear, adjusting the tooth setting on the cog and replacing the steering lines.

At mid-afternoon he noted that his yacht's batteries were still low and he could not contact Rio de Janeiro Radio with his suspect HF radio. At 5.55 p.m. he wrote: *Listened to a superb programme on the BBC World Service on the First Fleet to Australia under Captain Arthur Phillip*. A few minutes later he heard rain on his roof, and after allowing time for the salt to be washed off the mainsail, he put out his canvas rain-catching bucket. At 10.30 p.m. he logged happily: *Harvesting fresh water. About 18 knots from south at moment, but suspect rain causing temporary wind change*. The fall proved incessant and steady and it did not take long to fill both tanks.

Not long after, *Parry Endeavour* and her doughty skipper completed one year at sea in their attempt to circumnavigate the world three times. They were past the halfway mark, and though they had shared setbacks and misfortune, both of them were in good shape to spend another eleven or twelve months at sea, longer if necessary.

I managed to get through to Jon Sanders by radio telephone via a linkup with Rio Radio that night. He was in good spirits and philosophical about his collision two weeks earlier. "Realistically," he said, his voice faint but clear, "one can't expect to do laps of the world without something going wrong." He said he believed he and his yacht would have no trouble in completing three roundings of the world by his self-imposed deadline of 1 April 1988. (His intention then was to finish his triple-circumnavigation in Sydney Harbour for the Bicentennial celebrations.) "We should do it okay if there are no disasters with other vessels or serious injury to me," he added. "I'm pleased with my progress since the collision and I don't think my mast is going to be any problem. But I'm really bored with my diet. I dream of having a nice feed of steak and eggs or a shearer's stew with plenty of plump mutton chops."

Jon Sanders wrote on the top of page 445 of his third logbook on Monday 25 May 1987: *One year today. 200th Anniversary of US Constitution*. At 3.30 a.m. he logged: *More rain, wind light-moderate, pitch black night. All water tanks and jerry cans full of fresh water*. By breakfast time, however, squally winds were punctuating the pleasant breeze and the solo sailor put two reefs into the mainsail and dropped his jib.

That afternoon he squandered some of his fresh water in washing and rinsing his thermal cardigan and vest. The sky outside his cabin was bruised black and he put his rain bucket out to top up his containers. At 4.40 p.m. he noted: *Raining cats and dogs*. Fifty minutes later: *Caught 19 litres. Put rain bucket away. Tanks are full up*.

And so ended Jon Sanders' first year at sea.

14

Unwelcome Passengers

A wet sheet and a flowing sea,
A wind that follows fast,
And fills the white and rustling sail,
And bends the gallant mast.

Allan Cunningham,
The Songs of Scotland

AFTER a year at sea, *Parry Endeavour* was now running northwards before a fresh southerly breeze towards the Equator and Sanders' planned turning point, St. Peter and St. Paul Rocks, a day's sailing north of the line. His total mileage logged was 38,096 miles.

With his fresh water tanks full, he indulged in the luxury of washing three pairs of tracksuit trousers and a towel in sea water and detergent and rinsing them in sweet fresh water. They soon dried in the warm semi-tropical sun on the line he rigged up from the mast to the backstay.

Early in the afternoon of Wednesday 27 May, 600 miles off the Brazilian coast, he lowered his mainsail for servicing. It was a balmy, sunny day with little wind, and Sanders used a power drill to put stitches into the sail near the headboard. He needed the drill to get the needle through because of the many laminates of sail cloth in the top part of the sea-grimed sail. There was a chafe there caused by the topping lift. The rest of the sail looked in good condition. He was pleased to see that running repairs he had made to the sail a few weeks before rounding the Horn the second time on his voyage had held up well. *Superb*, he noted in his logbook. *Sail okay. The original massive repair I did nearly one year ago, when the bolt rope tore out of the sail and the sail tore away from the luff after a metal slide jammed, is in good shape. The mainsail has been in continuous use for over one year—must surely be a record for a single mainsail always attached to its station and in use.*

A major part of Jon Sanders' success as a single-handed sailor is his attention to detail and his forethought. He had learnt from two decades of long-distance solo sailing that preparedness for any eventuality should be the cornerstone of any long, lone voyage. His stitch-in-time philosophy had saved him time and time again from potential disaster.

The calm, warm conditions prevailed the day after his mainsail refurbishing, so Sanders got busy on other parts of the yacht. He logged at 1.45 p.m.: *Busy day. Replaced topping lift halyard and stripped, serviced and greased the two reefing winches located on either side of the main boom.*

Mid-morning on the following day saw him scrubbing the sides of the hull with a long-handled scrubbing brush. Later he scrubbed the foredeck to remove some of the green slime that had accumulated there. At four o'clock he removed the life raft, unbolted its holding locker, and detached then cleaned and sorted out the contents of the aft section. This "yukky job" left him a bit sunburnt.

He noted ominously in his log that, despite attempts to conserve it, he expected to be out of methylated spirits (used for priming the stove) months ahead of schedule.

At breakfast time on Saturday 30 May, with the wind NNW at eighteen knots, the sloop was close hauled before a big gradual swell from the south. Around noon Sanders sighted Isle de Trinidade on the starboard horizon, bearing 125 degrees on his compass, and it became clearer as the afternoon wore on. That night *Endeavour* encountered rough conditions with an occasional squall to forty-five knots as she bounced to windward.

By midnight he was forced to reef down as the squally NW wind buffeted his yacht. Just before dawn he logged: *Odd weather about, some black, low, lurking clouds across the sky. Wind west 25 knots*. But it came to nothing and by noon that day Sanders was basking in sunshine in a pair of shorts, which he even wore at night. *Getting tropical*, he noted.

During the afternoon he tried for ninety minutes to contact Brazil, Pacheco, Rio Salvador or Olinda radio on eight and twelve megacycles, but without success. At 4.35 p.m., however, he managed to get through to Olinda Radio in Recife, which asked him to stand by. Half an hour later Olinda tried to call him, but they could not copy him. He decided to wait for two days when he would be in closer range.

Although he was enjoying the balmy days and nights, Sanders was getting impatient with the wind. He expected to encounter the South-East Trades, which would push him along at a brisk rate, but the winds—what there were of them—were from the west and light. At 9.40 a.m. on day 374 (1 June) he logged: *Rather warm. Blue, oily sea—calm*.

As *Endeavour* lay becalmed, her skipper decided it was the ideal time to get rid of some unwanted passengers—the goose-neck barnacles. He had forgotten to pack swim flippers, facemask and snorkel, which annoyed him, but he knew that his progress would be much faster, when a breeze arrived, with a clean hull.

After climbing the mast to scrutinise the mirror-like ocean for tell-tale signs of sharks, he descended barechested into the tropical Atlantic. He did not attach a lifeline to his waist as he had done when he scraped *Perie Banou*'s barnacle payload during his double circumnavigation. This had almost proved fatal. The lifeline got tangled in the self-steering rudder, and every time the yacht rolled, it carried him under the hull, threatening to deal out a lonely death by drowning.

This time he dropped *Endeavour*'s jib, put a reef in the mainsail and flattened it right out. Then he centred the self-steering so that in the unlikely event of a sudden appearance of a breeze, the yacht would head into the wind slowly and stop. Sanders knew he would be able to keep pace—he is a strong swimmer.

In two sessions lasting a total of two hours, he wrenched off hundreds of the living gooseneck-shaped barnacles with his bare hands, inflicting dozens of cuts on his fingers. At 11 a.m. he logged contentedly: *Cleaned off 90 per cent of the goosenecks. Some big bunches. Went around the yacht. Most under the stern sections. A lot on the trailing edge of the keel also. Hull and rudder both look okay*. His legacy from this effort—two very red eyes.

The calm continued and Sanders spent an hour sanding some of his cabin woodwork for revarnishing. When darkness fell, he mused "Not only does the half moon reflect in the oily sea, so do the stars". *Endeavour* finally fetched a light south wind about eight o'clock the following day and as the sloop continued her passage northwards, the skipper varnished his cabin interior. He enjoyed the smell of the fresh varnish—any new aroma after a year at sea was a treat. Progress in these light conditions was hardly spectacular—just eighteen miles in twenty-four hours.

But it picked up dramatically next day (112 miles made good) as Sanders plugged away at making contact with Olinda Radio so that he could make radio-telephone calls to Australia. *Hooray*, he exulted to his logbook when, at 4 p.m., he eventually got through to his brother Colin, Dr. John Penrose and the author. It seemed whimsically incongruous to me, shivering at my desk telephone at home at 2 a.m. on a wintry 3 June while chatting to a sweaty lone sailor on the opposite side of the world about gooseneck barnacles.

He gave his position as 600 miles south-east of Recife. "I'm sailing in trade winds and it's warm and pleasant," he said. "I expect to cross the Equator in about a week and then I'll have a day's sailing to round St. Peter and St. Paul's Rocks, my turning point before I head south for the Cape of Good Hope."

He admitted being apprehensive about rounding the Cape of Good Hope again in mid-winter gales, but added he was feeling fit and well, if not a bit skinny.

By noon the following day the tropical South-East Trades were living up to their reputation as good sailing breezes and *Endeavour* was scudding across the Atlantic northwards. But all was not well on board the damaged sloop.

Noticing a foul smell from the port food locker in the galley, Sanders went through his remaining cans of food. To his dismay many of the cans had leaked through rust and some had swollen with evil-smelling gas. He had no choice but to throw overboard most, but not all, cans of tomatoes, spaghetti, baked beans, tinned fish, pineapple chunks and mushrooms. Then came the smelly and awful task of cleaning up the sludge at the bottom of the locker. *My choice of supplies is thinning*, Sanders wrote. *It is going to be a long time before I get a decent feed*.

It was, in fact, nearly nine months.

He made 160 and 149 nautical miles before the trade winds over the following two days—notations like "sparkling breeze", "lively yacht" and "steady progress" testify to the ideal conditions. At 2 p.m. on the second day he was startled to hear a whistle and a foreign voice on his channel 16 VHF radio, which meant there was a ship within twenty miles. He usually left the radio on listening watch. Soon after one o'clock the next morning he sighted the ship astern and travelling the same way. He switched on his mast tri-light and watched her passage carefully—there was no sign of activity—and within an hour the ship had drawn ahead.

Monday 8 June—day 381—was washing day on *Parry Endeavour*. It was so hot—the Equator was only 150 miles to the north—the solo sailor had all of his yacht's hatches open as he did his laundry the usual way, giving it a final rinse in fresh water.

In the early hours of Tuesday morning he was disconcerted to find the yacht kept running out of wind and putting itself about, so that the sails were on the wrong side for the next puff of wind. Still, he was able to make use of a pleasant sailing breeze to notch 145 miles in a day.

At 7 p.m. he noted in his logbook: *Over the Equator!* He was less than a day's sail from St. Peter and St. Paul's Rocks, his turning point, but, because he decided he would like to observe them in daylight, he lowered his genoa to slow the yacht down just before midnight.

He was delighted with his spot-on navigation when, at 8.05 a.m. next day, while enjoying his second cup of milky Milo, he spotted the rocks—a mere speck in the tropical North Atlantic. He wrote: *Rocks ho! How about that—Penedos de Sao Pedro e Sao Paulo dead ahead of the yacht. I navigated for them and found them. The tallest pinnacle is only 64 feet high. A little higher than the tip of* Parry Endeavour's *mast.*

He noted that his adjustment of course after his 7 a.m. sight had proved correct —"bang on". Just before ten o'clock he was within 200 metres of the rocks, from which position he had an excellent view, noticing the remains of an old lighthouse and an object that looked like a radar reflector. He also spotted a small, rather scruffy fishing boat anchored in the lee and decided he didn't want "that sort of company" close by.

Although a yachting hero to thousands of Australians, Jon Sanders rarely, if ever, looks for trouble. He believed it would be foolhardy to approach the fishing boat. On many of his long sea passages he had been warned about pirates operating in the guise of fishing boats. On this day he decided to increase sail and quickly put some distance between *Endeavour* and the foreign vessel.

In the fresh twenty-knot trade wind he was soon clear of the rocks and by mid-morning they were just tiny lumps on the horizon.

Later, in a mild evening with a full moon lighting up the seascape and the interior of his cabin, he sighted a ship two miles astern. As it closed on *Parry Endeavour*, he adjusted course downwind to give the ship a wider berth. Through his binoculars it appeared to be a naval ship and fairly fast.

After the usual muesli-weetbix and hot milk breakfast the following morning he logged: *Nice and mild, blue sky and sea. But I want rain. When I get that it will be southwards for Cape of Good Hope and onwards.*

Jon Sanders went looking for rain and he found it. At 8.20 p.m. he logged: *Golly, I caught 85 litres in 25 minutes. My new system of one reef in the mainsail and fold of sail into bucket works A1. Rain has abated for moment, but I filled all four plastic 20–litre jerry cans. Another shower like that and I can head south again.*

An hour later he reported more rain, and by nine-thirty he had filled all his tanks. It was time to bring in the rain bucket and go about.

Ten minutes later *Parry Endeavour* turned round at latitude 4 deg. 02.2 N and longitude 29 deg. 28.7 W and headed south to recross the Equator. Skipper Sanders felt pretty pleased with himself.

Sailing south-eastwards into the South-East Trades was a different proposition to sailing before them, and at 10 a.m. the following day, Saturday 17 June, the lone sailor logged: *Fresh 25 knot SE. Plugging to windward. Took some film of the yacht going to windward. Would like to make a bit of easting, but can only hold due south, but making good progress.*

He was forced to close all of the hatches because of the spray cascading all over the yacht. This made the cabin very muggy in the tropical heat. But when the wind lessened the following day he was able to open the hatches again and air the cabin. The Guinea Current was influencing *Endeavour*'s course—she was losing ten degrees heading to the west, and progress slowed. In mid-afternoon he sighted one of the biggest bulk carriers he had seen on the voyage. It crossed his sloop's track at a slight angle. That night he recrossed the Equator and was now back in the South Atlantic.

By the following day the Guinea Current was having a lesser effect on the yacht's progress and Sanders managed to make some east with consistent progress southwards. During a ten-minute radio-telephone chat with the author, he said he had decided to set a course for the region near the Rocks of Martin Vaz, 600 miles off the Brazilian coast, and then head south-eastwards towards the Cape of Good Hope. "I heard on my radio that the Cape had been experiencing gales up to eighty knots," he commented. If on schedule he would round Cape Leeuwin at the end of September, but he did not plan a mail exchange. "I might throw some mail to a boat from the Royal Yacht Club of Tasmania, because I've been writing a few letters," he said. "But I don't want to risk it by taking on any more mail . . . I'll do two laps without mail."

Even though Squadron Leader Clarke had ruled that letters and newspapers could go on to *Parry Endeavour* without disqualification, he was taking no risks.

15

Cape of Storms

Seas roll to waft me, suns to light me
rise;
My footstool earth, my canopy the
skies.
Alexander Pope, An Essay on Man

ABOUT three quarters through his second non-stop circumnavigation and well over halfway in his attempt to be the first man to complete three such girdlings, Jon Sanders nevertheless felt a trifle apprehensive as his sloop *Parry Endeavour* tacked southwards and a little to the east to round the Cape of Good Hope, which had given him a pasting seven months earlier.

But now on a sunny Friday, 19 June 1987—day 392 at sea—the former wool-classer was enjoying cruising in a deep blue sea with azure skies above. To air his cabin and saloon, he had both hatches open. Just before noon he sighted a big ship going past in the opposite direction, and he wondered where it came from. Her course would suggest Antarctica, between South Africa and South America! Here, way out in the mid-east section of the South Atlantic, he was seeing shipping he never expected to encounter. That night he spotted the lights of a ship passing about three miles astern.

Rain clouds brought a freshening easterly breeze and Sanders put out his rain bucket. He had plenty of water, but he had thousands of kilometres of "dry" ocean to traverse in the next few weeks. By noon he had caught enough rain to overflow all of his tanks and containers. By mid-afternoon the nimbus clouds gave way to thin cirrus.

Sunday morning saw *Endeavour* bumping to windward under blue skies etched with a few trade wind clouds. His distance-made-good for the previous twenty-four hours was a pleasing 139 miles, which brought his total to 38,445 miles. He had actually logged 40,802 miles. (When a yacht tacks it covers more water than when sailing in a straight line. Distance-made-good means the actual distance sailed towards a given point.)

As he got farther south from the Equator, he was revelling in the temperate weather, but he could do without the big swells now rolling his yacht from the south. When the wind backed to the north two days later, he was happy at being able to easily steer his preferred course, the rhumbline to well south of the Cape of Storms.

Soon after noon the following day he took out two of his yacht's bank of six batteries and replaced them with two Argos batteries, which had been steadily losing power over the previous four months. The main batteries had recently been indicating full charge thanks to the solar panels.

With the sea quiet on Thursday 25 June, Sanders busied himself with maintenance chores. He varnished his chart table, changed his mainsail (after a solid 397 days of continual use!) and spent hours removing shackles from slides and sewing tapes to them. Because of the metal slides between the top reef and the peak of the sail, the shackles had a dangerous tendency to jam on the slides and cause the sail to jam up the mast when reefing down.

Almost becalmed the following day he noticed some rain about, so he took out his canvas rain bucket in the hope of again topping up his tanks. Light rain started to fall about 6.30 p.m., but there was little wind and the sails were flapping annoyingly, prompting him before long to lower the jib and put a reef into the main to flatten it.

On his 400th day at sea—Saturday 27 June—*Endeavour* was "stooging along" under her mainsail, that is until a strong, humid southerly breeze sprang up, which saw the lone skipper hoisting a working jib for the necessary tacking. By breakfast time the following day the wind had piped up to twenty-five to thirty knots (SSW) and after his second cup of Milo, Sanders put three reefs into the mainsail. At mid-morning he logged: *Bumping to windward, rough as bags*. It did not improve during the day and at sundown he wrote: *Awful ride, tacked—perhaps the wind is more favourable to the west*.

At midnight things had not improved. He logged: *It is such a yukky rough night. Current against the wind, I suppose. Will now hoist storm jib and slow down*. After replacing the jib (and with three reefs in the main) the yacht rode much better, but Sanders wrote that the sea was "*phooey*". When the wind moderated at sunrise, he rehoisted the working jib and after breakfast he took two of the reefs out.

During the early hours of 1 July he heard something clatter to the deck, but by torchlight he could find nothing. At dawn he went on deck and found that the yacht's port runner had fallen down from the top of the mast. By 9.30 a.m. he had fixed it, but only after five climbs to the second spreader. He would have had second thoughts about this manoeuvre had the sea been anything but mild.

A few Cape Pigeons fluttered around the yacht the following morning as *Endeavour* neared the South African coast. On the next day he saw a lone whale and sketched the hump and tail in his logbook. At midmorning, while a school of silver fish with yellow tails swam around his yacht,

Sanders gave himself a short haircut with his mother's kitchen scissors.

In now calm conditions he went back to chores that could save him a lot of anguish later in the voyage. He serviced his working jib, which was showing the effects of the long voyage. But he was not worried. He still had a jib that he had used only once—when he sailed past Fremantle after his first circumnavigation five months earlier. *My sail wardrobe is in good shape*, he told his log. He also spent an hour scrubbing the side of his yacht with a long-handled brush to within half a metre below the waterline.

Before dawn on Saturday 4 July he wrote: *It could not be more windless, sea like glass with the stars reflecting on it.* Although he logged forty-one nautical miles for the previous twenty-four hours, he actually made good only twenty-eight.

But his daily runs improved dramatically when *Endeavour* fetched a steady twenty-knot northerly breeze on 5 July. At 4.40 p.m. the yacht passed a fishing float bobbing on the ocean. It was a glass sphere laced with rope—a collector's item in

Australia. But Sanders was not interested in picking it up.

More tins of food had gone off and burst, leaving a horrible black sludge for him to clean up. But at least the dumped cans lightened his load. He figured his freeze-dried food, though boring, would probably see him through another circuit of the world.

Conditions were perfect for flying a spinnaker the following morning, 7 July, so Sanders decided to hoist the kite. He took out his video camera to film the spinnaker in action, but the camera would not work. Nor would the spinnaker work effectively. At 11.40 a.m. he logged: *Spinnaker dropped. Certainly makes the yacht go faster, but the self steerer finds it hard to cope. It weaves a course as boat speed at times nearly cancels out wind pressure on vane*. That morning he scrubbed the foredeck with detergent to remove green slime.

More cans went overboard that afternoon. He logged: *Continued to clean port quarter berth stowage under bunks, dumping even more cans. Mainly tinned tomatoes, some baked beans and spaghetti. Will run out of those in due course.*

His menu for that day: Breakfast, two cups of Milo, muesli with hot milk. Lunch, Ryvita biscuits with peanut butter and jam, Milo. Supper, three satchels of freeze-dried rice, macaroni cheese and canned smoked fish, more Milo.

The pleasant northerly backed to south-west on 9 July and Sanders surmised it was because of rain clouds. By early after-noon light rain was falling on the yacht and Sanders had his rain bucket out catching valuable precipitation. But *Endeavour* was going nowhere. He esti-mated he caught sixty litres of water, enough to top up all of his tanks and containers.

After breakfast on the tenth, with *Endeavour* reaching nicely before a twelve to fourteen knot northerly, Sanders noted: *The barometer has been consistently high in recent days and suspect I am close to the centre region of the South Atlantic "high", which is usually stationary.*

While sailing briskly in a lively twenty-five knot westerly on Saturday 11 July, he heard on the BBC World Service that the

Australian Labor Party under Bob Hawke had won a third term of office. "Hope they don't fine me for not voting," he joked. In fact, the election had posed a bit of a quandary for the solo sailor—voting was compulsory, yet he was very much "sea bound" and had made no prior arrangements with the Commonwealth electoral authorities, not even to vote by radio-telephone. While Australian voters were going to the polls, he was about 400 nautical miles south-west of Cape Town.

Electoral officials ended up adopting the normal procedure for Sanders—a letter was sent to his Perth home asking why he had not voted. Fortunately, commonsense prevailed and Sanders escaped a fine.

Certainly the Federal Government appeared to be treating him well. When he left on his 658–day odyssey fourteen months earlier, it had waived his $20 departure tax!

Endeavour's progress on election day was slowed in the afternoon when the wind dropped and a fog rolled in over the yacht. That night before retiring to his bunk for a few hours' sleep, he noted: *Yukky-pooh, no wind in a sloppy sea*.

On the mid-winter Sunday, Sanders searched for words to convey the utter stillness he was facing. At 2 a.m. he logged: *As out of wind as out of wind could be*. The flapping of the mainsail was annoying him, so he left his bunk to put a reef into the sail to flatten it and prevent the noise. At 4.10 a.m.: *Ever so windless*. At breakfast time it was: *A painted yacht on a painted ocean*. Noon: *Clear over yacht and very calm, some fog clouds here and there*. 3.20 a.m.: *It is still a painted ocean calm*. 5 p.m.: *Still not a breath*. A puff of wind found the yacht at 6.15 p.m. and Sanders wrote: *I hope a little more comes*. It was a miserable daily run—eleven nautical miles made good, though in her meanderings on the still sea, *Endeavour* had logged forty-two miles.

It was a similar story the following day, when *Endeavour* made only twenty-seven miles, inching her way towards the Cape of Storms.

Then a healthy fourteen-knot north-west breeze sprang up overnight and put the lone sailor in a better mood. At 4 a.m. the yacht was running square with an eighteen-knot wind and the jib on the foredeck.

He made steady progress as the nor'wester got up to twenty-five-knots. At mid-afternoon he logged: *Working jib hoisted with full main. Sunny, scooting along*. The yacht's progress matched the description, for that day she made 110 miles.

The north-west breeze kept up on 15 July—day 417—and the sea-begrimed sloop notched a whopping 151-mile run. The noon entry: *Bit by bit getting windier. All blue sky, but hazy, zooming along*.

The solo circumnavigator's keen weather eye told him at 1.10 a.m. that he could be in for a tough day. He observed at that time: *Rather windy, 30-knot north-west. One reef and working jib, sailing fast. Suspect more reefs in mainsail might be needed soon*. The time for more reefs came an hour later, and Sanders got drenched with heavy rain as he tied the three reefs into the main at 2.30 a.m. His prudence could have saved the yacht from serious damage.

At 7.30 a.m., as Sanders was preparing hot milk for his Milo, a screaming line squall hit the yacht, capsizing it beyond 100 degrees—which meant the tip of the mast was below water level. In yachting parlance, a knockdown.

A locker in the cabin burst open and jars full of jam crashed on to the floor and broke, leaving a sticky mess for Sanders to clean up. His favourite winch handle was swept overboard along with buckets and other pieces of gear in the cockpit. The squall came with heavy rain and lasted about thirty minutes.

When he had recovered some composure, Sanders scribbled: *0830—hove-to in severe SSW gale. Jib down below, constant rain. Wind for about half hour was alarming hurricane strength*.

To his great relief the wind "moderated" to thirty to thirty-five knots at 9.30 a.m. A little after noon he hoisted the storm jib and logged: *Now experiencing a very rough ride. I may have to drop it as yacht sailing fast in a very rough ocean*.

Her speed was becoming perilous and Sanders decided to heave-to again. *Caution is the better part of valour*, he wrote after he had dropped the jib and turned *Endeavour* into the lumpy seas. The southerly gale continued to howl through *Endeavour*'s patched-up rigging all afternoon, varying in strength between forty and fifty knots, but at dusk it got even worse.

At 5 p.m. he wrote: *Gale severe, sea conditions reaching dangerous*. In the black of night, only 120 nautical miles from the Greenwich dateline of zero degrees and about 1000 miles due west of Cape Town, *Endeavour* rode out one of the worst gales her skipper could remember.

His first entry for the next day, 17 July: *Bad gale continues. 40–45 knots SW. Still hove-to*. As a bleak dawn cast a pale light on thousands of white horses racing on mountainous seas, Sanders detected a lessening in its fury. After breakfast, he logged: *Wind has moderated, but gale squalls in between. Still very rough. Have squared yacht and course a little. Will venture storm jib soon*.

The temperature outside the yacht was a bleak 8C, but with the wind chill factor it would have been around freezing point. A hail squall pummelled the yacht at 9 a.m. At 11.05 a.m. the shivering lone sailor reported a "full gale" of forty to fifty knots SW. At 3.20 p.m. he wrote: *Gale continues, bitterly cold outside. Makes your eyeballs ache. I just adjusted course and sails a little to more downwind. Lot of heavy squalls about. It is a rather bleak day*. Before dusk he changed course to the north-east to get a better ride.

Saturday 18 July—day 420—was an auspicious day for Jon Sanders. Not only did he cross the zero meridian from west to east longitude, he broke *Perie Banou*'s record of 419 days, twenty-two hours and ten minutes at sea continuously without stopping, set in his remarkable double-circumnavigation of 1981–82.

But records were the last thing he was thinking of when he logged just before 1 a.m.: *A bleak winter's night continues, squall after squall after squall with rain and hail. Barometer falling again. Running with wind aft of abeam to NE. Too rough to hold course of east which would need storm jib. Yacht then would go too fast into a very bad sea. At the moment sailing with storm reefed mainsail only. But not hove-to*. At breakfast time he added: *Gale is severe at moment—40 to 50 knots. Sky is so stormy*.

Later that afternoon he noted with wry

humour that a BBC sports announcer referred to the wind "howling in from the sea" on to a Scottish golf course at twenty-five knots. *Golly*, he logged, *I wish this gale would decrease to that*.

The cold, miserable South Atlantic day ended with a midnight barrage of big hail-stones on his cabin roof.

As he ate his Weeties with hot milk the following morning the seas were still lumpy, but the gale had abated and Sanders pondered the advisability of venturing a storm jib. After breakfast he decided on this course of action and went up for'ard to hoist his spitfire jib. Back in the comparative warmth of his cabin, he wrote: *Rough sea, wind fresh. Close to course but deliberately sailing a little freer so as not to knock yacht and me about too much*.

The storm had abated enough by mid-morning for Sanders to replace the storm jib with a working headsail, but he was keeping a keen eye out for squalls. It was still a rough ocean with occasional squalls at 4 p.m., but as daylight gave way to wintry dusk the wind dropped even further. Incredibly, by nine o'clock

Endeavour was nearly out of wind on a still-lumpy sea and the skipper took two of the three reefs out of the main.

Jon Sanders was amazed the following day when he took sun sights to find that *Endeavour* had made good 208 nautical miles. He had doubted his previous day's fix, surmising that his sextant had caught on one of its teeth. But at 3.55 p.m. on 20 July he logged: *Sight confirms yesterday's extraordinary fix. Amazing despite a big sea running now. I took two separate sights, worked them out separately and they came up with the same answer to a decimal point i.e. both 5.4 deg. towards the sun. Means my sextant aiming is good*. The yacht was making good progress running before a twenty-five-knot nor'wester with no jib and a mainsail with one reef.

Fast approaching the Cape of Good Hope on 22 July, with 134 miles made good, *Endeavour* was zooming along with one reef in the main and a working jib in a twenty to twenty-five-knot nor 'wester as Sanders tried for the first time to call Cape Town Radio. He could not raise the operator. The lean, sunbronzed sailor with the crew-cut hairstyle had noticed that his yacht was being set farther south than he dead-reckoned it was. After lunch he logged: *Compass check shows centre cockpit compass 10–15 deg. error—the one I was using*.

At mid-afternoon he wrote: *I am steering or hoping to pass Cape Aghulas* [South Africa's southernmost point] *no more than 30 miles to south. However, if wind forces yacht farther south I shall shape a course to pass at least at 38 deg. S. Important to keep clear of the SE tail of Aghulas Bank—very dangerous in gales. Near 35 deg. S gales could be less severe, but shipping might be a risk. At 38–39 deg. S gales more severe*. Ocean Passages of the World *suggests 40 deg. S. That is a long way south in winter*.

He noted two hours later that his Codan 4000 radio-telephone was playing up and he could not make radio contact.

The fickleness of the South Atlantic winds was amply brought home to Sanders the following day. At 12.45 a.m. he logged: *Oh dear, time for storm reef in mainsail*. After fully reefing the main, he settled back into his bunk. The wind promptly moderated. After breakfast he took advantage of the quiet conditions to strip and service his main halyard winch which had been jamming when lowering the sail.

By mid-morning he had made a decision on his course. He logged: *Decided to sail south of the Aghulas Bank, risk scary gales, but feel risk of collision with shipping the greater risk nearer to Cape Aghulas. I must give the south-east tail of the Aghulas Bank a wide berth as it is a dangerous region for breaking waves. Winter around southern Africa is not a lot of fun*.

His afternoon sight the following day showed that the Aghulas Current was having an adverse effect on the yacht. But Sanders was more perturbed about his three main Codan radios which had temporarily stopped working. He still had not made contact with Cape Town.

If he thought the hurricane-force winds of a few days earlier had been among the worst he had experienced, the gale that sprang up on Saturday 25 July was to test his fibre—and his yacht's sturdiness—almost to their outer limits. It was ominous a few minutes after midnight when he noted the wind rising and the barometer falling. At 3.45 a.m. he logged: *Storm jib down and storm reef is in main. More wind than thought at times. Running downwind, listening to Johannesburg Radio, okay music*. But the radio was switched off as the gales reached forty to fifty knots and Sanders had to heave-to again. By lunch time the gale was terrible. He scribbled: *Most severe gale for the voyage—awful*. At 4.20 p.m. *Endeavour* was heeled right over by an horrendous squall which Sanders estimated at sixty knots or more. *Big sea and a bad one*, he recorded.

Later in the afternoon Sanders got a piece of glass—probably from the breakages during the previous gale—in his foot and he extracted it with tweezers from his first-aid kit, not an easy task as the yacht gyrated wildly.

Just after midnight he logged with concern: *I wish this awful gale would go away. This yacht sure knows how to fall off big waves now and again, and the motion is violent*. Ninety minutes later he noted: *Frequent squalls between 50 and 60 knots. Yuk night. The only thing good about tonight is the music on South African Radio.*

Rain was pounding *Parry Endeavour*'s cabin roof as Sanders ate breakfast, and a little while later he noticed a lull in the gale, down to thirty-five to forty-five knots. This encouraged him to ease the storm-reefed main and ease course. *We are off—nearly on course*, he logged. *Huge seas*. By mid-morning the wind was down to twenty knots with squalls up to thirty-five.

His out-of-order radios had been worrying him during the boisterous night, and now, with the wind moderating, he spent several hours working on them. He reported: *Pulled Codan 4000 out and sprayed, trying to find fault with it, but found none. It still does not work for my efforts. My Codan 6801–S does not even switch on now.*

Jon Sanders had barely recovered from the weekend's gales when he found out with terrifying reality why journals for seafarers warn that to round the Cape of Storms in midwinter is folly.

At dawn on Monday 27 July *Parry*

Endeavour was running downwind before a lively nor'wester with three reefs in the mainsail and a bare forestay. The wind increased while he was eating breakfast, but at 9.30 a.m. he managed to get a sun sight in difficult conditions—the sun peeked through the clouds only spasmodically. At 11 a.m. he logged: *Wind gale at times, but barometer steady; hope it doesn't fall any further*. At 12.54 a.m. he exulted, *Hooray, got my noon sight in a gale!* He noted that the current was playing havoc with his progress and that he was farther north than he expected. By mid-afternoon he was again in the true gale—forty to forty-five knots and strengthening. At 4.05 p.m. he told his logbook: *Oh dear me, it is time to heave-to*. Fifteen minutes later: *Most terrible squall, well over 50 knots, whilst I trimmed the main and hove-to the yacht. Another pitch dark* [squall] *line approaching, too. Very rough storm. This is a bad gale region*.

Ten minutes later the squall he had sighted hit the yacht with heavy rain and fifty-knots-plus wind. Just before supper, at 7.35 p.m., he logged: *If only the weather would give me a break long enough to get round the Aghulas Bank and farther north where gales are less severe. This yacht will not run downward in a savage gale. I must heave-to at about 50 knots. Big waves whacking the yacht, which is scary. That aside, barometer is now going up. Such is winter where I am.*

Although Jon Sanders was a confirmed Christian, he seldom went to church and never prayed. But he thought of his Maker this day.

As *Parry Endeavour* lay head-to-wind in horrific seas this pitch-black Monday night he wondered how long the fibreglass foam sandwich hull on his yacht could take the pounding it was getting from rogue waves. About 9.30 p.m. he heard the roar of a breaking wave and braced himself. Another knockdown! The gallant yacht heeled over past the horizontal and slowly righted itself. Fifteen minutes later, Sanders recorded: *This is a terrible gale. Lost a sea brake. Broke free and I let it go. I also found self-steering lines have worked very loose. Thank goodness the self-steerer holds up. Its best protection is this wind angle.*

The storm showed no sign of abating and at 11.30 p.m. he logged: *Yacht just got put about by a huge wave. I've just got it back on the former tack. There are some lulls in the wind, but some very bad waves.*

The solo circumnavigator thought the gale was moderating at 2.40 a.m. the following day when he dared to ease the mainsheet and steer his correct course eastwards in a very rough sea, fully storm-reefed. But at five o'clock *Parry Endeavour* suffered her third knockdown of the storm. The problem, as Sanders identified it, was that his yacht steered badly downwind on the starboard gybe.

By mid-morning the gale had built up in excess of fifty knots again, and once more Sanders heaved-to, rationalising that it was risky running downwind in such a dangerous sea. At 11.15 a.m. a note of desperation entered his log: *Gee whiz, is there no let-up from this terrible weather?*

At 1.05 p.m. he gybed the hove-to yacht on to a starboard tack hoping that it would ride better. At 4.45 p.m. the yacht was again knocked down ninety degrees. Sanders heard the roar of the breaking wave from his cabin. At 6.40 p.m.—it was dark again—he wrote: *Jolly yacht came off a wave and put itself about*. He struggled to bring it back into the wind on starboard tack.

His final log entry on this horrific day was gloomy. *This most horrible gale in the most rotten of breaking seas persists*.

But persist it did, and at four o'clock the next morning, 29 July, he noted wearily: *This gale does not want to subside; it is not fair, the barometer is going down again*.

But soon after a pale sun sent streaks of light through the breaking seas, Sanders decided the gale had abated enough to risk easing the mainsail and getting on course again. By 7 a.m. *Endeavour* was careering along before the thirty to forty-knot gale, but her skipper found the self-steering would not handle the conditions. He decided to persevere with the tiny (fully-reefed) mainsail and if it would not steer, he would gybe and try the other tack. If that failed he would try running under bare pole—no sail at all.

He observed to his log: *Big sea. I chose the wrong tactic, or should I say* Ocean

Passages of the World's *recommendation to pass well south of the Aghulas Bank, even for sailing vessels from Cape Town in winter, was astray. I should have instead sailed 200 miles farther north near the coast of South Africa.*

At 7.40 a.m. he logged: *Hooray, made adjustment to self-steering line and yacht is self-steering okay in a big, spectacular sea. Should squalls come I will simply hove-to and hand steer. Wind at moment 30–35. Waves are huge, but not breaking heavily, just the white tops*. After a quick breakfast he wrote: *If I am where my dead reckoning says I am, I am now entering the Indian Ocean portion of the Southern Ocean. But this is unlikely as keeping track hove-to, especially with the Aghulas Current, is impossible*. At 9.45 a.m.: *Gale 35–45 knots. Still sailing, very rough. Self-steering just coping, with some broaches*.

By mid-morning *Endeavour* was surging along in big seas under a cloudy sky. At 11.40 a.m. Sanders logged: *Perhaps the sun might peek through at noon and I can attempt a sight (in this sea!)*. About an hour later he added: *I got some sort of a sight. That was clever. I am 45 miles farther south* [than he thought he was]. *Now, let's hope I can get a PM sight. Suspect now I might be farther west than dead reckoning, but hope not*. He failed to get a later sight as the cloud cover thickened. The yacht broached badly about five o'clock, but when darkness closed over *Endeavour*, Sanders sensed the worst was past. He wrote at 6.40 p.m.: *Things have moderated and going nicely with three reefs in main. Wind 30 knots, stronger at times. Better than last night*.

Sanders and his sloop had taken the worst that the wintry Cape of Good Hope could hand out. Now, for the first time in many days, he felt he could relax his vigilance a trifle.

16

Sailing into History

And bade betwixt their shores to be
The unplumb'd, salt, estranging sea.
Matthew Arnold, To Marguerite

THE rounding of the Cape of Good Hope for the second time in his epic triple-circumnavigation attempt had given Jon Sanders his worst experience of non-stop gale conditions in more than thirty years of making ocean passages—four continuous days in which the wind velocity did not fall below thirty-five knots. For much of the time the wind had been around fifty knots and up to sixty, perhaps seventy. His yacht had been knocked down—heeled beyond the horizontal—four times and Sanders was forced to heave-to in horrific seas for three full days and nights. This meant that he was facing in the wrong direction, a tactic that played havoc with his distance-made-good figures, but that was the least of the lone sailor's worries. He was not out to break speed records and the safety of his yacht and, of course, himself, had been his prime motivation for the heaving-to tactic.

Now, on Thursday 30 July 1987—day 432 at sea—he was all but round the Cape of Storms and Sanders had the feeling the worst was behind him. His first log entry that day, at twenty minutes after midnight, was: *Conditions have certainly moderated. Sea is sloppy. These damp conditions block my nose up and I am always coughing. It also causes a lot of mould in the yacht. Wind 25–30 W and cold, squalls to 35.*

The wind backed to the north-west and in the early hours of the morning, Sanders hoisted a storm jib and *Endeavour* started zipping along in a rough sea. She was inclined to broach at times, but not dangerously so. But his optimism was short-lived. Soon after a dreary dawn he logged: *Drat, the wind is close to gale and from the NNW. I am now very keen to angle the yacht's course northwards 70 degrees and well clear of the Aghulas Bank region 45 degrees to 35 degrees south parallel where gales should be less severe than where I am now. Then I shall sail due east along 35 deg. S. It is too rough now to harden up. There are some breaks in the sky, perhaps the sun may eventually show through and I will get a sight.*

Sanders got his morning sights in a very rough sea, clinging precariously to his backstay. After some calculations he logged: *Put position back much farther west as I suspected after finding the yacht much farther south yesterday. (It is most difficult to track where the yacht ends up when hove-to.) I made too much allowance for lee-way, but what of, and which way, the Aghulas Current? It splits somewhere.*

By noon *Endeavour* was sailing in a thirty to forty-knot NW gale again but handling it well. At 4 p.m. that day he tried again to reach Cape Town Radio by switching to the automatic tuner on his big Codan 4000 unit. He logged exultantly: *Hooray, hooray, got through to Cape Town, spoke to Colin, Hugh Schmitt, John Penrose*. In a twenty-minute radio-telephone chat, the solo sailor told me about his perilous Cape rounding.

Describing the seas as horrendous, he said: "You've read of waves like mountains, well, these were like that. There were waves riding on top of other waves which often caused them to break." As *Endeavour* bumped along in a thirty to thirty-five knot sou'wester, he told of his immediate plans—to sail well south of Western Australia's Cape Leeuwin and not have any more mail exchanges. "I'm feeling quite fit, but I've lost a lot of weight—I'm real bony," he said.

The last day of July saw *Endeavour* still sailing strongly—150 miles made good in the previous twenty-four hours—with a storm reef in the mainsail and a spitfire jib. By noon Sanders was out of the Aghulas Current and into much colder water—a 4.8C drop. At mid-afternoon he took two reefs out of the main, leaving one in, and his sloop continued to make good progress in a sloppy sea. Late in the afternoon he got through to Dr. Penrose on radio-telephone and spoke for fifty minutes, and he wondered how much this had cost his sponsor. Just before dusk he was surprised to see a ship astern of him travelling in the same direction.

At breakfast time the following day, 1 August, he logged: *Zinging along nicely with one reef in the main only. The farther north I creep (as I go east), the better everything is becoming.*

At noon Sanders was pleased to note that *Parry Endeavour* had made a record day's run—202 nautical miles. He also noted: *Back into a warm current—feels it too. Today 18.8C, yesterday 13.6C.* But the Indian Ocean was proving as fickle as the Atlantic he had just vacated. By 1.30 p.m. he was in yet another gale, with forty-knot winds and heavier squalls. Back on deck he went to storm reef the main and replace the working jib with the well-used spitfire. But by midnight the gale had died to a reasonable twenty-five to thirty knots and he rehoisted the working jib. At noon he wrote: *Now reached desirable latitude to cross Indian Ocean in winter—35 deg. 30 min. S.* By late afternoon the wind had dropped to a zephyr, and he logged at 8.50 p.m.: *Right out of wind, becalmed—better than going nowhere in a nasty storm.*

The stop-start-stop routine continued in the southern Indian Ocean as a gale sprang up the following day, 3 August. Sanders noted at 2.50 a.m.: *Lots and lots of wind, a gale in fact. Time to change down everywhere*. The gale blew all day with momentary lulls, and a little after midnight the following day he wrote: *Wind 30 knots NW, 35 at times. Storm reef in mainsail only*. But five hours later everything had changed. He logged at 5.45 a.m.: *Not much wind and yacht rolling like a pig. From gale to zilch in minutes.*

Endeavour must have sailed into the core of a mini-hurricane, because within two hours the yacht was being pounded by a thirty-five to forty-knot southerly gale. The 7.30 a.m. entry: *Gale reaching severe. May have to heave-to*. The gale increased to between forty and fifty knots and once more Sanders turned his yacht into the wind and heaved-to. At mid-morning he logged: *Gosh, wind to 40–50. I was hoping to avoid this severity near 35 deg. S, but not to be*. At 2.20 p.m.: *This sure turned into a yuk gale with winds over 50 knots at times*.

An hour later a giant breaking wave knocked *Endeavour* down beyond 100 degrees. After a light supper he wrote: *Oh dear, this gale continues. The barometer is zooming up, but the stupid gale takes no notice.*

Endeavour was still hove-to at 4.30 a.m. the next day, but by breakfast time it had moderated enough for the skipper to hoist his spitfire jib and put his yacht on a beam reach. It was an uncomfortable ride and twenty degrees off course, but at least roughly in the right direction. The gale came and went again during the day with some welcome lulls. Late that night before retiring briefly to his bunk he noted: *Yacht's main batteries are getting down a bit because of the mainly-overcast conditions in recent weeks.*

He was annoyed with himself the following day when he dropped and smashed one of the three thermometers he carried on board. It was the one he used for taking outside and water temperature readings. *Silly Billy*, he berated himself. Friday 7 August dawned quiet and windless and Sanders busied himself with neglected chores, like cleaning out the bilge in his saloon cabin, greasing the mainsail slides and three of his winches. He also end-for-ended his reefing lines to avoid excess wear in the same places. Late in the afternoon he scrubbed thirty-six tins of spaghetti that were damp and rusty and going off. Nightfall saw *Endeavour* becalmed.

The following day he varnished the tops and bottoms of all the tinned food that remained on board, mostly spaghetti and tomatoes, to arrest the rust. He finally got a quiet wind that was enough to get his sloop sailing again.

Predictably the wind rose to gale-force again, but there were welcome lulls. After lunch on 10 August Sanders noted: *Amazing. Wind is fresh 25 knots, sea choppy, one to one and a half metres, but no big swell. Can see horizon all the time. It must have been calm here before my arrival, also pressure is high—1025*. It became windier and rough the following day but *Parry Endeavour* recorded a fair daily run of 112 miles.

Jonathan Sanders' forty-eighth birthday —his second at sea on his gloriously mad adventure—came on day 445, 12 August 1987, as *Endeavour* sailed eastwards across the southern Indian Ocean towards Australia on his second circumnavigation of his current voyage. At noon he noted that his yacht had made fine progress over the previous twenty-four hours—164 nautical miles made good. He logged: *Will steer east, but with touch of north, preferred latitude 34.40 deg. S*. By 9 p.m. on his birthday he had put three reefs into the mainsail as the breeze built up to thirty knots.

With his rough winter rounding of South Africa fresh in his mind, and having sailed clear of the stormy region, he had chosen to set a course across the southern Indian Ocean at latitudes of somewhere between 33 deg. south and 34.30 deg. south—the equivalent of between Cape Leeuwin and Bunbury on the West Australian coast. The pilot books had warned him of tempestuous weather with dangerous fitful wind shifts south of 40 deg. in winter—and this was winter. The weather rapidly improves north of 40 deg., so the lone sailor decided to head north with as much easting as he could muster.

Coincidentally his birthday started off logbook number four of five used during the twenty-three-month odyssey. He noted: *Navigation in this logbook by celestial sights with sextant—usually the sun. The satellite navigator stopped working about four months ago, and the Brookes and Gatehouse speed and distance log stopped working long ago. Mileage used for navigation since and in this log is estimated by me*. (Sanders' estimates proved to be uncannily accurate.) His total logged mileage on day 445 was 46,085, though *Parry Endeavour* had made good 41,511 nautical miles.

The sailing shearer did not have the wherewithal on board his sloop for a birthday celebration, so contented himself with watching a video.

Two days after his birthday, Sanders was taking a pasting from a thirty-five-knot nor'wester, and at 2.30 a.m. he braved the stormy night to try a tactic he had never tried before on *Parry Endeavour*. He lowered the mainsail completely and furled it round the boom, and hoisted a spitfire or storm jib. *Presuming gale will increase*, he told his log. *Progress okay and more comfortable*.

By breakfast time the nor'wester had piped up to forty-five knots and *Endeavour* was handling the conditions reasonably well under the storm jib. When the gale moderated down to eighteen knots by mid-morning and light rain started to fall, he took his storm jib down and rehoisted the main with one reef in it. He wanted to catch some rain, but after an hour a break in the clouds put an end to his efforts.

Surprisingly the wind dropped dramatically and Sunday 16 August found him doing afternoon chores on his yacht —fitting new self-steering blocks and scrubbing the sides of the boat with a long-handled brush.

On her 450th day at sea *Parry Endeavour* was completely becalmed—time for more housekeeping and washing as the sloop rolled gently almost in the one spot. But two days later, just after putting his clock forward two hours, Sanders picked up a brisk wind, which rose to twenty-five knots at mid-morning and had him on deck after lunch putting three reefs in the mainsail.

His distance-made-good the next day was a pleasing 163 miles over twenty-four hours. He was now more than halfway across the southern portion of the Indian

Ocean. His supper that night: spaghetti bolognaise à la Sanders. He cooked the raw spaghetti and covered it with a blend of chilli con carne, tinned tomatoes and quarter of a tin of baked beans with parmesan cheese.

The wind dropped away again and while Sanders slept, the yacht's self-steering put it about. When he woke up at 3 a.m. he was heading the wrong way. At mid-morning when he had still not fetched a breeze, he logged: *In for a quiet day or two I suspect.*

He had guessed correctly again. Early the following morning he was so becalmed that he took down the number one jib, which was flapping badly with the roll of the yacht, and put a reef in the main to flatten it right out and stop it from slatting. At noon *Endeavour* was ghosting along with little wind, but helped by an easterly current. That afternoon he took advantage of the tranquillity by piling all of his sails on the foredeck to dry and scrubbing out the fo'castle. The wind fluctuated frustratingly between five and twenty knots all day and Sanders was kept busy making adjustments to the self-steering, which would not function properly in light conditions.

The breeze, or what there was of it, remained temperamental the following day. In the afternoon Sanders occupied himself by painting white the liferaft cover and his wind vane. At six o'clock he logged: *No wind, nothing, breathless, calm, oily sea, going nowhere—stuck in the middle of the Indian Ocean, "parked", stopped, halted and so on. Oh dear.*

The following dawn brought a light wind from the north-west and *Endeavour* was running quietly downwind with playful dolphins all around the yacht. Soon after lunch next day he spotted a ship to starboard—he could just see its bridge and yellow funnel—and he tried unsuccessfully to talk to it by VHF radio. He was still making fair progress in the southern Indian Ocean towards the south of Western Australia, and on day 460 (29 August) he picked up a local radio transmission—a warming reminder of the distant land that was "home".

He made the following observations on his navigational technique in his logbook: *0815: Sun between the clouds, otherwise mild, quiet progress. Got two sights with sextant. Generally it is a good yacht to take sights from—stable, sort of. The short mainsail boom makes for easier sight-taking either standing on the top cockpit hatch ladder step with support of cabin, or sitting on cabin with feet in cockpit hatch. Though this morning I took the sights from the stern pushpit (rail). If there is any speed on or yacht bumpy as often is, I wear a safety harness while taking sights. I am using the Tamaya sextant and keep my faithful Saura (which has accompanied me on every voyage) for stars or moon-sights. The index error of the Saura is greater. But I prefer not to tamper with it to try to correct it. Saura for stars because I can accurately take sights with telescope removed (easier to locate the star). I do not worry about stars or moon too often —just to practise.*

Usually in mid-ocean a morning or afternoon sun sight (subject to sun!) with meridian passage (noon). There is always a small risk of accident to self or sextant, which is why I do not over-extend myself. This is also the cautious manner I think I sail the whole yacht—lessen the chances of

Not all washing days were as benign as this!

Sanders' meals were simple, if not monotonous, but there were few dull moments with his faulty stove.

Sanders in fine voice after months at sea alone.

Parry Endeavour As she approaches Fremantle to clinch the record-breaking triple circumnavigation,

Water police draw up alongside the sea-begrimed sloop as Sanders waves to the huge crowd.

Just minutes away from finally setting foot on dry land, Sanders (circled above on his sloop) is caught up in a

tumultuous welcome as some 350 craft, big and small, escort him into port.

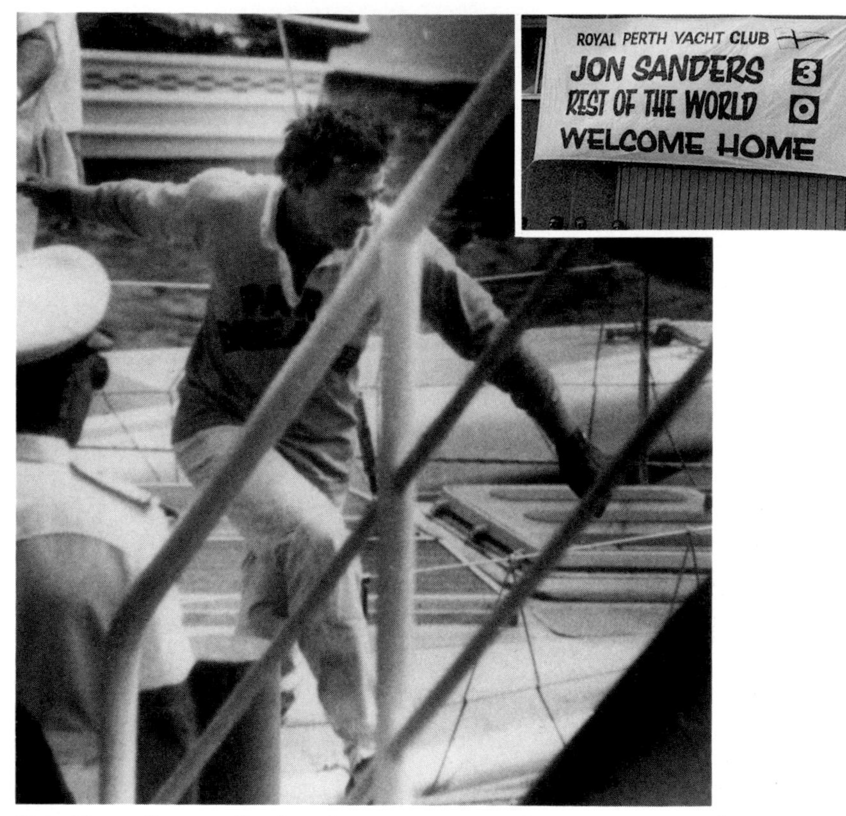

Sanders bounded ashore up a red carpet to where an official reception awaited him. The sign above tells its own story of how one man battled the odds.

In more serious mood, Sanders stands with Western Australia's Premier Peter Dowding.

Sanders holds aloft a banner newspaper poster in central Perth.

Thousands turned out to pay tribute to their maritime hero in a colourful ticker-tape parade through the city.

a slip-up. Approaching or near land I use all at my means to navigate. In rough weather it is the sun that is useful. The satellite navigator has long since stopped working. So, too, the B and G speed and distance log. I must estimate distance.

If the sun is about, I believe I am good at getting a fairly accurate sight in bad weather, when the sight can only be caught on top of the occasional wave. I am well practised.

Comments like "oily calm", "no useful wind about", and "sunny, good for solar panels" punctuated Sanders' logbook on Sunday 30 August as he tried to sail eastward.

On the first day of spring, showers fell, enabling him to top up his fresh water supplies. Unfortunately he was sailing into an east wind and every time a shower came he had to square the yacht away to better catch the rain, which meant sailing the wrong way. Craving fresh vegetables, he decided to try his luck at bean sprouts and opened a packet given to him by a friend, Billie Connor, before his departure fifteen months earlier. Sanders soaked some of the seeds in a container of fresh water and noted in his log: *Will take about a week or so to sprout I suppose. I will keep them damp with a rinse every day until suitable to eat—I hope.*

Light headwinds persisted and *Endeavour* was making little or no progress on 4 September. At breakfast time the following morning Sanders boated a small fish, which provided a nice change of diet for supper. He made a fish mornay with it, using sprouting bean shoots instead of parsley. The meal ended a pleasing day for the solo circumnavigator, because he had picked up a nice breeze on his beam and the yacht logged 124 miles.

On Monday 7 September—day 472—he changed his clock to Perth time and shouted *Hooray!* into his logbook. He was still averaging more than a hundred miles a day, highly satisfactory. That night he made himself a curry and rice dish, blending in his last can of baked beans, freeze-dried chilli con carne and savoury mince flavoured with curry powder.

The next supper was his first substantial feed of "*Parry Endeavour* bean sprouts". He ate them with Hawaiian chicken, mixed with freeze-dried rice and boiled spaghetti.

Running before a fourteen-knot westerly wind on day 473, he logged at noon: *Nice mild sunny day. Armchair sailing*. He was now closing fast on the Cape Leeuwin region and he heard his yacht's progress mentioned on ABC radio, as reported by his radio mentor Jack Seabrook, who was getting fixes on the yacht from the Argos satellite system. He had not spoken with the veteran radio man for months because his high-frequency set was not working.

Soon after nightfall on Saturday 12 September he managed to make radio contact with Albany by using his old Codan radio, usually used for transmitting and listening on his radio direction finder. Later he heard Jack Seabrook transmitting. Jack could not "read" him but "copied" enough to know that all was well on board *Endeavour*. Another radio message came through to say that a boat named *Portofino* was going to attempt a rendezvous with him off Cape Leeuwin for an exchange of messages, and that Richard Stainton and his other *Perie Banou* crewmates would be on board.

Portofino, a luxury power cruiser, was chartered by one of Sanders' minor sponsors, the Royal Automobile Club, through its chief executive, Roy Caldwell, who was a close friend of the solo sailor and whose son John sailed in the crew of *Perie Banou*. I was invited to join a select band of Sanders' friends and head out from Fremantle Sailing Club on the Monday evening, motor south overnight and rendezvous about noon the following day off Leeuwin. That was the plan. The execution was not so simple.

As *Endeavour* neared the 115 deg. E longitude line that would mark the end of two circumnavigations, her skipper was tacking the yacht to windward in big seas. At 9.45 p.m. on Sunday 13 September—he logged: *Changed from storm jib to working jib. Do not like this head wind. Rough sailing. Only 193 miles from Fremantle. If this wind holds—and it looks as if it will—I will tack in the morning and go south. I am making little true progress towards the south of Cape Leeuwin (to 35 deg. S).*

The wind moderated the following day and he was able to take the reefs out of his mainsail. At 8.25 a.m. he raced on deck when he heard an aircraft circling the yacht. It was an RAAF Orion anti-submarine turbo-prop aircraft and Sanders did not know that I was on board. The RAAF had allowed me to join them on a joint US-Australian naval exercise off Jurien Bay, 100 kilometres north of Fremantle, and then, if time permitted, they would try to locate *Parry Endeavour* and take aerial photographs for me. Having theoretically located two "enemy" submarines and sunk them, the pilot officer headed south to look for the sloop.

Flying low, we searched in a grid pattern for more than an hour without success; it was only after obtaining a more accurate fix for the yacht from the RAAF base at Pearce that we eventually buzzed her. On each pass the lone sailor waved excitedly.

His own log version: *Being buzzed by RAAF Nimrod—or is it Orion?—four-engined turbo-prop aircraft. Called on Channel 16, but no reply. Nice to see them*. A few minutes later he added: *Gosh, it certainly flew low and made lots of passes this way and that, but mainly down my port side.*

It seemed that everything was happening at once, for just a few minutes later he had sighted a whale about ten metres long surfacing 100 metres astern of the yacht. That excitement over, Sanders again had contact with the outside world when a ship called the *Gachau* and registered in Hong Kong passed close by, South Australia-bound. He could see Indian officers and Chinese crew on deck through his binoculars and when he radioed them they responded, exchanging greetings.

Sanders could now smell land, warm and sweet, and he even spotted two bush flies on board, brought out with the east wind.

Tuesday 15 September 1987 was an historic day for the annals of sailing in general and for Jon Sanders in particular. It was the day he sailed into history beyond his 1981–82 double circumnavigation, a voyage itself which set a dozen new records for single-handed sailing.

Sanders woke up at 2 a.m. that morning and logged: *Wind only five knots on a calm sea. The yacht is way off course. I wonder for how long (been asleep).*

At eight-thirty he looked across his port bow and saw Australia again—Cape Leeuwin. "Hooray!" he exulted. After some careful position plotting he wrote on top of page 1269 of logbook four: *Two laps completed! Congratulations me*. He logged below: *Today I have crossed my second outgoing track at 33 deg. 44 south, 113 deg. 56 east and thus I have tied the second knot and completed two true circumnavigations of the world solo*. His mathematics had improved dramatically from the days when at school he got two per cent for the subject in a Junior Certificate exam. He worked out that his time for his two circumnavigations was 447 days, twelve hours and fifty-eight minutes. His first rounding (west-about) had taken 249 days and twenty-four minutes, while his second globe-girdling (east-about) 228 days, twelve hours and thirty-four minutes. He had sailed 49,402 nautical miles or 91,493 kilometres.

While Jon Sanders was entering all this in his log with some elation, there were some glum faces on board the luxury power boat *Portofino*. With two motors crippled by fuel filter problems we had been searching the now lumpy seas off Cape Leeuwin all day without sighting *Parry Endeavour*, and we faced the prospect of a 500–mile round trip in vain.

Skipper Iain Graham rightfully decided in the interests of safety to head back to Bunbury, about a hundred kilometres away. We were limping north-eastwards on one barely functioning motor when we turned our heads to the cloud-strewn western horizon to admire the sunset. Suddenly Des Piesse, the veteran boatbuilder who had done the strengthening work on *Parry Endeavour*, exclaimed: "What's that to the left of the sun?" Then we all saw it—a tiny triangle of begrimed sail. "It's Jon!" we shouted almost as one.

With some trepidation our skipper helmed *Portofino* towards the sliver of sail, which gradually got bigger as *Endeavour* and our boat converged. Sanders heard the cruiser while he was enjoying a hot drink, and quickly came on deck to wave to us excitedly. Soon we were within hailing distance and Sanders dropped his jib as the sun sank below the horizon.

"What a lovely surprise to see you all," he yelled.

Our skipper dared not cut the ailing motor, so we circled *Endeavour* slowly while we shouted greetings and questions at the lone sailor. This became hazardous in the lumpy sea, so we asked him to go below to his VHF radio to continue the interview while we moved away a little from his yacht.

Perhaps stirred by the warming contact with old friends, Sanders' thoughts lingered on food. "I'd give anything for a country roast dinner . . . roast lamb with mint sauce and lots of spuds, sweet potatoes, peas and onions," he said. But this was fantasy—he knew all too keenly that he barely had enough food to last the voyage.

He said his sloop was sailing as well as the day he left Fremantle, and reckoned it could do "four or five laps". But he would not hear of a new long-range radio being placed on board his yacht. "It would immediately disqualify me under the rules of single-handed sailing laid down by the *Guinness Book of Records*," he pointed out.

How did he feel to have notched another world record to add to the dozen he set during his 1981–82 double circumnavigation?—"It's terrific to have done the longest lone voyage in the history of sail," he replied. "I've just written in my logbook, 'Today I tied the second knot'. But it's great to be on the homeward lap."

The interview over, Sanders talked briefly to his crew members, Richard Stainton, John Caldwell and Derek Baxter, who were exuberant at having found their skipper-hero. "I couldn't think of anyone else I'd like to meet in the middle of the ocean," he told them.

Jokingly, they offered him a beer. "I haven't had a beer for 480 days and I'd love a cold can with you," he yelled.

As he rehoisted his genoa to continue his odyssey, he called: "I'm sure Betty Fitzhardinge [wife of his blue-water sailor friend Bill Fitzhardinge] will cook me that roast dinner when I return, and I can hardly wait."

Two minutes later the sea-stained sails of *Parry Endeavour* were ghostly triangular shapes against a darkening Cape Leeuwin sky. Jon Sanders was alone again —naturally.

17

Storm Bay . . . and Some Sprouts

They change their clime, not their disposition, who run across the sea.

Horace, The Epistles, Book 1

IT was an unexpected delight for Jon Sanders to see some of his mates and crewmen in that remote rendezvous off Australia's greatest cape, and when he was finally alone with his thoughts, he logged: *It was lovely to see them all and hear the news . . . Margaret Connor* [daughter of sailing colleague Dennis Connor] is *getting married and even worse, so is Jill Farrell —so who am I going to take out now when home?* (The confirmed bachelor enjoyed a platonic friendship with Jill Farrell and often escorted her to official functions.)

Those of us on *Portofino* were glad to limp back to Bunbury to escape a rising sea; the thought of our single sick engine failing was not a comforting one. Meanwhile *Endeavour* sailed into a relatively calm sea with winds down to eight knots from the west.

It was to prove short-lived, for two days after the rendezvous a gale typical of Leeuwin sprang up and by 4 p.m. Sanders had to reef down the main. At 8.50 p.m. he logged: *Oh dear, winds 45–50 knots. Hope it quietens, do not want to heave-to*. After ten minutes of worried thought he added: *Think I will hoist storm jib and lower the main*. On this blustery night he donned foul-weather gear and safety harness and clipped himself to the lifeline on deck for the tricky chore. Fifty minutes later he wrote: *Mainsail down and furled on boom. Storm jib up. Lightning about. 35–45 knots west*. At 10.10 p.m. he logged in some pique: *Went up on deck to secure a winch handle and copped a wave as I went below*.

The westerly gale continued all night, but moderated enough during the morning for Sanders to hoist a fully reefed mainsail. By 4 p.m. he was able to take two of the three reefs out of the main and hoist a working jib.

Worried about radio contact for his third rounding of the world, he took apart his 6801 radio and sprayed it with an anti-moisture treatment, hoping it would revive, but it still did not work. But at seven-thirty he got through to Royal Perth Yacht Club on his faulty VHF radio, on which he could transmit (poorly), but not receive. His radio mentor, Jack Seabrook, relayed messages to him from Curtin University's Tim Pauley and his Aunt Sheila. Seabrook had to transmit to *Endeavour*'s radio direction finder, which could receive but not transmit.

Sanders entered the Great Australian Bight in a perfect eighteen-knot sailing breeze, and on that first day made a healthy 123 miles. The winds backed to the north and increased to thirty knots, enabling him to boost his progress in the next two days to more than 150 miles. As he approached the region south of Port Lincoln on South Australia's Eyre Peninsula, he kept a radio sked with his old friend Geoff Boyes at the Royal Yacht Club of Tasmania, using his VHF radio to transmit and his radio direction finder to receive.

He found it a source of comfort having local radio stations within range so that he could listen to the various breakfast and other programmes. On the one hand, it was an advantage being able to keep up with the Australian and overseas news; on the other, the explicit advertisements played havoc with his jaded tastebuds, by now thoroughly accustomed to monotonous and predictable menus.

As he passed south-east of Adelaide he encountered fickle winds that fluctuated in both strength and direction, but he was making good 130 and more miles a day. Sunday 27 September found him in near windless conditions, poor for sailing but good for scrubbing the sides of his yacht. He felt he was fighting a losing battle with the grime.

At 9 p.m. he logged: *Wind has dropped out again. Sails flap, yuk. I was rather hoping to clear Maetsuyker Island* [south of Tasmania] *tomorrow afternoon. No hope now—no progress at all. I spent the last couple of hours packaging up all the letters I've written to Colin to post, plus my echo charts, still and movie films for John Penrose, all to be passed over in*

Storm Bay [near Hobart] *whenever I get there*.

It was bitterly cold in the Southern Ocean when Sanders finally got a breeze, which turned out to be an easterly—just what he did not want. At noon on Monday 28 September he logged: *Got a sight of the sun between the clouds and found I am a mere 0.1 of a mile north of my dead reckoning*.

As he slowly tacked towards the western coast of Tasmania the following cold, wintry day, he left one reef in the main, the better to catch rain that now threatened astern of the yacht. At noon he wrote: *Fresh, cold SW wind has arrived. No sun, so no noon sight, just when I needed it*. The adrenalin always flowed within Jon Sanders when he neared land that could pose a navigational problem or a lee shore hazard.

Three hours later he logged: *Land ho port side—Tasmania!* An hour later a rain squall with thirty-five-knot winds hit the yacht and lasted two and a half hours.

Now off the south-west corner of Tasmania, Sanders decided to give himself plenty of sea room. Although the wind was dropping, the sea was still very rough. But the elements were perplexing the lone circumnavigator. His logbook tells the story—*2205: Gosh it is annoying. Not much wind now, lots and lots of it at other times. 2215: Squalling now, 30–35 SW. What a night. 2305: Bumpy, yukky night.*

It was to be an eventful day at sea the following day, day 494. At 4.05 a.m. he sighted the loom of the Maetsuyker lighthouse on his port bow—just as he expected. He immediately tacked away to give himself more sea room.

As dawn streaked the horizon ahead of *Parry Endeavour*, Sanders caught sight of Tasmania's South-West Cape off his port bow. Ten minutes later he could make out Maetsuyker Island dead ahead. He was nearly out of wind in a big, sloppy sea.

Soon after eating his hot porridge, he logged: *Hooray. Got through to Hobart radio on 2201.* He had long telephone chats with his brother, crewman Richard Stainton and the Parry Corporation's Malcolm Bailey, who had been appointed to oversee his voyage on behalf of a busy Kevin Parry. During the morning his attention was drawn to some impressive looking rocks sticking high out of the water.

Early that afternoon as he sailed around navigational hazards that would be tricky in darkness, he radio-telephoned me as he watched Eddystone Rock through his starboard cabin window. He was quite aghast about a suggested plan to put a radio expert from the Royal Yacht Club of Tasmania on board *Endeavour* to repair his HF radio, as this would have disqualified him immediately as a solo circumnavigator. "I'll be telling them tonight that there'll be nobody allowed on my yacht," he declared. "One lone circumnavigator was disqualified when he took a wreck survivor on board, and another was ruled out because someone threw him a can of beer."

That afternoon Sanders was forced to heave-to when a thirty to forty-knot gale lashed his yacht. He had three reefs in the mainsail when he logged at 5 p.m.: *Nasty gale, not even forecast*. Fifteen minutes later he sighted Tasman Head. In the late evening he snatched an hour's sleep while hove-to, but woke up in time to log: *Local gale continues. Cape Bruny light bears 307 deg.*

Half an hour after midnight, he elaborated: *Gosh, I really do not need this gale, gusting to 45 knots WSW. Forecast for Hobart tonight 6C.* The wind moderated as quickly as it had sprung up the previous morning and at 2.55 a.m. he braved the cold to venture on to the foredeck to hoist a working jib. In the darkness he was keeping a keen eye out for shipping. He sighted a ship or a fishing boat out to starboard at 3.15 a.m. and ninety minutes later another passing ahead of the yacht. The wind faded further as Sanders ate a quick breakfast. With his rendezvous with the Royal Yacht Club of Tasmania vessel planned for that morning in Storm Bay, he was alert and apprehensive.

At 9 a.m. a Cessna aircraft buzzed the yacht with press photographers taking pictures from the windows. Down below the object of their attentions was becoming frustrated—in just half an hour the vagaries of the wind had him way off course now, and as a result he was late in handing over his letters and echo-sounding graphs.

It was not until noon that he kept his rendezvous with the Tasmanian Yacht Club motor sailer *Lullaby II*. Nothing whatsoever came on board *Parry Endeavour*, Sanders noted.

At 4.20 p.m., away from civilisation again, he found himself nearly becalmed, with the yacht rolling awkwardly. He waited two hours for a breeze to spring up and when it did, he got too much. At 11 p.m. he logged: *Lots of wind now, near gale. Put all reefs into mainsail. Wind chill factor outside nearly freezing. 30 knot WSW*. Ten minutes later: *Cancel near gale, make it read gale, 30–40 WSW*.

The gale was behind him and *Endeavour* made good progress during the small hours of the following morning. Despite the near calm of the previous day, he made good 135 nautical miles. The high winds had moderated by breakfast time and Sanders took advantage of his proximity to Hobart to make more radio-telephone calls through his VHF radio. From these he learnt of a splurge of publicity about the rendezvous given in eastern states newspapers and television, and in his home state.

Well clear of the Tasmanian coast the following day, Saturday 3 October, he wrote at mid-morning: *Mainly sunny, bit winterish. Fairly big sea typical of Roaring Forties, moderate wind, 20 knots W.* It was a favourable wind for progress and he was able to make 150 miles that day. In the afternoon he wired up to a second Argos transponder he had fitted to his cabin roof a few days earlier as a backup to the transponder on his transom. He logged: *Tomorrow I will connect all power leads up and the number two, like the number one, will run off the 24V batteries and solar panels fitted specially for them. The number two has been on its own power for past three days (own power has 60 days life). Was advised by Geoff Boyes over radio that both transponders are working okay.*

It was of great comfort to Sanders, because he knew that once he got out into the South Pacific he would be lucky to be able to report his daily positions. At least Curtin University and his friends back home would know where *Endeavour* was and that all was well from the multiple daily position reports picked up by satellite and sent to a computer in North America for relay to Toulouse, France, and on to Curtin's Centre for Marine Science and Technology. Even if he fell overboard the yacht's subsequent erratic course would alert the authorities that all was not well on board the yacht. But this, of course, would be of little help to the lone sailor.

More running repairs were necessary on the Sunday when his self-steering line broke at mid-morning. Sanders had to drop the jib and heave-to to make the repairs. He rove through a new self-steering line and by 11.20 a.m. the yacht was on course again. That afternoon he became the yacht's handyman again, soldering wires together and crimping terminals on the spare Argos. Amphometer tests showed that the current was drawing properly after he connected the second Argos to the batteries. That evening as he ate supper he noted the barometer was falling and, when he kept a faint sked with Geoff Boyes, he was told a strong sou'wester was headed his way.

A south-west front did in fact pass over the yacht that night, but by mid-morning the next day it had dropped to a light following breeze. Late in the afternoon Sanders did more running repairs—he fixed the broken tape leach cord in the working jib, replaced a broken hank, and stripped, serviced and greased the mainsheet winch. After supper he received an interesting message relayed from Geoff Boyes. An Australian astronaut-oceanographer, Paul Scully-Power, would like him to keep an eye out for any eddies in the ocean twelve to twenty kilometres in diameter, as observed from a satellite.

On his 500th day at sea without stopping, tying up or mooring and without taking on any provisions, Jon Sanders awoke at 3.25 a.m. to find his yacht being jostled by a strong nor'wester of up to thirty-five knots, and he left his warm bunk to put a further reef—the third—in his mainsail. For such a milestone, the day was to prove a particularly rough one, though the wind moderated briefly at mid-afternoon. At 8.25 p.m. he noted as he finished supper: *Rough, cold, bleak winter's night*.

At breakfast the next day he heard the

forecast for Foveaux Strait, which separates Stewart Island from the south coast of New Zealand's South Island. The wind was expected to increase to forty to forty-five knots from the west. At mid-morning he wrote apprehensively: *Rough sea, strong wind. Three reefs and storm jib. Zooming along. Hope pending heavy gale forecast for south of New Zealand is not too bad. Steering a course to give Stewart Island and The Traps a wider berth in what might be a bad night tonight.*

Despite the wintry conditions, he managed to get a noon sun sight—a valuable fix in a hazardous region. By late afternoon *Endeavour* was running under a storm-reefed mainsail only, and at eight o'clock Sanders decided to gybe the yacht to port for safety. *Better err south, off-course, than risk coming close to the coast and The Traps unawares this night*, he explained to his log. Two hours later he wrote: *Amazing. The wind has dropped to only 15 knots. I am now well under-sailed, but barometer is very low at 992 and gale warning is out. Will leave sails as is.*

The gale that was forecast south of the Land of the Long White Cloud did not eventuate, much to Sanders' relief, so after breakfast the following morning he hoisted a working jib, but left the three reefs in the mainsail, a wise precaution with the wind at twenty-five to thirty knots with squalls much higher.

His kerosene stove was still giving trouble, and his reward for an hour's patient servicing was an unscheduled fire and black smoke throughout the cabin. But he persevered and two hours later managed to get the burner working properly.

Strong winds with gale-force squalls continued all afternoon with the yacht making good, but bumpy progress. The gale abated overnight and at 12.40 a.m. when Sanders went on deck to take two reefs out of the mainsail, it had started to rain. He quickly rigged up his canvas bucket under the main, in which he left a single reef to help catch the rainwater. At 12.55 a.m. he wrote one word in his logbook: *Hailstones!* The hail gave way to light rain, however, and the solo sailor's bucket was harvesting it. The fall was constant over half an hour—sufficient to fill one tank and meet his needs for six days.

Cold, but sunny and mild conditions prevailed that day and Sanders revelled in the nice change, busying himself cleaning out his galley and scrubbing down the sides of the yacht.

Saturday 10 October saw *Parry Endeavour* well out into the South Pacific and making north-eastwards. In yet another gale (of thirty-five to forty knots) and with the main fully reefed, he logged at 12.50 p.m.: *Grey bleak winter and rough. It is yukky, plus cold. I am sailing freer to lessen the bad ride and so 50 deg. off course. Making north—for warmer conditions—and some east*. Two hours later: *Constant rain. Shame it is so rough, cannot catch it*. Just before supper he noted: *The bad weather is getting badder. I may have to heave-to*. His last entry for the day at 8.45 p.m. was: *Awful weather continues. Still going bash, crash. Wind whines so*. Soon after midnight came a gloomy postscript: *Gale continues, rough as bags*.

In near freezing conditions, the gale gradually moderated during the small hours and at mid-morning Sanders took all reefs out of the mainsail. By four o'clock he was nearly out of wind, and in these mild conditions he was able to relax. Having watched only one video in the past eight months, he now decided at supper that he would "spoil" himself and watch another, *Educating Rita*. Alas, his expectations went unfulfilled, for the video machine began, somewhat perversely, to pull the tape out. The same happened when he tried other video cassettes too. Sanders had purposely not been using the video in order to conserve battery power in the southern waters. But he could not help but feel cheated that his vigilance was so rewarded.

The video contretemps was offset to some degree by the pleasant sight of dozens of small dolphins splashing about his yacht in the early evening darkness, "squeaking or miaowing like cats".

The following day as *Parry Endeavour* sailed across the South Pacific towards another appointment with Cape Horn, Jon

Sanders gave himself a special treat—a feed of yacht-grown bean sprouts, vitamin rich and a welcome addition to a dreary diet.

18

Endeavour 3, Cape Horn 0

Break, break, break,
On thy cold grey stones, O Sea!

Alfred, Lord Tennyson,
Break, Break, Break

NOW well into the Southern South Pacific on his way to a third (for this voyage) encounter with Cape Horn, Jon Sanders found himself becalmed at breakfast on Tuesday 13 October. After his porridge and hot-milk cocoa he replaced his port genoa halyard —the one that had been doing most of the work—with a new one and checked his topping lift halyard. His only entry for noon when he usually took a sun sight was: *No sun and no wind*.

Slightly bored, he tried feeding a brace of Cape Pigeons that had adopted *Parry Endeavour*. He logged: *When I throw them something to eat, one chases off the other—a real bully. Needless to say, I tried to feed the nice one. I think they are a pair (one must be a wife-basher!).*

Eventually, around mid-afternoon, a breeze found the yacht and rain began to fall steadily. As night closed in the solo sailor let his yacht stray off course, the better to catch rain off his sails. His final entry for that slow day was at 10.45 p.m.: *Gybed yacht. Wind north 20—25. Rain bucket in. Caught about 100 litres or so. Put three reefs into main as barometer tumbling, 991.*

The variable wind, which rose and fell from between seven and twenty-five knots, had Sanders guessing. At breakfast the following day he logged: *The wind is varying, now only seven knots N. With such a low barometer, will I get caught out if I increase sail?* If he had been sailing with a crew Sanders would not have worried. With two or three experienced crewmen on deck reefing the mainsail and dropping or replacing the genoa, a skipper could feel secure. But being alone meant that he had to think ahead and try to second guess the weather's vagaries.

After breakfast he took two reefs out of

the main and hoisted the working jib. It was disconcerting to have such windless conditions in a rough sea. His sails were slatting everywhere and the yacht was rolling all over the place—the proverbial calm before the storm.

Just before ten o'clock rain and gale squalls arrived, which meant it was time for reefs. Sanders admitted to his log that he had been "caught out properly". He reported: *Winds over 60 knots. Had to reef the main and get the jib down—it was awful. Silly me—all the clues were there. Wind south, severe gale, off course, running downwind on the only angle the self-steerer will cope with.*

The southerly gale persisted all afternoon with lumpy seas, but at sunset it started to moderate—down to thirty to thirty-five knots—and Sanders wrote: *Ventured into adventure land and hoisted working jib. Now zooming. Bloody cold outside.* He added after supper: *Sailing fast in a very rough sea, working jib, three reefs, wind well off of abeam 25–35 SW. Oops, no sooner wrote that, than got 40-knot squall.*

The beefy southerly continued overnight

and did wonders for his distance-made-good—135 miles compared with fifty-eight the previous day. At noon he managed to get his first sun sight for three days, and, as he suspected, he was twenty-eight miles farther south than his dead reckoning put him. He had expected to sight Chatham Island, a big island off New Zealand's east coast, jutting over the horizon that morning, and when he did not he assumed he was farther south than he reckoned. He decided to shape a course—wind permitting—to the 43 deg. S mark and run along that parallel.

He recorded an extra 15 October the next day as he was about to cross the International Date Line. He was now out of range of New Zealand medium wave radio and so had to rely on the BBC World Service, Radio Australia and Voice of America for his news and entertainment, at least until he could pick up the British Forces Broadcasting Service off the Falkland Islands. During the afternoon, Sanders did some stock-taking of his stores and reported: *Enough porridge (16 x 750g.) and two packets of Weeties for breakfast for the rest of the voyage. There are enough (186) D cell batteries to keep my SW radio going eight hours (and more) for every day of the voyage. Did some spring cleaning in forward sleeping section of the saloon. Keeping things clean and tidy is a non-stop job, which one gets behind with in bad weather.*

The solo circumnavigator did not expect so much wind now that he had reached 44 deg. S, but the following day he fetched yet another gale, between thirty-five and forty knots from the south, with stronger squalls. Just after lunch a hailstorm rat-a-tat-tatted a drumbeat on his cabin roof. Late in the afternoon he logged: *It is getting rougher, sailing freer for better ride*. At 8.45 p.m. he added: *Wow, gale most severe at moment—only a temporary squall, I hope*.

It was no passing squall. At one-thirty the following morning Sanders had to leave his warm bunk and change course downwind in heavy squalls and rough seas.

The cold, bleak southerly had been playing havoc with Sanders' chest complaint, pleurodynia, which flared in consistently damp and cold conditions and caused intense pain on the right side of his rib cage, front and back. He had diagnosed it himself from a book he carried on all his voyages, *The Ship Captain's Medical Guide*. Now it was bothering him a lot, and he had no medication for it.

By mid-morning on Sunday 18 October he decided he had erred from his course far enough north and it was time to try to sail due eastwards along the forty-third parallel for several weeks before heading south-eastwards towards the Horn.

It was on-again, off-again sailing as *Endeavour* plied eastwards. Even the lone sailor's log entries hinted at boredom. *Usual view outside*, he noted on 19 October, *grey sky and sea and odd wandering albatross gliding here and there*.

The following afternoon he logged: *Appear to be sailing in the effects of an adverse current. Yesterday I thought I detected a movement in the water, with small waves cresting slightly—a possible swirl*.

The wind continued to rise and fade and it was still bitterly cold. At mid-morning on Friday 23 October he noted: *Cloud thinning, bit of blue sky here—but cold, brrr. Not good for my pleurodynia. The yacht appears to be sailing slower, I presume because of the dirty sides and bottom.*

With more sun hitting the solar panels, *Endeavour*'s three banks of batteries started to register healthy charges on his Brookes and Gatehouse volt indicator. He logged: [the volt indicator] *showed 13.60V for all six ship's batteries, the highest in more than three months. The two separate Argos batteries continue to show a small, but steady decline in voltage and are getting low. The small 24V solar panels do not quite cope. I have just changed the 24V solar panel regulator to the Argos system in case this is the reason for the decline. If the sun is out tomorrow and the ship's batteries show at least 13.6V, I will swap two batteries with the Argos batteries.*

The weekend of 24–25 October saw *Endeavour* scooting along before a stiff westerly gale with squalls of up to fifty knots and more, even intermittent hail and sleet. Sanders had no chance of switching batteries.

The gale had not abated by Monday,

and the sloop could only self-steer downwind. It got so rough that Sanders lost a bucket with some washing in it from the cockpit. The gale moderated by late afternoon on a day in which *Endeavour* made good 131 miles.

During the windy, showery Tuesday Sanders took advantage of a lull to swap two of his yacht's twelve-volt batteries for the two Argos batteries, which had lost much of their charge. The yacht's batteries were fully charged by their solar panels, while the Argos batteries—used to power the Argos satellite reporting system—were down to 10.8V. Had they become too weak to allow the transponder to emit its beep to the satellite, *Endeavour* could have become the subject of an alarm and a costly sea search.

By mid-afternoon the wind was back to gale force and at 5.15 p.m. Sanders wrote: *Wind 25–35 W, barometer falling. I guess I'd better put some more reefs into the mainsail*. Fully reefed that night he logged: *Oh dear, we are in another gale, some bad waves about*. The gale continued all of the next day, varying between thirty and forty-five knots, but *Endeavour* was running before it with only a fully-reefed mainsail—no jib. The waves were big and some were breaking, causing the yacht to surf at times. But progress was a healthy 133 miles.

Mindful of his water situation, but unable to put off his accumulated laundry any longer, Sanders spent Thursday afternoon on an improvised washing session. He warmed up some sea water and, using buckets inside his sink, washed most of his dirty clothes and bunk linen in salt water, to which he added some baby shampoo. Then he rinsed them sparingly in the first run-off water he had stored in jerry cans for that purpose (it was slightly brackish). He strung a line from mast to backstay, no easy task in thirty-knot winds and a rough sea. It was an even more difficult chore to hang out the washing, which comprised two sheets, three flannel shirts, a pair of track suit pants, five pillowslips, a windcheater, a pair of thermal socks and five pairs of jockey shorts.

In these cold regions Sanders rugged up. A typical "ensemble" would be a pair of wool socks, thermal long johns with cut-off jeans, a thick sailing shirt, long-sleeved thermal T-shirt and a navy blue naval jumper with epaulettes.

Later on he brought the washing in, still damp, to finish off drying inside the cabin. As the wind again approached gale force, Sanders fully-reefed the main for a rough night at sea.

Cabin dampness was a continuing problem, especially when accompanied by near-freezing cold. In cold regions Sanders usually slept on a fleecy sheet over an opened sleeping bag on top of his bunk cushions. Over him he spread a woollen rug and a sleeping bag he used as a doona. He lamented the thinness of his bunk cushions, which allowed his boney hip and ribs to come hard-up against the bunk boards. This tended to inflame his pleurodynia, because it allowed dampness to get through.

Scrubbing mould within the yacht was a non-stop job, and the lone sailor did it just whenever the weather permitted. But apart from condensation, mainly under the side decks, not the cabin roof, Sanders was pleased to find the saloon dry of leaks, except for the cockpit hatch in the stern cabin. *This yacht is amazingly leak-proof and seldom needs pumping*, his diary records.

On Saturday 31 October—day 526—as *Endeavour* made good progress before a thirty to thirty-five knot west-nor'-wester, Sanders noted that his number one water tank was empty and his number two was just over half full. He also had three full jerry cans. He calculated that, with normal use, this would last him forty-five days, or roughly 4500 miles. With another 7000 miles to go before he reached a region of reliable rainfall, north of the Equator in the North Atlantic, it was obvious he needed another good steady fall.

In mid-afternoon he logged: *Hoping the sun will glow through the leaden sky for afternoon sight. Folded all my washing which was hanging in the cabin. Now dry —I hope (it is a damp world I live in).*

On the Sunday morning he wrote just before breakfast: *Hooray, got morning sun sight. Gosh, it has been five days without an a.m. or p.m. sight (though noon meridian passages have been obtained)*. He noted that since he left Storm Bay, Tasmania, *Endeavour* had averaged 124 miles a day.

That afternoon the wind moderated and the clouds cleared to allow the sun to beam down on the sea-stained sloop. Sanders felt grateful for the change, brief though it was. At ten-thirty next morning he noted gloomily: *All the nice blue sky is fast disappearing—grey again!*

He decided to take advantage of the moderate conditions to check and service the self-steerer ready for the Cape Horn region. In order to attach new steering lines he had to heave-to for half an hour. That night, though racehorses held no interest for him, he tuned in to the Melbourne Cup broadcast on Radio Australia and heard No. 8, Kensei, win.

Fog increased around *Parry Endeavour* the following day as Sanders undertook preparations for his third encounter with the Horn. He lowered the mainsail and checked the stitching, then greased the slides and the main halyard winch with his concoction of vaseline and engine oil. While doing this he almost dropped some vital winch parts overboard, but just managed to save them. During the quiet afternoon he put several new stitches in his working jib where he found chafing, and oiled the hanks.

The fog and zephyr breeze gave way to a gale the following morning before dawn. At 11.35 a.m. he logged: *Presently sailing east to longitude 110 W, will then shape a course to pass south of Tierra del Fuego and Cape Horn, which is 2046 miles from present position as the crow, oops, albatross flies.*

On day 531—Guy Fawkes Day—he noticed during the morning some dieselene leaking into the bilge. He rigged up the pump tap from his toilet to a length of plastic tubing, took it into the cockpit and pumped the diesel fuel out of the starboard tank into a bucket, from where it was dumped into the sea.

After breakfast the next day he perused his *US Ocean Pilot* chart, which showed that *Endeavour* was now in an area of icebergs, and that they were more likely to drift farther north in November than in any other month.

At noon he changed his course from due east to south-east to pass south of Tierra del Fuego.

At 6.20 p.m. he observed in his log: *My*

bedding in these latitudes is always so damp and so are the charts. I keep them on my bunk under the bunk cushion. No wonder I have pleurodynia. Never mind, soon it will be sticky tropics in the Atlantic.

For something different for lunch, he made a scone loaf in his oven, topping it with cheese he extracted from a packet of freeze-dried macaroni cheese, supplemented with some Parmesan cheese. His supper was curry and rice mixed with savoury mince and chilli con carne. He also indulged himself with a scone and golden syrup.

Consistently making good around 130 miles a day, *Parry Endeavour* was fast closing on the Tierra del Fuego region. At breakfast time on a foggy 10 November, Sanders heard on a BBC World Service programme that an iceberg the size of Cyprus had broken away from Antarctica, and he found it hard to stop wondering where it was. He had a little grouch to his log about matches: *I have trouble, as always in these regions, getting my matches to strike, despite them being labelled "waterproof". They're not even damp-proof.*

On 13 November *Endeavour* was out of the Roaring Forties and Sanders personally was entering the screaming fifties for the fifth time in six years. He was about to make his fifth run to Cape Horn (the third on this current voyage) 935 miles to the south-east.

At 11.30 a.m. he noted: *Hoisted storm jib. Meant to hoist working jib, but accidentally hanked on spitfire—that will do.* It proved to be the better choice of sail.

The spate of sunshine in recent days and the long days—sunrise was at 3.30 a.m., sunset 8 p.m.—had topped up his yacht's batteries through the solar panels. It was still bitterly cold, however. *Blue sky and blue with cold!* he told his log. Late in the afternoon the wind started to rise and all signs pointed to a gale that night. By midnight all three storm reefs were in the mainsail as the gale developed. At daybreak the following day, he logged: *Heavy gale. Wind 35–45 knots NW and raining.*

It was too windy to catch the rain, and when the gale moderated the rain ceased.

Endeavour made good 144 miles. The wind dropped right away to a puff and Sanders lamented, *Too much wind yesterday and not enough today*, as the sloop rolled unpleasantly in the southern Pacific swell. *One does not expect to be out of wind on the Chilean side* [of South America], *but out of wind I am. My US Pilot chart says zero per cent calm in this region—liar! My US. Pilot charts often tell lies!*

At midnight it was still so calm that Sanders could hear dolphins squeaking around his yacht. At breakfast he logged wryly: *Those monitoring my Argos positions at Curtin University will notice my lack of progress over this last day. They will probably think I've been stuck in some diabolical gale (instead of a diabolical calm*). But by mid-afternoon *Endeavour* was sailing briskly again per favour of a following (south-westerly) twenty-knot breeze. The yacht's daily run was only thirty miles, but there was a dramatic four-fold increase the following day as Sanders found himself in near-gale conditions.

By Wednesday 18 November he was

about 180 nautical miles west of Ile Noir—Tierra del Fuego. At breakfast he could faintly hear the British Forces Broadcasting Service from the Falkland Islands. He had difficulty getting his morning sight of the sun, because in the rough seas the mainsail kept obscuring his vision as he perched on the stern rail. At noon he calculated he was 355 miles from Cape Horn and 125 miles west of south-eastern Tierra del Fuego.

The wind strengthened to thirty knots during the afternoon and the seas were steep and close together. A little after midnight on Thursday he logged: *Sailing downwind fast. Think I will put one more reef into sail and thus take some of the load off the rudder and self-steerer, though the yacht is steering well.*

Having braved the icy wind to put a second reef in the main, he logged: *2 a.m. and there's dawn in the sky!* He was in a good frame of mind, but little did he know that this pale dawn was to usher in the worst storms he had ever experienced in three decades of sailing. As outlined fully in Chapter 1, over the next four days he would endure a hurricane, four knockdowns and waves bigger than he had ever seen.

Half way through this terrible storm—at breakfast time on Saturday 21 November—Sanders noticed a self-steering line had broken and quickly repaired it. At mid-morning he wrote self-assuringly in his logbook: *All blue sky and cold, good progress now, 30 knots WSW.* At noon: *Position found 24.1 miles south of dead-reckoning. Not surprised after yesterday's hurricane. 31 miles WSW of Ramirez* [island], *should pass that about 5.30 p.m. May have to gybe to avoid the rocks etc*. At mid-afternoon he sighted Diego Ramirez Island clear on the horizon off the port bow. Then he got a bearing on Bartolome and Gonzalo Islands, which prompted him to log: [the bearing] *advances my position seven miles—I guess my morning sight in rough conditions plus the favourable current known to be in this region, pushed on by yesterday's hurricane . . . sounds reasonable*. The wind dropped out that day and Sanders could hardly believe he was in the same region as that which thoroughly chastened him the previous day.

Just after dawn on Sunday he calculated that he should be due south of Cape Horn at 3.40 a.m.—a magic moment for any sailor whether a skipper or crewman or single-handed. The world's most infamous cape has held a strange fascination for mariners for centuries, and Jon Sanders harboured great respect, even awe, for its now familiar outline.

By five o'clock the wind had piped up to thirty-five knots north-north-west, and after breakfast Sanders fully reefed the main and hoisted his spitfire jib. He wrote: *I am now under the lee of Cape Horn Island and the Hermite Group 30 miles NW. I can expect more manageable seas. I shall sail a more northing to get more protection from Tierra del Fuego way to the north-west from which direction the wind is coming.*

Endeavour was in a full gale again by 11.15 a.m. when the wind changed to west-south-west and squalled up to fifty knots. After a nervous lunch he logged: *Dropped jib and yacht just broached. Change of wind to WSW exposes yacht to full fetch of sea*. But by 4.40 p.m. the gale had moderated to thirty knots—a breeze that would send any weekend sailor scurrying for a haven, but which was a welcome relief for Jon Sanders. It dropped away further and swung to the west by sunset.

By midnight his sails were flapping desultorily and the lone sailor was moved to write: *Gale by day, floppy sails by night. I hope I can clear the eastern side of Estados before the next gale because of the tidal stream in the region*. He wondered if he would be able to sight Estados in the hazy conditions. Although he could not see land, he smelt it—"as sweet as a young lady's fair hair, a little different, but just as nice".

When the expected daily gale did not arrive by breakfast time, he replaced the storm jib with the working jib. He noted after returning to his cabin drenched that he had some rheumatism in each hand caused by the cold water.

The wind did pipe up mid-morning and by noon *Parry Endeavour* was being buffeted by a thirty-five-knot gale. Sanders had one surprise in store—he found in the shambles of the aft cabin (caused by a knockdown in the hurricane) a rusty tin of Milo.

The north wind on *Endeavour*'s nose prevented Sanders making the northing he wanted. He realised he was getting too far east, into risky iceberg territory.

Just before dusk he sailed through some tidal current which whipped up metre-high waves that were breaking in unison. The wind was quickly rising and at 8.50 p.m. he logged: *Oh dear, it is a gale again*. At 11 p.m.: *Strong north bang-on-the-nose headwinds continue. Course now due north to pass by the Falklands*.

Frustratingly the wind stayed in the north and it was extremely cold. Sanders could not stop thinking about icebergs. At 6.45 a.m. on 24 November—day 550—he got the British Forces Broadcasting Service on his medium-wave radio, which put him in a better frame of mind. He liked their programme, and the emphasis on popular music. It went down well with his porridge and hot-milk Milo. The Falklands forecast was for a wind change to the west, which pleased him.

The sun shone weakly through the

clouds at noon and the lone circumnavigator got a sight with his sextant. He logged at 12.15 p.m.: *I'm not making good progress. Perhaps I should shape my course to pass the east side of the Falkland Islands.* Ocean Passages for the World *warns of ice risk not far on the east side. On the other hand, I pranged a trawler on the western side last time. Hmmmn.* After an hour's deep thought he came to a decision. He told his logbook: *Shall pass to the east and force myself to keep good lookout. Twilight and dawn are not far apart. I should be in range of Port Stanley VHF—just perhaps radio-telephone.*

Decision made, he promptly replaced the storm jib with a working jib and was soon laying his new course, for better or for worse. The waves were not as big as they had been the previous day, but they were steep and closer together, causing *Endeavour* to bury her nose in them amid cascades of green water. That night he tried to call the Falklands, a British fisheries inspection vessel or a British Navy ship on his VHF radio, but he got no reply.

As he turned in to his cosy bunk, he

noted the wind had got up to gale strength. At 10.30 p.m. concern crept into his log entry: *Oh dear, the wind is increasing still further and it is so cold. But up there I must go to change storm jib*. An hour later he added wearily: *Wrong jib; now the wind has dropped to 20 knots. Maybe temporarily*.

He deferred going on to the foredeck in the bitter cold again, and it was the right decision. Soon after midnight he logged: *Wow, 45–50 knots rain squall—glad I did not change up again. Black outside*. The breeze moderated as quickly as it had risen, but Sanders decided not to venture out into the cold, black night. It was 6.8C outside and the fresh wind made it seem even bleaker.

As he breakfasted in sunny conditions the following morning with *Endeavour* zooming along, Sanders little realised the day ahead had some unexpected excitement in store for him. At nine o'clock he heard the unmistakable drone of an aircraft and, rushing to his companionway hatch, he saw an RAF surveillance aircraft circling *Parry Endeavour*. He logged excitedly: *Aircraft—it is a Hercules I think—*

made lots of passes. I got photos and I presume they did, too. Minutes later: *Just flew low by—about 100 ft.—yet again.* At 10 a.m. he added: *The aircraft is flying at about 500 feet, still going round and round —they will get giddy!*

At 11.35 a.m. a Royal Navy Sea King helicopter was hovering over his yacht and Sanders went to his VHF radio in his cabin. He logged: *They said they had received emergency call from London. I suspect those in Perth asked for a checkup on me in the interests of safety. Anyway, they picked up three letters, one each for Kevin Parry, Hugh Schmitt and a part-finished letter to* [aunt] *Sheila. Sea King helicopter 25 said that they would log that nothing came on to the yacht. It was nice to see them. They advised that they knew of no icebergs in the region.*

The Sea King dropped a weighted bag on a rope to the sloop's starboard stern corner which Sanders caught easily and placed the letters inside, together with two press clippings for the 'copter's information.

In mid-afternoon Sanders received a radio call from the British fisheries inspection vessel *Falklands Right* asking for his position. *It seems they are going to intercept*, he confided to his log. An hour later, 4.15 p.m., the fisheries vessel approached from astern and a further hour after he sighted it he was having a VHF radio conversation with the skipper and his crew. He logged: *They sailed close down my starboard side, we are taking photos of each other*.

The fisheries men gave him the welcome news that there were no fishing vessels operating on the east side of the Falklands and only seventeen at this time of year on the other side. As *Endeavour* sailed on alone again under the lee of East Falkland Island, thirty miles to the west, Jon Sanders was still not aware of the drama on the other side of the world that resulted in that visit from the RAF Hercules and Navy helicopter.

19

Alarm Stations!

I will go back to the great sweet
mother,
Mother and lover of men, the sea.

A. C. Swinburne,
The Triumph of Time

WHEN Jonathan Sanders heard the thwack-thwack-thwack of the Royal Navy Sea King helicopter over his yacht at 11.35 a.m. on 25 November 1987, he was totally unaware that he and his yacht were a source of great concern, even alarm, back at home.

Unknown to him the Argos satellite reporting system (registration number PTT 2764) on *Endeavour* had gone into a distress mode. This was quickly picked up in Toulouse, southern France by the Argos scientists who immediately telephoned Dr. John Penrose at Perth's Curtin University after first sending an urgent telex to him.

Penrose learnt that the position of the yacht when the Argos went into distress mode was 53 deg. 498 S, 59.569 W.

Dr. Penrose and his assistant Tim Pauley immediately telephoned the Canberra Sea Safety Centre to tell them of the alarm. They also called Parry Corporation officials and the Falklands' Governor in Port Stanley. Next they telephoned Port Stanley harbour master Captain John Jackson, who asked them for Jon Sanders' course. They asked the captain to respect the lone sailor's rules for single-handed circumnavigation—nobody was to board *Parry Endeavour* except in dire circumstances.

The Curtin officials started telephoning at 3 p.m. as soon as they heard from Toulouse. By 10 p.m. they had word that all was well on the sloop; Captain Jackson got through with the advice that the yacht had been sighted from the air and that Sanders appeared to be in no distress.

Dr. Penrose asked Captain Jackson to tell Sanders to leave both of his Argos transponders activated in case further spurious distress calls emanated from PTT 2764. Forty minutes later the harbour master called again to report that the navy helicopter had found the solo sailor fit and well and unaware that his Argos was in alarm mode. He added that a ship was due shortly to rendezvous with *Endeavour*.

The Canberra Sea Safety Centre also confirmed the aerial sighting of Sanders and the helicopter contact. An official told Dr. Penrose that during the recent Sydney-Osaka yacht race several Argos transmitters gave illusory alarms, followed by a genuine one. Just before midnight Dr. Penrose telephoned Britain's Falmouth Maritime Rescue Co-ordination Centre; their news, passed on from the Falklands, confirmed that the alarm was spurious and the Argos switches were normal.

By midnight the weary Curtin University scientists had notified everyone concerned that Jon Sanders was alive and thriving after 551 days at sea. But John Penrose was awakened at 3.15 a.m. by a call from the Canberra centre reporting a mayday message from Falmouth. The boffin thought it was a mistake, but asked for a check. Fifteen minutes later the Canberra official again called to report that

Falmouth had advised they were in error —it was the previous day's message.

Meanwhile the Australian Embassy in Buenos Aires had been alerted and asked to contact the Argentine Coast Guard for help in what seemed like an emergency. The officials swung into action and called on the coast guard for help. The coast guard base in Comodoro Rivadavia on the Argentine coast was asked to keep a lookout for the yacht. The coast guard would not send a search vessel because Sanders' last position was ten to twenty miles inside the restricted British military and fishing zone.

The next day Dr. Penrose received another telex from Argos in Toulouse reporting that a Sea King helicopter had "lowered a crewman to the deck" of the yacht. Although he doubted this had happened, he was concerned lest the *Guinness Book of Records* authorities heard of this and believed it. It would disqualify Jon Sanders as a solo circumnavigator. However, Falmouth came to the rescue the same day with a telex message which read: *Statement that crewman lowered by Sea King incorrect. Contact with yacht made on FM channel 16. Skipper Jon Sanders requested that we stress that no-one was lowered to his vessel as this would invalidate his world record attempt. His mail was collected by lowering a hi-line with bag. Nothing was transferred from aircraft to yacht.*

A postscript to the drama caused by the false alarm came nearly four weeks later when Dr. Penrose received an international telegram from the lone sailor, who had dictated it to a passing ship named the *Redestos*. It was sent through Cape Town Radio and was somewhat garbled. It read: *All iswell withyawt Iaminjoy good spirit looking arrival Australia, kind regards, John Fanters.*

Unaware of the drama that had caused a flurry of anguished calls across Australia and across the world, Jon Sanders was sailing blithely ahead in the South Atlantic. On Thursday 26 November, day 552, he logged at breakfast time: *Forecast from British Forces Broadcasting Service for Falklands says west winds. I've got a north wind—that's not fair. I want a west wind, too, it's more favourable.* He put a second reef in his mainsail and sailed close-hauled as near to north as he could, but the wind constantly headed his yacht.

At 11.55 a.m. he noted: *My VHF radio makes a splutter now and again indicating someone is transmitting—out of range*. The sloop was bumping into a mild gale of up to thirty knots and a fog rolled over the scene early in the afternoon. At 3.40 p.m. Sanders logged: *Still hard on the nose, bash, crash*. But the wind veered slightly to the west and by nightfall *Endeavour* was back on course but still close-hauled and burying her bow in green seas. Her skipper had set a course for Isla Martin Vaz, a Brazilian-owned island about a thousand miles north-east of Rio de Janeiro.

The yacht was still rigged for a gale when Sanders awoke at 4 a.m. but the wind (by now a westerly) was down to about thirteen knots. He dashed on deck to take out two of the three storm reefs and replaced the spitfire jib with a working genoa. The breeze dropped further and by midday he was becalmed. He busied himself doing chores and scrubbing the sides of *Endeavour*, which were so soiled the sponsors' advertisements were illegible.

A light wind from the north-west found the yacht late in the afternoon, bringing a light fog with it. But at sunset Sanders heard an ominous weather forecast on Falklands Radio—a depression near Cape Horn and a severe force ten to eleven gale warning. He decided forthwith to tie a storm reef into the mainsail. Reefing down was easier in daylight and he did not want to be caught out as he had before. After completing his neat reefing job, he admitted: "Bit ridiculous now."

When he awoke at 1.30 a.m. *Endeavour* was in a full gale—thirty to thirty-five knots—and he proceeded to drop the jib and heave-to in a head wind. By daylight the gale had not worsened and the wind had backed to the north-west. Sanders hoisted his storm jib and got his yacht sailing again. At 6.30 a.m. he logged rather sheepishly: *Storm jib down, working jib up. Wind 25–30 NW. There was no severe gale. I was a little cautious. I guess all the nasty stuff is at Cape Horn.*

Endeavour was making good progress under a sunny sky and in a brisk nor

’wester, only to be buffeted around 11 a.m. by a gale again. Back came the storm jib, and the sloop broached twice early in the afternoon as she ran before the strong, quartering sea. At six o’clock Sanders decided to drop his jib and run square with the wind and sea to stop the yacht broaching. The gale had not let up and he sailed *Endeavour* twenty degrees off course for a better ride.

The gale moderated during the early hours of the morning, and at breakfast time Sanders logged simply: *The gale has gone*. He noticed that the water temperature had shot up from 6.3C to 10.3C and surmised that he had picked up the Brazil Current.

Next morning in a freshening NNW wind Sanders noticed that the barometer was falling—a familiar harbinger of gales for the region. He got busy tying all three reefs into the mainsail while it was easily manageable, and no sooner had he completed the task in darkness when the wind increased to twenty-five to thirty knots, accompanied by light rain. Just after dawn the wind veered north-east, a true headwind, and as it piped up to a mild gale Sanders ran up his spitfire jib. After midday conditions moderated and he rehoisted the working jib in place of the smaller one. Late in the afternoon, as conditions became foggy, he took out two reefs from the mainsail.

When it started to "spit" rain, he put his rain bucket under the mainsail optimistically. At 6.45 p.m. he logged: *Dribble dribble, I am catching rain water. I am way off course whilst doing so*. His efforts yielded some fifteen litres of brackish water for washing and about thirty litres for drinking.

Back on course by sunset, *Endeavour* was giving her skipper a rough ride in a lumpy South Atlantic, and later that night he put three storm reefs in the main to give the yacht a slower and more comfortable motion.

At noon on the following day, 1 December, Sanders logged with some satisfaction: *Freak. My moon observation was 0.1 of a minute* [one-tenth of a mile] *from my dead reckoning*. That afternoon he gave himself a "skinhead" haircut, figuring that his appearance should be acceptable by his scheduled arrival home in about four months.

Wind fluctuations at this stage were causing him considerable extra work, reefing down when the wind increased, then taking them out just hours later when it moderated. He felt loath to leave his warm cabin in the dead of night for this chore.

As 3 December dawned clear and sunny with a light breeze, Sanders had his yacht sailing with a full main and working genoa. After lunch he undertook more cleaning and scrubbing in the back cabin, resolving to start on the fo'castle cabin mould next. He also oiled all hanks on the working jib, storm jib and other fittings (he oiled the self-steerer every day, except in gales).

At breakfast time the following day—day 560—*Endeavour* was ghosting along on a smooth sea in a zephyr. There was too little wind for the self-steerer to be effective, but the sloop was steering a straight course without her skipper touching the big Huon pine tiller. The sails were not flapping because the sea was so smooth.

Becalmed completely after breakfast, Sanders decided to make adjustments to his self-steering lines. While doing this necessary chore he scrubbed weed off the Servo rudder. Using his last scrubbing brush, he was angry with himself when he lost it overboard. *It was so calm*, he told his log, *I thought I could drop the mainsail and swim after it*. But no, the water is a bit cold. Instead he steered the yacht around in the calm, oily sea and recaptured the scrubbing brush. As he returned to work on the self-steerer he noticed a five-foot shark near the yacht.

After a light easterly wind found the yacht, Sanders got on with his chores in his cabin, unbolting his stove and scrubbing it and then scrubbing the galley and navigation area. More strenuous work called late in the afternoon when the wind picked up, and before sunset the solo circumnavigator had to go on deck to storm reef the main. At sunset he logged: *Having a rough and bumpy ride. I have eased the course a little to stop the bumping*. Soon after darkness fell on the lonely South Atlantic, *Endeavour* was in a full gale. Sanders recorded at 10.35 p.m.:

Dropped jib, hove-to. I suspect this weird weather will switch to the south or south-west with a hurricane squall line—like I got caught out in the South Atlantic last lap. So I choose now to heave-to and wait and see.

It was a prudent tactic. The gale strengthened and heavy rain fell. But after breakfast next day, from fifty knots the wind now completely stopped, and the yacht rolled unnervingly.

As quickly as the wind dropped away, it picked up again and before nine o'clock *Endeavour* was in a thirty-knot south-easterly, running before it with a fully-reefed main. The barometer was falling, so Sanders optimistically put out his rain bucket. But fog rolled in instead.

Less than half an hour later he wrote: *Mad weather—out of wind. Yacht rolling like yuk*. Becalmed in a lumpy sea, Sanders took down the working jib which was flapping annoyingly, and did the best he could in a confused sea. The fog persisted all day, but soon after 7 p.m. a light south-easterly stirred *Endeavour* into desultory action. Rain started falling soon afterwards, a promising downpour which almost filled the number one tank by midnight. At least his fresh water worries were over—for the time being.

Late on Sunday afternoon, 6 December, a thirty-five-knot squall caused him to reef down. His methylated spirits supplies, which he had been carefully conserving for the past year, finally ran out and he had to prime his stove with kerosene. This sent clouds of acrid black smoke through the cabin.

Two quiet, sunny days followed and Sanders grabbed the opportunity to work on the mould in his cabins. He also sand-papered the timber furniture in his cabin ready for varnishing or oiling.

In the mid-morning calm on 9 December he oiled the teak in his cabin, lowered the main to grease the slides and dismantled and greased the main halyard winch. In the afternoon he varnished all beams, his chart table and the trim around the benches in the navigation-galley area of the saloon. He also did some more scrubbing out of the aft cabin and fore saloon.

On Friday 11 December *Endeavour* was still out of wind, so Sanders got to work on the green weed and slime that had turned black on the deck, and varnished toe rails. The yacht at that point, he noted was on the same parallel (32 deg. 55 S) as the coastal town of Mandurah, about an hour's drive south of Fremantle.

Sanders got so warm scrubbing the deck after lunch he decided to cool off in the calm sea (but not before checking for "bities") and at the same time rid his sloop's underhull of joyriding gooseneck barnacles. After an hour he climbed back on board well pleased with his efforts, and resumed scrubbing the deck till his back ached.

On the Saturday—day 568—*Endeavour* was joggling along into a light headwind in summery conditions. But by mid-afternoon Sanders had found the breeze he did not want, an eighteen-knot north-easter right on the nose. That afternoon his keen nostrils smelt land. He logged in some puzzlement: *No doubt, but outside I smell something upwind—but there is no land that way except for the small island of Trinidade, 800 miles away. Compass check, no land, but wind is north and yacht sailing in a NW direction towards*

Brazil. Could he be picking up the scent of land from hundreds of miles away? Incredible, but Sanders trusted his sense of smell.

Just before midnight he logged: *Raining and as black as ink outside. And it's got windier and rougher and yukkier*. After a bumpy night going to windward, *Endeavour* sailed into a mid-morning lull, but it was short-lived. At noon he wrote: *All overcast, bopping to windward in a 20–25–knot north wind. Time for a wind change. Doesn't it know these are the variables. No sun for sight, tomorrow I suppose*.

The annoying headwinds continued overnight, but dropped to eight knots about breakfast time. At 9.50 a.m. he wrote: *Out of wind, becalmed*. At mid-morning he used his long-handled brush on the sides of the yacht and sandpapered the weed away from the yacht's name. Just after failing to get a noon sun sight, he logged: *No wind and no sun. Spitting rain, put rain bucket out, might catch some, might not. Completed scrubbing all decks and cockpit. Now whipping ropes, because I have shortened those that are too long*.

The calm continued, and Sanders' exasperation began to show. *Such a waste of time*, he wrote at 9.20 p.m.

He tested his navigation lights that night and found that his tri-light on top of the mast no longer worked and nor did his steaming, deck or strobe lights. The light on his pulpit had been smashed along with the pulpit in the collision with the trawler. Only one (of two) red-over-red "Not under command" lights on the mast worked, and only one of the two stern lights was operational. He would henceforth have to be extra careful in shipping lanes, though he had no plans to sail near any busy maritime thoroughfares.

With Christmas only ten days away, the solo circumnavigator was making steady but unspectacular progress north-eastwards towards the Equator. At noon on 15 December he logged: *Today's noon fix shows Brazil Current has helped and progress over the past two cloudy days better than I thought on my dead reckoning*. Despite the flukey winds, *Endeavour* had made good ninety-six miles.

As the yacht sailed into the low twenties

of latitude the weather became semi-tropical and by 17 December Sanders was past the influence of the Brazil Current. From now on, he told himself, it would be a south-setting current—against the yacht. He continued his refurbishing of the interior of the sloop by sandpapering and oiling the teak in the foward section of the saloon, a difficult task in the humid and bumpy conditions.

On this day his mother, Dorothy Lucy Sanders, who had indirectly inspired his history-making voyage, passed away aged eighty at a Perth nursing home. Because his HF (long-distance) radio was not operational, his family could not advise him of his mother's death, and it was not until three days before the end of his voyage three months later that he heard the sad news.

At 3 a.m. the following day Sanders, noting it had become quite rough and windy, put more reefs into the mainsail to improve his ride. Just before breakfast a heavy shower of rain swept over and he caught a pleasing sixty litres. After it cleared he set up his bean sprouts' equipment for his biggest and last crop so that he could enjoy some fresh vegetables on Christmas Day.

Late in the morning he sighted a ship on his starboard beam, closing fast. By 11.30 a.m. it was heading straight for *Endeavour* and Sanders tried to get through on his VHF radio, but there was no answer. He decided to tack. The ship—he could just make out its name, *Redestos*, with his binoculars—passed about 150 metres in front of the sloop. When eventually he did make contact on his VHF set, he sent the telegram mentioned earlier in this chapter—the one signed "Fanters". The telegram in its ungarbled state read: *All is well with the yacht and I am in good spirits, looking forward to arriving in Australia. Kind regards, Jon Sanders.*

Pleased with the break in his of-late humdrum existence, Sanders busied himself with his laundry that afternoon, indulging in the luxury of rinsing in fresh water. His yacht made a better daily run this day—143 miles.

On the Sunday before Christmas he made some calculations and came up with some arrival times for the end of his voyage. He reckoned he would be south of Cape Leeuwin—tying the third knot—on 28 March 1988, pass through King George Sound by Albany on the south coast of Western Australia on 31 March, and arrive at his intended final destination, Sydney Harbour, on 20 April. He was not to know his plans would be changed only days before he arrived off Leeuwin.

Sanders calculated he had 10,006 nautical miles to go before he reached Cape Leeuwin after his third circumnavigation. He had sailed a total of 55,978 miles and logged 60,638 miles in 576 days.

On 20 December he logged just after midday: *My dead reckoning over the past 24 hours has been extremely good—1.8 miles out on my morning position line and correct to a decimal point with my latitude at noon. All with no log (estimated speed and distance only) and self-steerer that zig-zags with different wind pressures while I sleep.*

Endeavour sailed into gale-force squalls the following day with gusts up to thirty-five knots. Sanders was enjoying the balmy tropical days but he could do with less wind on this day. He wrote at mid-morning: *Days and days with a northerly component in the wind. Here's hoping it does not go south down these latitudes when I'm coming back and going the other way. It is rough and humid at the moment. Lots of water over the deck. Wind is strong to near gale.*

He added a few minutes later: *Bean sprouts are sprouting nicely*. His last entry for the day: *This has turned into such a bad and uncomfortable night. Wind 35–40 NNE, raining*.

After an unpleasantly rough night *Endeavour* was way off course at breakfast time and bumping against a strong head-wind. The yacht was in the region of the South-East Trades but was battling strong NNE winds. In mid-morning Sanders sighted what he thought was a big fishing trawler with a dark hull and white topsides. He could not make out its name.

The adverse wind moderated to Sanders' relief late the following afternoon and he took the last reef out of *Endeavour*'s main. At 9.10 p.m. he logged exultantly: *Hooray, wind at last has backed to the east-north-east—going east*.

At dawn on Christmas Eve the lone

sailor was happy with his progress under the easterly. After lunch he listened rapt to the beautiful Kings College (Cambridge) choir on the BBC World Service before finishing the teak oiling and varnishing in his for'ard cabin.

At 2 a.m. on Christmas Day he logged somewhat melancholily: *Happy Xmas me all alone—with sunburnt, cracked, chapped bottom lip—very sore.* At 11 a.m. he wrote: *Blue sky, consistent east wind. Tropical but okay. Took reef out of main. I am listening to Xmas carols specially taped for me by Noel Semmens* [former Commodore of Royal Perth Yacht Club] *who is a truly nice friend*.

The solo circumnavigator settled down to prepare himself a special Christmas treat for supper that night. He had found a small bottle of Bacardi rum placed on board by his young crew in a "survival kit" before he left twenty-one months earlier. He decided to break his long "dry" for the festive season and mixed himself a rum with water. Then he ate with great relish a big plateful of Hawaiian and Californian (canned) chicken mixed with Surprise beans and a liberal helping of fresh, green sprouting beans. For dessert he had stewed prunes and custard followed by two cups of coffee. Not the most memorable of Christmas dinners, but one that Jon Sanders vowed he would never forget as he spent his second Christmas at sea alone.

20

Homeward Bound

The longest way round is the shortest way home.

Proverb

JON SANDERS' lonely Christmas would have been more bearable if his HF radio had been operational and he could have called home. But it had long since ceased to function because of condensation that had crept into it around the cold, bleak Cape Horn region. He was sailing in radio silence, no longer able to report his position to his radio mentor, Jack Seabrook, and catch up on all the news at home. He still had his normal broadcast radios, however, and he was receiving the BBC World Service loud and clear. The solo sailor knew when he set out on his triple circumnavigation attempt that he would have to spend two Christmases alone at sea, so there was no point in feeling sorry for himself. And he knew that once he spent a day above the Equator to satisfy the rules of the *Guinness Book of Records*, he would be able to swing his big Huon tiller and head *Parry Endeavour* southwards, homeward bound. But he could not do this until he had all of his water tanks topped up to see him through some notoriously dry regions across the South Atlantic and Indian Ocean.

On Christmas night he had received a surprise present from his yacht. Around 8 p.m. he sighted a ship's light ahead of him off his starboard bow. He switched on what was left of his yacht's navigation lights, including the strobe, which had not functioned for six months. The strobe actually worked, though none of the other lights on the mast did. Sanders was particular about running navigation lights or the strobe, in the area from 6 deg. S to above the Equator and back because this was a busy corner for shipping between Europe and South America, and Northern America and Southern Africa.

The trades persisted on Boxing Day and the day after but *Endeavour* was now in the Guinea Current which set her to the west and affected daily progress. Still, on the twenty-seventh Sanders made a healthy 138 miles.

Taking advantage of the pleasant sailing conditions and the warmth, Sanders occupied himself in painting two spare wind vanes and the life raft recess cover. He also daubed parts of the stern cabin and forward cabin to finish the tin of white paint. At 9.05 p.m. he noted rather testily: *Not had supper yet. Stove broke down and I've just got it going again—I hope.*

At breakfast time on Monday 28 December—day 584—*Endeavour* was only one degree, or sixty miles south of the Equator and sailing smoothly in a low sea.

All was not smooth, however, in the galley. During the morning Sanders' stove stopped making gas and poured out fiery liquid kerosene which smoke-filled and blackened the cabin. He logged ruefully: *I wish I had the stove I originally prescribed. I wish a lot of things had just been left to me.*

That off his chest, he prudently checked that the current from their batteries was flowing through the two Argos transponders, one on his transom, the other on the cabin roof. He explained in a log entry: *I want confirmation of being north of Equator. I shall continue to one degree north. I am very close to doldrums and expect to catch rain tonight*.

At three o'clock he crossed the line. But he failed to catch rain that night.

The next morning, however, *Endeavour* was sailing under heavy rainclouds and the solo sailor rigged up his canvas bucket and put a reef in the main, the better to harvest the rain. But it was true doldrums weather —very overcast, confused bits of wind coming from various directions, and rain about but not actually over the yacht. With the sails flapping annoyingly he observed: *On my previous two roundings north of the Equator I've hit the rain in the equatorial trough before running out of wind. This time I've run out of wind before getting the rain. I can see* [rain] *further north and north-west*.

At noon he was 106 miles north of the Equator in a variable wind. The cloud had dissipated. Then *Endeavour* sailed into a patch of rain and Sanders caught thirty litres of fresh water from one sharp, heavy shower. At 3.25 p.m. he logged: *Fine drizzle. Do not need Scotch mist, I want RAIN*. He could see lots of fish jumping out of the water, but they completely ignored his lure and fishing line.

Late that afternoon a sea bird about the size and colour of the Australian wattle bird perched on his tiller and Sanders was careful not to frighten it. He liked its company. At 8.40 p.m. he wrote: *Oh dear, it does not rain. Bird still perched on the tiller. He or she is most welcome.*

Still sailing slowly northwards in his pursuit of rain, Jon Sanders noted at breakfast time on 30 December: *Looks like rain astern but not ahead. I've been creeping north, but the equatorial trough is near the Equator this month. Have I passed the rainy section, or is it farther north?* After breakfast: *Heavy cloud upwind, will dawdle along and see what it brings. Guinea Current has set the yacht west. I do not believe my first sight this morning, so crossed it out and did another —the first was confirmed by the second— exactly the same. The bird had gone before I woke this morning—but it left its messages!*

It was too overcast for Sanders to take a noon sight of the sun, but it did not worry him, because he was going nowhere in particular. He sighted two whales about 150 metres away off his starboard side, but he could not identify them. Light but steady rain started falling just before seven o'clock, adding another thirty litres.

Jon Sanders got all the rain he wanted for the remainder of his voyage on New Year's Eve. He had caught a little in the small hours—still not enough. It was still a game of hide-and-seek.

At 11.15 a.m. he logged: *My US Pilot Atlas for the region north of 5 deg. N shows I am into NE trades, so perhaps I should now turn south again as I am fetching steady NE winds and swell*. Ten minutes later he turned the yacht round—he was homeward bound.

At 1.48 p.m. precisely it started to rain and the canvas bucket was catching it. At 2 p.m. he reported: *Number one tank full*. Ten minutes later: *It's raining and raining and raining*. At 2.30 p.m.: *Number two tank nearly full and it is pouring*. Five minutes later: *Number two tank absolutely full. All water tanks and containers full.*

Enough fresh water to get to Australia!! Just before 3 p.m. he wrote: *It can stop raining now*. He added in jovial mood soon after 3 p.m.: *Out of wind and the rain has stopped, I think. Homeward bound!!*

That night he was in a mellow mood listening to New Year's Eve festivities on the BBC World Service as *Endeavour* plied southwards about 150 nautical miles north of the Equator. He even forgot to wish himself a happy New Year, having slept through the dawning of 1988. His first log entry for New Year's Day—day 588—was: *Steady 20-knot east wind—oops, north-east*. Early in the afternoon he sighted a ship, hull down, cutting across his stern and he called it on his VHF radio to wish someone a happy New Year. But all he got was a foreign language he could not identify.

As *Endeavour* made slow, quiet progress south the following day Sanders knew he would not be far away from St. Peter and St. Paul's Rocks, his planned turning point before he decided to keep plying northwards on his quest for rain. At 4.30 a.m., just before dawn, he logged: *It is too dark to see the rocks. I should have the number two* [jib] *up, but perhaps I will just stooge along—I don't want to bump into them in case my dead reckoning is out*. (Later: *It was!*)

At 6 a.m. he reported: *There is a fish about two feet long with yellow tail swimming with the yacht. Wish it would hop on to my lure—yum*. He sketched his impression of the fish and added: *Similar to fish I have been seeing lately*.

His noon sight placed the yacht at 54.8 minutes north of the Equator (29 deg. 13.3 W longitude) or 8.8 miles west of St. Peter and St. Paul's Rocks at 2 a.m. that day. He noted: *Guinea Current is strong hereabouts and the variable (in strength and direction) wind meanders my course and plotting*. Early in the afternoon he wrote: *Not a single cloud in the sky. A light wind, sailing quietly along in a very mild sea*. At 4 p.m. he logged: *Once more south of the Equator. (I spent five days this last time north*.)

Late that night as he scanned the horizon for ships' lights, he saw a brown sea bird perched on the stern rail of the yacht. Twenty minutes after midnight on

Sunday 3 January he logged: *Yacht gliding southwards. Bird still enjoying the ride on the stern rail.*

At 4.20 a.m. he wrote: *A second bird was on the yacht, but I accidentally frightened it away.* Two minutes later: *The second bird has now landed on the back rail, making two on the rail hitching a free ride—lazy things!* At daybreak the birds had flown.

At noon he observed: *Gosh, the Guinea Current is not only pushing me west, it is zooming me south.* His distance made good for the day was 152 miles, which increased to 160 the next day as he moved out of the Guinea Current and into the Brazil Current.

Endeavour continued to make about 150 miles a day as she plied southwards, but her skipper was finding it difficult to lay a course in the direction he wanted to go—south-easterly towards the Cape of Good Hope. *Yacht falling off to the west*, he wrote, *but expect the wind to draw to the east and north-east in the next day or so—the norm for the region.* At 12.45 p.m. he logged: *Gosh the wind has backed to the south—that's really coming from the wrong way*. But to his relief it was only a temporary shift, probably caused by a stray patch of cloud.

The wind was such that he might as well have been back in the Variables. At 3.40 p.m. he was becalmed briefly before continuing way off course. At 4.50 p.m. a squall hit the yacht and he hoped it would not blow out his number one genoa. When the breeze got up to twenty to twenty-five-knots (SSE) he decided it was time to change to a working jib. But an hour later he wrote: *Stupid weather, now becalmed*.

By Wednesday 6 January *Endeavour* had fetched an easterly wind and was sailing nicely on course, and Sanders had the luxury of having all of his hatches open to air his saloon and cabins. Similar favourable conditions prevailed the next day and he hauled all his sails from the forepeak on to the deck and scrubbed out the forepeak. He wanted to get his yacht home in reasonably clean condition.

The steady easterly was still taking the sloop on course into the South Atlantic the following day when Sanders decided to take an inventory of the food he had left. His stock-taking showed he had 154 sachets of freeze-dried dinners and fifty-four cans of meals. He had lots of powdered milk, enough Weetbix for fifty days, six big packets of porridge and five packets of Weeties. A few packets of dried fruit and vegetables also remained. He noted: *At present rate of consumption, that is okay. Not luxury, but okay. As long as the mast stays up I'm okay for food, and as long as I do not rupture a water tank, okay for fresh water too.*

The Sunday of 10 January saw the lone sailor unable to get a noon sight because of overcast conditions. Noting that his Argos batteries were a little low in power, he swapped two of his fully charged ship's batteries over. "That should give the Argos enough charge till we get home," he told himself. Now, more than ever, Jon Sanders was speaking his thoughts to keep his voice box exercised since he was no longer using his out-of-order HF radio.

On his long lone voyages, Sanders enjoyed the satisfaction of navigating accurately with his sextant and on this trip he had had plenty of practice with his satellite navigation equipment out of commission. On this Sunday evening, with the lonely island of Trinidade hovering near to his course, he tried to get two star sights to fix his position—having missed his noon fix. He logged at 7.45 p.m.: *Sight on star Aldebaran puts yacht 3.1 miles away, which is okay, but overcast and I could not identify the only southern star that I needed for a fix. I'm wondering about Trinidade, of course, should see it after daylight tomorrow.*

At 5.15 a.m. he wrote smugly: *Daylight. Sure made a good job of finding Ilsa Trinidade—dead ahead of the yacht. I've changed course to pass to the west of it. Long way off yet. I have passed by Trinidade 10 times going north or south over the past 12 years and sighted it maybe four or five times.*

Half an hour later he expanded: *Wind is sufficiently free to enable me to go closer to the wind at good speed, so perhaps I will head to pass east of Trinidade—between it and Martin Vaz—and have a gink* [look] *at the two as I go by. It appears my dead reckoning for longitude is close, 29 deg. 22.7 W, but suspect I am farther south on latitude by some distance, no doubt helped by the Brazil Current.*

After breakfast he logged: *Island about five and a half miles starboard bow, very mountainous and rugged with one spectacular pillar rock. Squared the yacht for a moment to photograph*. Half an hour later: *Through binoculars can see some buildings on some gentle slopes and others near the NE foreshore*. At 8.45 a.m.: *Ilsa da Trinidade now abeam approx. three miles. Can observe through binoculars hole in rock, marked on chart (Islands in the South Atlantic) as a natural arch*. A few minutes later his radio erupted in a babble of foreign voices and he assumed he had been spotted from the island.

Eventually the rocks of Martin Vaz appeared through the haze abeam to port on the horizon. He expressed disappointment that his cameras were playing up. He was out of AA batteries.

On Tuesday 12 January he was well clear of the islands, having made good 150 miles for twenty-four hours. The following day was his 600th at sea without stepping foot outside his sea-stained sloop and without stopping. His total mileage was 59,138 (63,577 logged). It also marked the last page in his fourth logbook. On that page at breakfast time he noted his estimated day of arrival at King George Sound (off Albany, Western Australia) as 23 March—seventy days away.

At 2.30 p.m. he logged: *Unscrewed the port quarter berth lee cloth and gave it a good scrubbing to remove mould and now hanging to dry. Steady, mild-to-moderate east wind—nice with full main and number one jib. My course from the Equator was south to pass near 30 deg. S, 28.30 W, then I shall head to 40 deg. S, then 40 deg. S, 20 deg. E, which is 300 nautical miles south of South Africa, about 2755 miles from here. Then a further 4650 miles to King George Sound rendezvous, then on to Sydney*. (Sanders had planned to reprovision in King George Sound after completing his record-shattering triple circumnavigation, and then sail on to Sydney for the Bicentennial celebrations. But these plans were changed dramatically.)

His first entry in his fifth logbook, on Thursday 14 January, was at breakfast time when he logged: *Nice fine morning with cotton wool bud type trade wind clouds. It was a comfortable night's sailing in a mild sea. Wind now 14 knots NE, full main and number one genoa. Sliding along nicely*. But the wind died and at 1 p.m. he was becalmed. With time on his hands, he adjusted the self-steering lines and fitted a new block for the steering ropes.

Endeavour found a nice sailing breeze the following day, but there were lulls and near-calms to keep the daily run to ninety-seven miles. The flukey wind persisted that day and Sanders logged at 7.45 a.m.: *Off course, sailing SSW. Preferred course SE, but I can only make south on this gybe. I think it best to sneak southwards to find stronger winds. I'm too close to the summer South Atlantic high where calms and light winds prevail*.

At dawn the following day he found greater strength in the wind and knew that his strategy of sailing due south had paid off. At noon he logged: *Sea temperature has dropped 2C since noon yesterday. Sailing nicely on course*. Similar conditions prevailed for two days with the wind piping up to twenty-five knots under an overcast sky and then fading to less than ten knots. But his daily runs were well over the century.

On Wednesday 20 January he wrote at breakfast: *Beautiful fine blue sea and sky morning and a most favourable 18–knot NNE breeze*. When the wind backed to the west he poled out his working jib and the yacht made steady progress towards the south-east.

On Saturday 23 January *Endeavour* sailed into rough, windy conditions and Sanders put two reefs in his mainsail—only to take them out later in the morning. At 11.21 a.m. he logged: *Just passed by 75 metres distance a large ship's mooring buoy adrift—gosh*. At 5.35 p.m. he noted: *Sea has become a dark, murky colour indicating colder water—18.3C. Passed a large clump of matted weed (kelp) with birds standing on it. A bird perch in mid-South Atlantic!*

A handy following breeze stayed with the yacht next day and Sanders went to work on the green slime, which again was growing on the foredeck. Late in the afternoon the clouds rolled over and the wind changed to the south-west, but progress was still good. For supper that night he ate two pouches of freeze-dried smoked fish with parsley sauce and his only comment in his logbook was *Ugh*. He was to tell the author later that if he never ate any more lasagne or freeze-dried smoked fish in his life, he would be eternally happy.

On the overcast morning of Monday 25 January he heaved-to to renew one of the self-steering lines and adjust the other. And, noting that the supporting staunchions were starting to wear, he put new bolts into them. Sailing gently along that afternoon, he scrubbed out the stern locker as best he could. He noted at 4.45 p.m.: *The wind is so light that I am shaping a course farther south than preferred to keep the yacht sailing properly*.

Sanders was now rationing his food supplies, and was looking forward to a resupply after he had completed the third circumnavigation (only then did the rules permit him to take on some supplies).

After he passed south of South Africa, he intended to allow himself either a packet of dried apricots or prunes or dried beans or peas each day extra. He was now eating two cereals a day—porridge with hot milk for breakfast and Weetbix and milk for lunch.

Apart from the monotony of cooking, he found little joy with his troublesome stove, which continued to emit clouds of black smoke. After each use, he had to wipe over the roof beams to get rid of the smoke stain.

On 27 January the sloop took advantage of a twelve-knot south-westerly, but this dropped out and Sanders had time to observe some odd-looking water beetles and a few jellyfish. He netted a couple of the beetle-like creatures and after examining and photographing them, noted: *They're not really beetles, some type of wee marine thing. They have a very hard shell. Perhaps snails would be a better description—with transparent flippers*.

It was too overcast for him to get a sun sight at noon the next day, but he knew almost exactly where his yacht was—only half a day's sailing from the Greenwich Meridian and around 38 deg. 29 S latitude. By mid-afternoon the barometer was steadily dropping and the ever-conservative Sanders noted: *All the symptoms of a gale on its way*. But by 4 p.m. the wind had backed to the west and the clouds were scattering.

At 7.30 p.m. he logged: *All overcast again with steady fresh westerly. Just passed to east of 0 meridian*. It was day 615 and he reminded himself that, all going well, he would be in home waters in less than six weeks.

When he finished breakfast and took his morning sight on the twenty-ninth, Sanders noticed the wind had got to a half-gale—thirty knots—from the south-west and a short while later the yacht broached, sending things flying about in the cabin.

Progress was poor on Saturday 30 January—the sails were flapping, the sea was sloppy, and he was well off course. *Should be on the other gybe, but self-steering will not work properly on starboard tack in light airs,* he wrote.

On the last day of January the sloop was sailing well again under a full main and working jib in the early hours, but when it piped up to near gale-force at breakfast time Sanders put three reefs in the main. He got a rough noon sight through the clouds. At 5 p.m. he observed: *Good progess, but slowly the barometer falls and the wind increases. I shall change the working jib for a spitfire after supper.* But the wind moderated and backed to the west and out came the mainsail reefs.

He was now at 40 deg. S latitude and almost becalmed in the region of the Roaring Forties as he ate lunch. Cape Town lay about five hundred miles to the north-east, but Sanders had no intention of sailing anywhere near the shipping lanes that circle the Cape region. He would stay well south, knowing that it was summer and the possibility of horrific gales was remote.

But near-gale winds prevailed on 2 February—day 620—and after lunch he tied three reefs in the mainsail. Late in the afternoon he dropped his working jib and allowed the yacht to run downwind in a freshening thirty to thirty-five-knot nor'wester with three reefs in the main. Just before he retired the wind moderated, so he went on deck to rehoist a working jib. He was "zooming" again.

Jon Sanders felt like a horse that was eager to get back to its stall for a feed of oats now that he was homeward bound.

He took advantage of every new puff of wind to make sail changes.

Soon after noon the next day he did another stocktake of his food supplies. He had been rationing himself to about half of what he would normally eat for supper and had noticeably become thinner. But, he told himself, the enforced diet was doing him no harm. In fact he felt fitter than when he left Fremantle all those months ago. He worked out that on an estimated average daily run of 110 miles he would be off King George Sound—4728 nautical miles away—in forty-three days.

He logged: *I have 83 pouches freeze-dried meals (plus about 40 pouches of smoked fish in parsley sauce—which I loathe). I have 49 Maggi (tinned) meals, a total of 132 pouches of freeze-dried or Maggi meals, not including smoked fish—yuk. This equals three per day for supper. (One pouch or Maggi container is not enough for a meal—three are required.)*

Plus: One packet of dried fruit or peas or beans per day specially kept for the Indian Ocean. I can now increase my supper ration by more than double—hooray—and I've got smoked fish for emergencies. I should have enough breakfast cereal for breakfast and lunch—porridge, Weetbix and Weeties—just enough, and powdered milk for five cups per day, a quantity of flour and some pouches of custard mix. It's looking good. Good suppers from now on. My main concern is that the stove will not hold out.

That night he celebrated his stocktaking with a formidable repast—at least by the standards of the previous three months. He cooked up together curry and rice and chilli con carne and blended stewed apples and apricots and ate them with custard for dessert.

After an uncomfortable night bumping and corkscrewing, the lone sailor fully reefed his mainsail before breakfast as the wind steadily increased. At 8.45 a.m. he wrote: *Took morning sight which advances* [dead reckoning] *position close to 30 miles. Took a second sight which confirmed big advance. The nasty sloppy sea yesterday afternoon clearly was a strong current. I should not have complained—it was very favourable.* At 10.30 a.m. he added: *25-knot west wind, good progress. Sun is out and yacht surrounded by lots of grey dove-like sea birds with the dark stripe on their wings —nice.*

At noon he was in a happy mood as he logged: *Hooray. I have passed to the east of 20 deg. E* [longitude]—*now in Indian Ocean. Water temp has done a plunge since yesterday*. He did some quick maths and came up with some *Parry Endeavour* statistics.

From Cape Leeuwin, Western Australia, to his present position on his first east-about circumnavigation *Endeavour* took 182 days. On his second east-about rounding—his current (third) circumnavigation—it took only 133 days, forty-nine days quicker. Of course his first circumnavigation times cannot be compared with his second and third, because he went west-about on his first lap.

That night, to celebrate crossing into the Indian Ocean—home waters, but a long way from home—he had another special menu for supper. He mixed tinned Hawaiian chicken with Californian chicken and had Surprise beans with it. For dessert he stewed some freeze-dried apricots and apples and covered them in custard. He retired replete and happy.

"I'm now on the home stretch," he told himself.

21

Home is the Sailor

> Home is the sailor, home from the sea.
> *Robert Louis Stevenson*, Requiem

NOW into the Indian Ocean and the "home straight" Jon Sanders was not sorry that the longest voyage in history was almost over. It had been demanding on him physically and mentally, and, though he was probably fitter than when he set out on 25 May 1986, he was mentally tired—but alert—and yearning for the companionship of his young crew and his many other sailing friends. Although he had always been something of a loner, enough was enough, he told himself. With his ETA in Sydney Harbour still more than two months away—about 10 April—he was not getting too excited. But little did he know that his epic voyage was going to be shortened to finish in Fremantle, his starting point, and that he was only an ocean away from setting foot on land for the first time in 658 days.

Now on Friday 5 February—day 623—*Parry Endeavour* was sailing in light-to-moderate SSW breezes under a blue sky and on a blue Indian Ocean that was furrowed by a long, gentle swell.

The sloop was almost becalmed at dawn the following day, but while Sanders breakfasted a light westerly sprang up and pushed his sloop towards Australia and home. The solo circumnavigator was still exercising every day, when it was not too rough. He would do leg and toe stretching exercises, "jog" on his rump while sitting, run on the spot—holding on to the chart table—to a count of 150, exercise his stomach and perform simple isometrics.

On Sunday 7 February he noticed the ocean had got considerably warmer—22.2C compared with 16.4C the previous noon and 12.8C three days earlier. That night after a supper of canned lasagne mixed with freeze-dried savoury mince and rice and stewed dried apricots and custard, Sanders lay in his bunk and listened to the squeaks of dolphins playing around his yacht.

The winds were again light and contrary the following day and it reflected in his daily run of eighty-four miles. At noon, he logged: *Gosh, the current has set me way north. Little wonder, I am in light airs. I do not understand . . . yes I do. At noon yesterday sea temperature 22.2C and today at noon 15.7C. I am 43 miles farther north now. Big currents. I've just been zapped up to the north—would prefer east.*

At breakfast the following day he noted: *Sea unbelievably quiet with weeny breeze from NE. The birds are having a fine time*. It was evident the yacht was floating much higher now—all the stores were nearly eaten, most of the water drunk and all the diesolene had been pumped out long ago.

Jon Sanders did not like pumping diesel fuel into the ocean, but he was more than a thousand miles from the nearest land mass when he unloaded his tanks and it was like a proverbial drop in the ocean. It would dissipate within days. As a fervent member of the Keep Australia Beautiful Council, he figured in television commercials before he set sail, entreating boating people to "stow it, don't throw it". Whenever he was near land, anywhere in the world, the lone sailor would stow his garbage and dispose of it when well out to sea again.

The lightness of the yacht had helped her to sail faster in lighter breezes; she also tended to surf down waves with a strong following breeze. As well, Sanders had lost much of his conservatism and was almost racing the yacht. In the early stages he nursed *Endeavour*, reefing down the mainsail when there was any likelihood of a "blow"—only in recent months did he push her to her limit, making frequent sail changes to get the utmost speed.

But by Tuesday 9 February he did not have a wind to push his yacht. At 6.45 p.m. he logged: *Becalmed—just wouldn't it*.

The following day was mild and sunny, and he stripped, cleaned and greased five of the yacht's fifteen winches. "That should see me through to Sydney," he told himself.

His Argos batteries had lost some of their power, so he switched them with two of his bank of six ship's batteries—the last time he would have to do this task.

In the light, flukey mid-February

breezes he was making less than a hundred miles a day, but he was in no great hurry.

At 1 a.m. on 13 February a steady fifteen-knot south wind found the yacht, as did some patches of fog, and Sanders was pleased to be on his way again. It was too overcast or foggy for him to take a morning or a noon sight. At mid-afternoon he logged: *Oh dear, some holes in the wind*. He continually tacked, hoping to find a better breeze, but at 11.05 p.m. he gave up, logging: *Becalmed, going nowhere*.

The calm day resulted in a daily run of only sixty miles, his lowest for months. But by noon the following day, *Endeavour* was making steady progress eastwards in a fifteen-knot NNW wind. Day 633 dawned foggy and overcast and later in the morning fine rain started to fall. The yacht had reached 42 deg. south and Sanders altered course to sail due east when possible. He missed his noon sight again, but logged at 5.35 p.m.: *Got PM sight in hazy conditions, advances yacht oodles. Foggy now and breeze has stopped*.

Endeavour made a pleasing 138 miles for the twenty-four hours.

Before dawn on 17 February Sanders awoke to find a gale buffeting his yacht and he quickly reefed down the main. But by mid-morning it had moderated enough for him to take two of the three reefs out. His daily run average had picked up considerably with a week of fairly strong winds. His average since *Endeavour* left the southern tip of South Africa was 121 miles.

The strong winds continued on 19 February with squalls up to thirty-five knots. Sanders was kept busy reefing and unreefing his mainsail. He had made good 197 miles noon to noon—probably the best run yet for the period.

On Sunday morning (21 February) the wind was piping up to twenty-five knots and increasing, so he put three reefs in the main. At 4.40 p.m. he logged: *Wind has reached gale force, 30–35 knots NW. Think I will change to storm jib*. By 6 p.m. the gale hit thirty-five to forty knots and he decided to drop the storm jib and run under fully-reefed main. Late that night the gale was up to forty-five knots and he considered heaving-to to ride it out. But soon after midnight it backed to the west and moderated. As he was untying the reefing lines to unreef the main, the breeze suddenly swung to the south-west and Sanders suspected it would build up again. It did, and by daylight *Endeavour* was in the thick of a severe gale.

At breakfast time Sanders logged: *Broached a short time ago, heavy gale continues.* It was too rough to bother with a noon sight—*not strategically important* he told his log. *Endeavour* was now halfway across the Indian Ocean and not getting things her own way.

Late in the afternoon the yacht was surfing and crashing in the high gale, broaching three times during the day. At midnight the gale still roared on. At 3 a.m. the yacht surfed down another breaking wave and gybed itself.

Sanders had had enough. He got out of his bunk and turned his yacht into the seas —hove-to—hoping the gale would abate by the morning. But forty minutes later he noticed some lulls between the squalls and decided to square the yacht away again and run with the gale. He was hit by a squall while on deck getting the yacht sailing again, but the gale moderated a little while later.

After breakfast he logged: *Took two reefs out (one in). I'm game, there are still gale squalls with rain*. By late afternoon the worst of the gale had gone and *Endeavour* was rolling in a lumpy sea.

Still making good progress towards Australia on the afternoon of Thursday 25 February, Jon Sanders heard on Radio Australia about the attempt by Sydney-sider Kay Cottee to become the first woman to circumnavigate the world alone and non-stop. He told his log: *That's nice—I've got company somewhere in the Atlantic behind me!*

Squally winds in the early hours of the twenty-seventh increased to a steady gale (thirty to forty knots) by 11 a.m. At mid-afternoon he logged: *It is a proper gale. I have got wind 40–50 knots NW at the moment*. At 5.50 p.m. he wrote: *Sudden wind change from NW to SSW with rain. Sending yacht headlong into head sea. Gybed*.

The gale gradually lessened but it had propelled *Parry Endeavour* 172 miles in twenty-four hours. Late at night on

28 February—day 646—he logged: *Not much wind. Temporary fade, I hope*. Next day he noted that his Argos system must be working, for he could get on medium wave the Perth radio station 6WF, which reported his position.

The lone sailor was still unaware that his mother had died and he thought of her almost daily, wondering whether she was still alive. He could bring her closely to mind, sitting at her kitchen table working on her novels till the early hours of the morning.

On the first day of March Sanders shaped a course for south of Eclipse Island near Albany's King George Sound where he intended to reprovision *Endeavour* for the last leg to Sydney. By then he would have "tied the third knot" as he put it, and he would be able to take on all manner of exotic foods for his jaunt to Sydney.

Still yacht-proud, he spent hours scrubbing out his galley and chart table area as his sloop was almost becalmed. The following day brought a weak breeze from astern (west) of his yacht, but it was slow going as he scrubbed his decks and toe rails. At 8 p.m. he wrote: *Running quietly downwind with poled-out number one jib on a lovely moonlit sea.*

The following day, 3 March and day 650 at sea, he advanced his clock to West Australian time—GMT plus eight hours. He had made only eighty miles the previous twenty-four hours, but he was not over-worried. It was pleasant sailing and it allowed him to catch up with his chores. His busy day included scrubbing down the sides of the yacht and the back cabin, cleaning the stove and climbing the mast to unbolt a fitting that had been catching on the mainsail slides.

By 6 p.m. next day *Endeavour* was sailing briskly again under a fourteen-knot north-north-east breeze, close hauled and twenty degrees off course. At 11 p.m. Sanders logged: *Plenty of wind now; may have to hoist smaller headsail. 25 degrees off course.* His distance-made-good, because of the previous day's calm, was only thirty-five miles. The following day it was a rollicking 133 miles.

His first entry for Sunday 6 March—at one minute after midnight—read: *Quite windy. Perhaps I should put second reef into mainsail.* He did this, but at dawn he took it out again and recorded: *Less wind, overcast, heavier line of cloud to west, might be more wind or squall in this, will not further unreef until its effects are known*. Early in the afternoon rain fell and he caught about eighteen litres before the wind backed to the south-west and increased to a forty-knot gale. He gybed, brought in his rain bucket and put three reefs into the main.

Sanders believed he had enough water to take him to Sydney, but he wanted to be sure. He would not have bothered if he had known his voyage would end in exactly one week.

The solo circumnavigator unreefed the mainsail the following morning when conditions moderated. Sailing on a sloppy sea more than five hundred nautical miles south-west of Cape Leeuwin, he was puzzled when he heard 6WF breakfast announcer Ted Bull refer to an article by this author in the *Daily News* saying that he might be completing his voyage at Fremantle. *Gosh, what's going on?—rendezvous is off Albany*, he told his log.

He found out what was going on when he made weak radio contact with Jack

Seabrook at Royal Perth Yacht Club at 7.20 a.m. He logged.: *My managers, Parry Corporation, Curtin University and Australian Bicentennial Authority, and the West Australian public want me to finish at Fremantle. I confirmed I will finish at Fremantle. I picked up Jack on my radio direction finder on 2524 and got my radio to work—just—in reply. Now steering 42 deg. T = 53 deg. C* [towards Fremantle].

He could hardly believe he was just six days away from his home port and the end of the longest non-stop voyage in history. He was brought sharply back to reality just after eleven o'clock that night when he was poling out his number one genoa in the dark. It got caught round the forestay and it took Sanders some time to unwrap it. He decided not to pole it out. It was the first major sail foul-up for the voyage, remarkable considering the many sail changes he had made in horrific conditions—gales and even hurricanes.

The following night he spoke again with Royal Perth which told him that a naval patrol vessel would rendezvous with him the next day with former senior State Shipping Service captain Roy Marsh on board.

He could not arrest a surge of excitement within him as he neared his home port and what he knew would be a huge welcome. How would he handle it? He wondered whether he should be composing a speech for his arrival.

Jon Sanders' welcoming committee had decided to send Captain Marsh, a longtime friend of the lone sailor, to meet *Parry Endeavour* in mid-ocean to outline plans for the welcoming festivities planned for four days hence—Sunday 13 March. Two journalists, including the author, and a photographer and TV cameraman were invited to go on board the patrol ship *HMAS Geraldton* for the rendezvous.

Meanwhile, on board *Parry Endeavour* at 5.45 p.m. on Wednesday 9 March Sanders was cursing his faulty stove. He logged in great frustration: *I give up. I cannot get the stove going and the cabin is now full of black smoke and smoke-stained. Cold meals and drinks from now on*.

On board *HMAS Geraldton* we scoured the lumpy horizon for hours during the afternoon for a glimpse of a triangle of sail, and the crew scanned radar screens in the hope of picking up a blip. The seas were big and some of the permanent crew were seasick.

Soon after dusk the duty watch officer spotted a tiny orange "blip" on the radar screen, and we hoped we had found *Endeavour* after eight hours of searching. An hour later we sighted what we assumed was the stern light of the yacht, which appeared to be blinking off and on. It was the constant pitching of the yacht in the lumpy seas that gave us this impression. We tried calling *Parry Endeavour* on VHF radio, channel 16, and Sanders' familiar voice crackled over the airwaves.

Let Sanders' log tell the story: *Sked with Royal Perth and* HMAS Geraldton, *which is 18 miles astern of me. Should draw near 2030 to 2100 hours*. At 7.45 p.m.: *Lights astern* HMAS Geraldton. *They have called me on channel 16 but did not hear my reply*.

Finally at 8.45 p.m. we got through loud and clearly to *Endeavour*. The lone sailor logged: *Good contact with* HMAS Geraldton *on channel 16, spoke with Roy Marsh and Hugh Schmitt. My dear mum died—oh dear, sad. I was not there and I feel awful now*. It was a melancholy duty to have to break the sad news of his mother's death, but his committee, including Captain Marsh, thought it better to notify him then than when he stepped on Australian soil for the first time in nearly two years.

Jon Sanders' thoughts were with his mother when he logged simply at 11.25 p.m.: *Wind is 30–35 SE, rough*. Before retiring with his thoughts to his bunk, he changed down to a storm jib in the lumpy seas.

Soon after midnight he was out on the spray-swept foredeck again changing back to a working jib. At 3.05 a.m. he wrote: *Rough and bumpy. Warship* Geraldton *is maintaining station a mile or two out to starboard*. An hour later he again ventured on deck to change back to a storm jib. Even so close to home he was sailing his yacht professionally and with great care.

At dawn on a cold, bleak and blustery 10 March *HMAS Geraldton*'s captain, Lieutenant-Commander Lynn Walton, brought his ship to within 150 metres of *Parry Endeavour* to allow media cameramen to get shots of the lean, sunbronzed circumnavigator, who waved obligingly for us.

I had been up since before dawn radio-telephoning a story through to the *Daily News*, which splashed a fine front-page picture by Peter Ramshaw, radiogrammed from a foam-flecked sea 180 miles off Cape Leeuwin.

Interviewed in the pre-dawn darkness on his VHF radio, Sanders told me he had spent a restless night with many thoughts about the passing of his mother. "I was thinking about her a lot . . . both of my parents died while I was away. I've lived with my parents all of my life and we were very close. They supported me, even financially, on all of my voyages . . . they got a lot of fun out of it too."

With the final demise of his stove, he had eaten freeze-dried lamb and green peas cold the previous evening. He was looking forward to a reunion with his brother and sister and their families, his aunt Sheila, who kept every press clipping on his voyage, and his loyal crew of *Perie Banou*.

At mid-morning we parted company after a final wave. The crew and media corps on board the patrol boat were suffering in the huge seas—how much worse must it have been on board *Endeavour*?

It was bad for Sanders. He logged soon after noon: *Gale, 35–40 knots SE continues*. At 6 p.m. as the yacht was still being tossed in her home waters, he recorded: *Gale is severe, 40–45 knots*. Fifty-five minutes later he decided the gale was so strong the proper tactic would be to heave to and ride it out. He had plenty of time—two and a half days to reach Fremantle for the Sunday 13 March welcome home.

While hove-to off Leeuwin, Jon Sanders heard the voice of Western Australia's new Premier, Peter Dowding, on the Royal Perth radio during a sked with Jack Seabrook. He logged: *Peter Dowding wishes me the best of luck, looks forward to my arrival. He said there was something in my honour, but I could not catch it*.

The gale continued and Sanders knew he was almost home when he caught a whiff of bushfire smoke—even though he was ninety-five miles from land.

Maritime history was about to be made as *Parry Endeavour* again made headway northwards towards Fremantle under fully-reefed mainsail and storm jib. At precisely 10 p.m. he logged with immense relief: *Tied third knot of three true circumnavigations at 33 deg. 51 S, 114 deg. 12 E. Also same position at 0630 Tuesday, 15 Sept. 1987.*

He did some quick calculations and worked out that the world's first triple, lone, non-stop circumnavigation had taken 655 days, eight hours, fifty-eight minutes and eighteen seconds. He had sailed an incredible 70,752 nautical miles, though his distance-made-good was 66,265 miles. His first rounding (west-about) had taken 249 days, his second (east-about) 228 days and his third (also east-about) with a lighter yacht only 178 days.

On the ABC news he heard that winds of up to ninety kilometres an hour had been recorded at Perth Airport the previous night. That afternoon a helicopter from Perth's Channel Seven buzzed around his yacht and he obligingly waved.

At dusk the lone sailor sighted the flash of the Rottnest Island light, bringing home one step closer. He had spent so many happy weekends sailing to and from the island and it held many special memories for him.

Forty-five minutes later he wrote: *Quick flashing light six points starboard side. I wonder what that is*. Before retiring for an uneasy sleep, he logged: *Rottnest light bears 50 deg. T, Fremantle Sailing Club marina light bears 86 deg. T fix. Echo sounder 25 fathoms. Will drop jib, run out to sea then stooge back in—killing time*.

Jon Sanders could have ended his epic voyage the following day, Saturday 12 March, but he knew that a tumultuous welcome was being planned for the Sunday—and the thought of it sent the adrenalin coursing through his sinewy frame. He spent an uncomfortable day being buffeted by a strong easterly near-gale at the back of Rottnest Island, occasionally being buzzed by media helicopters. Late in the afternoon the wind died at last and Sanders prepared himself a cold meal for his last supper at sea after 658 days.

Knowing that he would be met by Marine and Harbour and police craft to be escorted into Fremantle Harbour the following morning, Sanders "parked" his yacht with two reefs in the mainsail between Fairway Buoy, which marks the entrance to Gage Roads and the shipping lane into the harbour, and some pylons known as "the Windmills" overnight. Just before dawn the power yacht *Portofino* loomed up alongside *Endeavour* with his old friend Roy Caldwell, chief executive of the Royal Automobile Club, on board with a band of media people.

Sanders had slept little the previous night. Excited, nervous and a trifle apprehensive, he donned his Sunday best for what was to be the greatest day of his life. He put on a specially-laundered pair of white yachting pants and a gold rugby shirt with the name of his yacht emblazoned across the chest, and a pair of grey deck shoes he had kept in a locker the whole voyage for the occasion. He tried to slick back his unkempt raven hair, which had grown unevenly after his last rough haircut out in the Atlantic two months earlier. He "dressed" his grimy yacht in Bicentennial, Curtin University, RAC Insurance, Royal Perth Yacht Club and Australian national flags, and on one of the backstays was the Christ Church Grammar

School football jumper he had carried as a talisman, and often wore, on all of his long voyages.

Jon Sanders knew his welcome would be big, but he did not imagine in his wildest dreams just how tumultuous it would be. His last log entry for the voyage on page 728 of logbook five read simply: *Many, many spectator and welcoming yachts*. He was soon swept up in a maritime welcome little short of that accorded to *Stars & Stripes* skipper Dennis Conner and crew after winning the America's Cup.

An estimated 350 craft from sailboard and dinghies to ocean-going yachts and luxury power behemoths surged around *Parry Endeavour* as she was escorted by a protective wedge of Marine and Harbour Department, police and yacht club vessels. His young crew shouted excitedly to him as *Perie Banou*, in command of Colin Sanders, followed *Endeavour* closely on a sparkling sea that had been whipped up into a maelstrom by the spectator craft.

"How do you feel?" his brother yelled to the remarkably fit-looking circumnavigator. "Nervous" was the shouted reply. "Like a beer?" called his crew. "Later."

As the flotilla neared the harbour entrance Sanders waved to tens of thousands of cheering well-wishers, including thousands of hero-worshipping schoolchildren standing on the north and south harbour moles. Police estimated a total crowd of about 130,000 on the sea and shore.

A cacophony of ships and yachts' sirens, hooters, horns and whistles blasted the normal mid-morning quietude of Fremantle Harbour as *Parry Endeavour* crossed the finish line just inside the harbour mouth at precisely ten hours, seventeen minutes and fifty-five seconds of day 657. Sanders estimated his voyage had taken 657 days, twenty-one hours, eighteen minutes and ten seconds—close enough to 658 days.

Few people heard the finish gun. Boat after boat came as close as they could to *Endeavour* to give the skipper and his yacht three cheers. First on board were Royal Perth Commodore Ian Cameron and his wife Nola, closely followed by customs and quarantine officials. Their first impressions were how neat and clean the sloop's decks and cabin interior were.

As *Endeavour* was towed slowly up to a pontoon moored alongside Victoria Quay especially for the homecoming sailor, cheers erupted from about ten thousand welcomers on the quay. As soon as the yacht nudged the green-carpeted pontoon, Sanders took his first step on shore since 26 May 1986. It was a somewhat shaky step and the modest sea hero faltered for a split second. But he almost bounded up the red-carpeted steps from the pontoon to the quay where a naval band was playing nautical tunes like "Sailing", "Life on the Ocean Waves" and "Anchors Aweigh".

Jon Sanders stood with his arms folded as Premier Dowding made a welcoming speech, announcing that a new state ship would be named after him and that an honour parade would be held through Perth streets the following Thursday, which would be proclaimed "Jon Sanders Day".

Former Premier Sir Charles Court, the official time-keeper for the epic voyage and a close friend of the circumnavigator, described Sanders as "a great hero who has always been a respectful and humble man." He said the solo sailor knew first-hand the potential dangers of his voyage —the horrendous seas, the whales, gales and ships lurking in the night. "But he still went ahead with it—that's true bravery," he declared.

Speaking in clear, but emotional tones, Jon Sanders responded: "After all the calms and fickle winds, after all the storms and tempestuous gales, frightening sometimes, after clearing the world's mighty capes more than once, after sailing across a lot of oceans more than once, you can imagine my moment, you can imagine my hour, when I stood on the cockpit ladder and looked forward, as I've done so often before—and there, dead ahead of the yacht was the Rottnest Island lighthouse. Home once more.

"I had just completed the longest non-stop voyage under sail in the history of this planet—and probably any other planet—and it would be an emotional experience after all of that time just to come ashore, let alone to be received in the manner in which I was by the oodles and oodles of spectator boats by what seems to be tens of thousands of people and even the honourable Premier—we've got a new one—what happened to the other one. . .?"

When he had finished thanking his committee and sponsors, Jon Sanders was given three cheers by an emotional crowd before being whisked away for a quick hot shower followed by an impromptu media conference.

22

The Aftermath

See, the conquering hero comes!
Sound the trumpet, beat the drums!
Thomas Morell, Joshua

STILL a trifle confused and bewildered—but not overawed—by the fabulous welcome, Jon Sanders faced the media with considerable aplomb. Some of the questions he fielded were quite fatuous, but he responded in good humour. Excerpts:

How did he feel being on dry land after 658 days on a heaving home?—"A little bit wobbly, but I get the same feeling after a weekend sail to Rottnest."

What were his first impressions of his home port after twenty-three months away from it in isolation?—"Nothing is normal any more . . . [former Premier] Brian Burke is an ambassador in Dublin and we've got a new Premier."

Was he ever afraid?— "No, I specially cancelled those thoughts out, but there were plenty of times when I was apprehensive."

Did he ever consider quitting his voyage, especially after his collision near the Falklands?—"It never crossed my mind."

He paid tribute to his sponsor: "Kevin Parry is someone who makes other people's ideas of dreams come true."

Sanders claimed that his alcohol-free lifestyle at sea helped keep him alert and fit throughout the voyage. "It probably pays to be on the wagon for a few years. Besides, the yacht was jam-packed full. There was nowhere to store the alcohol given to me, so I chucked it overboard."

He said he had heard on his radio that a man named Brian Burke had been appointed as the new Australian Ambassador to Ireland. "I thought that was funny because he had the same name as our Premier," he said amid laughter.

After the media conference he again boarded *Endeavour* which was towed out of the harbour again and around into the Challenger Harbour to Royal Perth Yacht

Club's Fremantle annexe, where hundreds of yacht club members waited to fete him. And where he had a tearful reunion with his aunt Sheila (Kenworthy), his late mother's sister. "He looks better than I thought he would," Mrs. Kenworthy said. "But he's very skinny, isn't he?"

The sailing hero quaffed his first beer for nearly two years and was called on board a luxury power yacht for a roast lamb dinner, cooked specially for him by past commodores. Later he ate a juicy barbecued steak for the benefit of a cameraman.

He told sailmaker Rolly Tasker: "Your sails were superb, Rolly." Later Tasker said: "Jon has arrived back with his sails in remarkably good shape. Many racing yachtsmen could not sail far past Rottnest without blowing out sails, but Jon has been three times round the world . . . that is a fantastic feat."

Sanders sought out veteran boatbuilder Des Piesse and told him: "You did a great job, Des . . . I blessed you many a time in big storms." Said Piesse later: "It was the right man on board that yacht that counted."

The emotionally drained navigator paced himself carefully as he drank a few cans of his favourite beer, Swan lager, that afternoon and, after a quiet family dinner of cold meats and salad, he retired early to a soft bed at his aunt's home.

Next morning a refreshed and alert Sanders was awake before dawn and I joined him for breakfast. He told how he woke up at midnight with severe pains in his thighs. "I lay awake for two hours with the pain," he said as he ate cereal with fresh cow's milk. "I reckon it must have been all the walking and jumping on and off boats yesterday—the pain of getting back my shore legs."

He said the previous day's welcome home had been the happiest day of his life. "It really brought a lump to my throat," he said. He was "completely cured" of his penchant for sailing round the world alone. "Enough is enough. Next time I will take my crew and stop off at nice ports."

After 658 days at sea his only immediate plans were—to go sailing. He said he was looking forward to a twilight sail on the following Thursday on *Perie Banou*, with his crew doing all the work.

But first he was given a ticker-tape parade through Perth city streets, a humbling event that Jon Sanders says he will never forget. A State Government advertisement in the morning newspaper asked Perth people: Jon Sanders made it three times around the world—can you make it to his parade?

Perth people braved shimmering heat in their thousands to honour their maritime hero. It was Jon Sanders Day and crowds lined city streets five deep to cheer him. More than fifty vehicles took part in the parade, carrying sports stars, including the West Coast Eagles football team and the Perth Wildcats basketballers—teams unheard of when Sanders began his voyage. The sailor hero rode in the back of a 1947 red MG-TC sports car driven by Royal Perth Yacht Club past commodore and close friend, Noel Semmens, with an escort of eight mounted policemen. Behind him came *Perie Banou* and *Parry Endeavour*, with her free-loading gooseneck barnacles still clinging in death.

Mothers, schoolchildren—they were

given a day off school—office workers, builders' labourers and elderly pensioners were united in a cheering, flag-waving crowd as Sanders rode by waving cheerfully, but with his steel-blue eyes misted over. As the procession arrived at the Perth Esplanade and he walked along an avenue of wildly cheering children, he could not form words. Asked how he felt, he shook his head and touched his heart. It was obvious that he felt sad that his parents were not there to share his greatest moment.

As calls for a knighthood came from his admirers, Jon Sanders went quietly about resuming a "normal" life—if anything he does is normal. His late mother had told him, "Son, who wants to be ordinary? Why don't you be original?" It is most unlikely that this extraordinary sailor, this self-effacing man-of-the-sea will ever settle down to anything resembling a normal life. For all this writer knows, he might already be planning yet another remarkable voyage. What can one say but "Smooth sailing, Jon Sanders."

Epilogue

Warren Jones, A.M.

SOME people fail to grasp the magnitude of what Jon Sanders has just done. To sail alone and non-stop three times round the world—the longest surface voyage in the history of the planet earth—must rank with the deeds of Scott of the Antarctic, the astronauts Carpenter and Armstrong and the explorer Mawson. In my book the only Australian heroes who can be compared with this modest hero of the sea are our explorers of the early and mid-nineteenth century. Jon Sanders is certainly the Australian hero of the twentieth century.

The courage, mental strength and self-discipline of this home-grown Western Australian defy imagination. I have a pet theory that knights originally were men of conquest and valour and that King Arthur knighted men for bravery and outstanding deeds. If King Arthur had looked down from his cloud when Jon Sanders sailed into Fremantle Harbour on 13 March 1988, he would have been saying, "I wish Jon Sanders was sitting at my round table."

In my involvement with five America's Cup challenges, I have seen many talented and courageous sailors, men who refused to acknowledge defeat when it was staring them in the face, determined men of great moral fibre and dedication to a cause. But to my mind, this middle-aged man with salt in his veins stands out. He is heroic and he has mastered our oceans.

Without decrying Sir Francis Chichester, I believe the pioneer circumnavigator himself would be the first to acknowledge that Jon Sanders' epic voyage far eclipses his magnificent voyage on *Gipsy Moth*. I believe it even transcends the scaling of Everest by Sir Edmund Hillary—there was no Sherpa Tensing on *Parry Endeavour*.

The enormity of the challenge this lone

sailor conquered cannot be comprehended by ordinary men or women, I'm afraid. He pressed on through tremendous seas, often in pitch darkness, and he did it knowingly. He was very much aware of what he was going in to before he set out. I have sailed in strong company in some extremely heavy seas and high winds and my heart was fibrillating. Yet the seas Jon Sanders encountered in rounding Cape Horn and the Cape of Good Hope in the middle of winter were five times as high—and he faced them alone.

Weeks before this self-effacing but brilliant sailor finished his epic voyage, I wrote to Prime Minister Bob Hawke and the then State Premier Brian Burke, asking them to seek dispensation from the Australian Labor Party to put party policy to one side and to ask the Queen to knight this brave Australian. My request did not bear fruit, unfortunately, but to me Jon Sanders has already amply substantiated the credentials that are demanded of the great knights of this or any other time.

I salute him as a great Australian who, in my opinion, has no peer in this century for courage and achievement, a man who is an undubbed knight of valour and conquest.

Appendix

Records

DURING his triple circumnavigation Jon Sanders set the following records which have been ratified by the *Guinness Book of Records*:

First single-handed to complete five circumnavigations (two having been completed by Sanders in *Perie Banou* in 1981–82).

● First single-handed to complete three non-stop circumnavigations consecutively.

● First single-handed to complete a total of four non-stop circumnavigations (the first in 1981–82).

● First single-handed to complete more than one non-stop circumnavigation.

First single-handed to complete five Cape Horn roundings (one east-west, four west-east).

First single-handed to complete four Cape Horn roundings during non-stop circumnavigations.

First single-handed to round the five southernmost capes four times.

First single-handed to complete a circumnavigation using the east-west route (i.e. Cape Horn plus two other capes—Leeuwin and Good Hope).

First single-handed to complete four circumnavigations using the west-east route (i.e. Cape Horn plus the four other capes—Good Hope, Leeuwin, South East, Tasmania and Southwest, New Zealand).

First small yacht (less than 15.5m) skipper to complete five circumnavigations, crewed or single-handed.

Longest distance ever sailed continuously by any vessel (71,023 nautical miles or 131,535 kilometres).

Longest period ever spent alone at sea (657 days 21 hours 18 minutes).

Believed first yachtsman to complete five circumnavigations via Cape Horn (as crew or single-handed).

First yachtsman to circumnavigate non-stop via the Horn west-about and east-about.

- First yacht to complete three consecutive non-stop circumnavigations.

Ulverscroft Large Print Books Ltd.
The Green, Bradgate Road
Anstey
Leicestershire
LE7 7FU
England

GUIDE
TO THE COLOUR CODING
OF
ULVERSCROFT BOOKS

Many of our readers have written to us expressing their appreciation for the way in which our colour coding has assisted them in selecting the Ulverscroft books of their choice.

To remind everyone of our colour coding—this is as follows:

BLACK COVERS
Mysteries

★

BLUE COVERS
Romances

★

RED COVERS
Adventure Suspense and General Fiction

★

ORANGE COVERS
Westerns

★

GREEN COVERS
Non-Fiction

NON-FICTION TITLES
in the
Ulverscroft Large Print Series

No Time for Romance	*Lucilla Andrews*
Life's A Jubilee	*Maud Anson*
Beautiful Just! and Bruach Blend	*Lillian Beckwith*
An Autobiography Vol.1 Vol.2	*Agatha Christie*
Just Here, Doctor	*Robert D. Clifford*
High Hopes	*Norman Croucher*
An Open Book	*Monica Dickens*
Going West with Annabelle	*Molly Douglas*
The Drunken Forest	*Gerald Durrell*
The Garden of the Gods	*Gerald Durrell*
Golden Bats and Pink Pigeons	*Gerald Durrell*
If Only They Could Talk	*James Herriot*
It Shouldn't Happen to a Vet	*James Herriot*
Let Sleeping Vets Lie	*James Herriot*
Vet in a Spin	*James Herriot*
Vet in Harness	*James Herriot*
Vets Might Fly	*James Herriot*
Emma and I	*Sheila Hocken*
White Man Returns	*Agnes Newton Keith*
Flying Nurse	*Robin Miller*
The High Girders	*John Prebble*
The Seventh Commandment	*Sarah Shears*
Zoo Vet	*David Taylor*

MYSTERY TITLES
in the
Ulverscroft Large Print Series

Henrietta Who?	*Catherine Aird*
Slight Mourning	*Catherine Aird*
The China Governess	*Margery Allingham*
Coroner's Pidgin	*Margery Allingham*
Crime at Black Dudley	*Margery Allingham*
Look to the Lady	*Margery Allingham*
More Work for the Undertaker	*Margery Allingham*
Death in the Channel	*J. R. L. Anderson*
Death in the City	*J. R. L. Anderson*
Death on the Rocks	*J. R. L. Anderson*
A Sprig of Sea Lavender	*J. R. L. Anderson*
Death of a Poison-Tongue	*Josephine Bell*
Murder Adrift	*George Bellairs*
Strangers Among the Dead	*George Bellairs*
The Case of the Abominable Snowman	*Nicholas Blake*
The Widow's Cruise	*Nicholas Blake*
The Brides of Friedberg	*Gwendoline Butler*
Murder By Proxy	*Harry Carmichael*
Post Mortem	*Harry Carmichael*
Suicide Clause	*Harry Carmichael*
After the Funeral	*Agatha Christie*
The Body in the Library	*Agatha Christie*

A Caribbean Mystery	*Agatha Christie*
Curtain	*Agatha Christie*
The Hound of Death	*Agatha Christie*
The Labours of Hercules	*Agatha Christie*
Murder on the Orient Express	*Agatha Christie*
The Mystery of the Blue Train	*Agatha Christie*
Parker Pyne Investigates	*Agatha Christie*
Peril at End House	*Agatha Christie*
Sleeping Murder	*Agatha Christie*
Sparkling Cyanide	*Agatha Christie*
They Came to Baghdad	*Agatha Christie*
Third Girl	*Agatha Christie*
The Thirteen Problems	*Agatha Christie*
The Black Spiders	*John Creasey*
Death in the Trees	*John Creasey*
The Mark of the Crescent	*John Creasey*
Quarrel with Murder	*John Creasey*
Two for Inspector West	*John Creasey*
His Last Bow	*Sir Arthur Conan Doyle*
The Valley of Fear	*Sir Arthur Conan Doyle*
Dead to the World	*Francis Durbridge*
My Wife Melissa	*Francis Durbridge*
Alive and Dead	*Elizabeth Ferrars*
Breath of Suspicion	*Elizabeth Ferrars*
Drowned Rat	*Elizabeth Ferrars*
Foot in the Grave	*Elizabeth Ferrars*

Murders Anonymous	*Elizabeth Ferrars*
Don't Whistle 'Macbeth'	*David Fletcher*
A Calculated Risk	*Rae Foley*
The Slippery Step	*Rae Foley*
This Woman Wanted	*Rae Foley*
Home to Roost	*Andrew Garve*
The Forgotten Story	*Winston Graham*
Take My Life	*Winston Graham*
At High Risk	*Palma Harcourt*
Dance for Diplomats	*Palma Harcourt*
Count-Down	*Hartley Howard*
The Appleby File	*Michael Innes*
A Connoisseur's Case	*Michael Innes*
Deadline for a Dream	*Bill Knox*
Death Department	*Bill Knox*
Hellspout	*Bill Knox*
The Taste of Proof	*Bill Knox*
The Affacombe Affair	*Elizabeth Lemarchand*
Let or Hindrance	*Elizabeth Lemarchand*
Unhappy Returns	*Elizabeth Lemarchand*
Waxwork	*Peter Lovesey*
Gideon's Drive	*J. J. Marric*
Gideon's Force	*J. J. Marric*
Gideon's Press	*J. J. Marric*
City of Gold and Shadows	*Ellis Peters*
Death to the Landlords!	*Ellis Peters*
Find a Crooked Sixpence	*Estelle Thompson*
A Mischief Past	*Estelle Thompson*

Three Women in the House
Estelle Thompson
Bushranger of the Skies *Arthur Upfield*
Cake in the Hat Box *Arthur Upfield*
Madman's Bend *Arthur Upfield*
Tallant for Disaster *Andrew York*
Tallant for Trouble *Andrew York*
Cast for Death *Margaret Yorke*

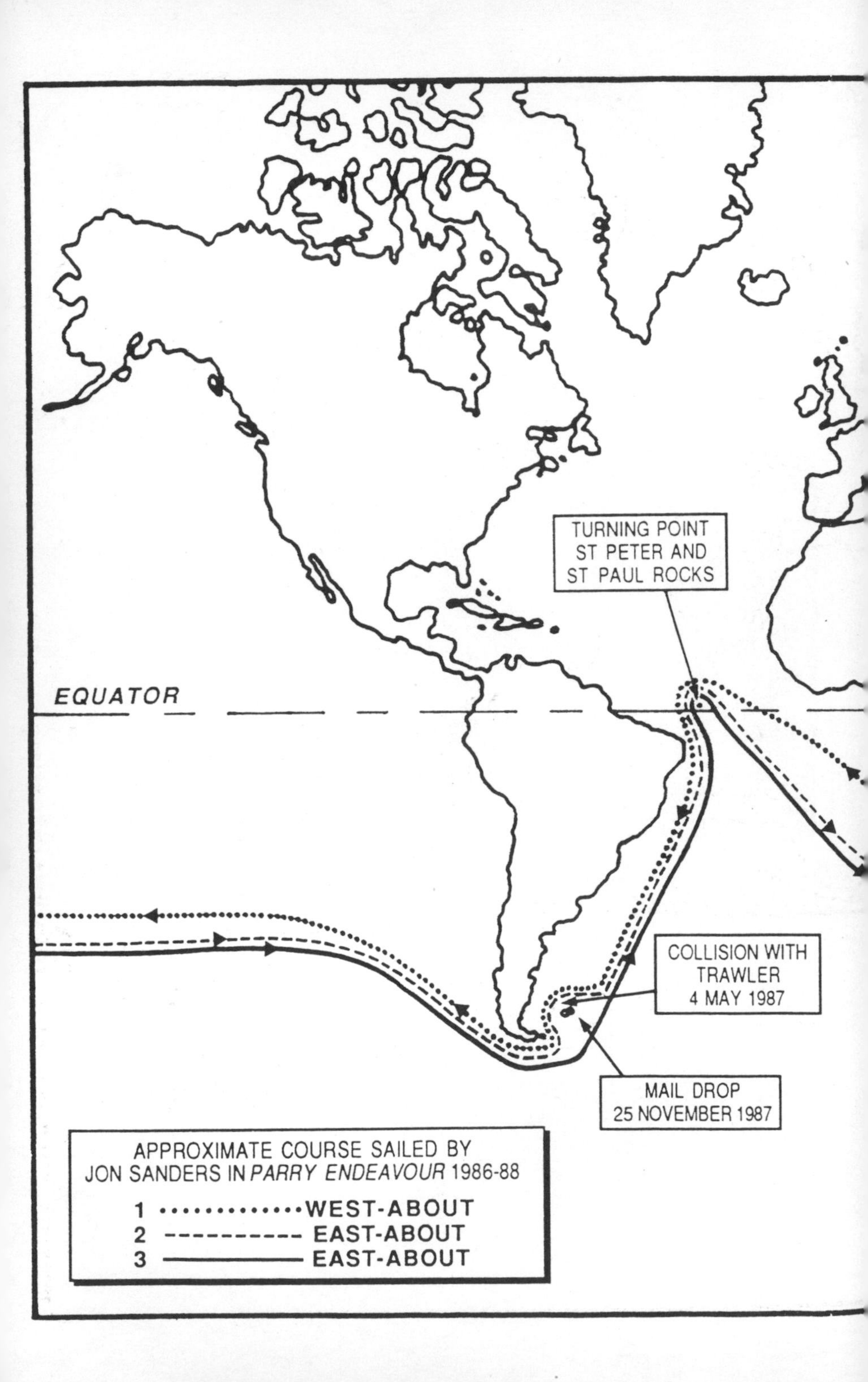
TURNING POINT
ST PETER AND
ST PAUL ROCKS
EQUATOR
COLLISION WITH
TRAWLER
4 MAY 1987
MAIL DROP
25 NOVEMBER 1987
APPROXIMATE COURSE SAILED BY
JON SANDERS IN PARRY ENDEAVOUR 1986-88
1 WEST-ABOUT
2 EAST-ABOUT
3 EAST-ABOUT